# McGraw-Hill's

# *Praxis I*
## PPST
## Practice Tests

# McGraw-Hill's

# *Praxis I*
## PPST
# Practice Tests

Laurie Rozakis, PhD

New York   Chicago   San Francisco   Lisbon   London   Madrid   Mexico City
Milan   New Delhi   San Juan   Seoul   Singapore   Sydney   Toronto

*The author wishes to thank her longtime editor and friend, Charles Wall, for his help and support over the years. In addition, McGraw-Hill Professional's editing and production team made invaluable contributions to this book, doing their best to catch any errors. Thank you, all!*

# Contents

# Welcome to *McGraw-Hill's Praxis I PPST Practice Tests*

Congratulations! You have chosen a Praxis study guide from America's leading educational publisher. You probably know us from many of the textbooks you used in school. Now we're ready to help you take the next step and become a licensed teacher.

You know the old saying, "Practice makes perfect." There's a lot of truth in this nugget of wisdom, especially when it comes to standardized tests like the Praxis. That's because the more you prepare for it by taking model tests, the better you will do on the actual test.

By taking practice Praxis tests, you will

- Become more familiar with the Praxis format, so you can work your way through the tests with greater speed and accuracy—this will help you earn a higher score
- Discover what skills are tested on the Praxis, so you can concentrate on those specific areas—these are the skills you'll need on test day
- Learn your strengths, so you won't waste valuable study time reviewing material you already know
- Learn your weaknesses, so you can concentrate your valuable study time on learning the material you really need to know
- Reduce test anxiety by being better prepared

This book gives you three Praxis reading, three Praxis writing, and three Praxis mathematics practice exams. Taking these tests can help you boost your skills and speed. The in-depth instruction in the answer keys will help you learn new material and review information you'll need. You'll also find valuable tips and strategies for the various types of questions on the Praxis.

## WHY CHOOSE THIS BOOK OVER OTHER PRAXIS PRACTICE TEST GUIDES?

In addition to being published by America's leading educational publisher, this book was written by the experienced classroom teacher and test prep expert Laurie Rozakis, PhD.

Dr. Rozakis taught high school for more than a decade and is now a full professor of English and humanities in the State University of New York. A master teacher, Dr. Rozakis was awarded the highly prestigious New York State Chancellor's Award for Excellence in Teaching.

She is also a noted test prep expert who frequently delivers seminars on test preparation to students and teachers around the country, and she has published widely in the field. Some of her other test preparation books include

- *McGraw-Hill's Praxis I and II* (now in its third edition)
- *Be a Super Test Taker*
- *Get Test Smart!*
- *Master Guide to the AP Exam in Literature and Composition*
- *Master Guide to the AP Exam in Language and Composition*

Learn from the best!

McGraw-Hill Education, a division of The McGraw-Hill Companies, is a leading global provider of print and digital instructional, assessment, and reference solutions. McGraw-Hill Education has offices in 33 countries and publishes in more than 65 languages. With a broad range of solutions—from traditional textbooks to the latest in online and multimedia learning—we engage, stimulate, and empower students and professionals of all ages.

# McGraw-Hill's

# *Praxis I*
## PPST
## Practice Tests

# PART 1

## Getting Started

# CHAPTER 1

# Overview of the Praxis Tests

Created and administered by the Educational Testing Service (ETS), the Praxis tests (The Praxis Series: Professional Assessment for Beginning Teachers) can help you achieve two goals:

1. **Earn a license to teach.** Many state education agencies use the Praxis tests as part of their licensing process. According to ETS, approximately 80 percent of the states that include tests as part of their process use The Praxis Series for this purpose, replacing the National Teacher Examination (NTE) that was used previously.
2. **Gain entry to a teacher education program.** Some colleges and universities use selected Praxis tests to qualify candidates for entry to their teacher education programs.

## THE THREE PRAXIS TESTS

The three Praxis tests are as follows:

1. Praxis I: Academic Skills Assessment (PPST)
2. Praxis II: Principles of Learning and Teaching (PLT) and Subject Assessments
3. Praxis III: Teacher Performance Assessments

Which tests do you need to take at which times in your teaching career? *Always* consult with your state education department for specific requirements, as these vary from state to state. The following chart provides basic guidelines.

| Praxis Test | When to Take It |
|---|---|
| Praxis I: Academic Skills Assessment | • when you are entering a teaching training program<br>• when you have graduated from college and seek to earn a state teaching license |
| Praxis II: Principles of Learning and Teaching and Subject Assessments | • when you have graduated from college and seek to earn a state teaching license |
| Praxis III: Teacher Performance Assessments | • when you are a beginning teacher |

Each Praxis test is different. Let's look at them all, so you better understand the entire program and its specific uses for you at each stage in your career.

# Praxis I: Academic Skills Assessment

This is a test of *basic knowledge*, what the test makers have determined is the fundamental information that all teachers should possess. As a result, you will be tested in three areas:

- Reading
- Writing
- Mathematical skills

This book covers the PPST. The practice tests cover the material on the PPST reading, writing, and mathematics tests.

# Praxis II: Principles of Learning and Teaching and Subject Assessments

This test has two parts. Principles of Learning and Teaching assesses your knowledge of teaching methodology. Subject Area Assessments evaluate your knowledge of specific subjects you will be teaching, such as social studies or biology.

## Principles of Learning and Teaching

This is the test you take to get licensed to teach a specific age group. For instance, I have a New York State teaching license for grades 7 through 12. Here are the three age groups for which you can be licensed to teach, according to the Praxis:

- Grades K–6
- Grades 5–9
- Grades 7–12

## Subject Area Assessments

Praxis II also includes subject area (content) assessments. These are the different subject areas that a person can teach, such as biology, French, and mathematics. For example, I am licensed to teach in one subject area—English. This means that I can teach English to students in grades 7 through 12. Currently, Praxis II includes more than 100 content tests. The following list shows some of the areas tested by Praxis II:

*Elementary Subject Assessments*
- Curriculum, instruction, and assessment
- Content area exercises

- Content knowledge
- Curriculum, instruction, and assessment (K–5)

*Subject Assessments*
- Art
- Biology
- English language, literature, and composition
- French
- Mathematics
- Music
- Physical education
- Physics
- Science
- Social studies
- Spanish
- Special education

Thus, you might take Praxis I as an admission requirement for a college of education. After you graduate, you might take Praxis II: Principles of Learning and Teaching for grades 5 to 9 and then Praxis II in social studies. When you passed all these tests, you would be licensed to teach social studies to students in grades 5 to 9. Later, you might complete a master's degree in special education, take Praxis II in that subject, and earn that certification as well. Candidates seeking multiple certifications at the same time can take the Multiple Subjects Assessments for Teachers (MSAT).

## Praxis III: Teacher Performance Assessments

This test has three parts:

- Direct classroom assessment, in which you are observed teaching
- Interviews
- A portfolio review

Thus, Praxis III involves direct classroom teaching experience.

To find out which Praxis test(s) to take, click on State Testing Requirements on the ETS website at www.ets.org/praxis.

In addition, always check with your university and state education department before you sign up for a Praxis test to double-check the ETS information. Make sure you are taking the appropriate test at the appropriate time in your career.

## SCORING SCALE

Each state sets its own passing scores. As mentioned earlier, always check with your state education department to find out the passing score in your state.

## FORMAT OF THE PPST

The PPST is offered in paper-and-pencil format as well as a computer-based format. Both measure the same academic skills.

How does the paper-and-pencil version of the PPST compare to the computerized version? Which one should you take?

On both the paper-and-pencil version and the computer version:

- The items are the same format.
- The same skills are assessed.
- The scoring is the same.
- The questions are linear. (The questions vary in difficulty, but this does not depend on the answers you give. Thus, this is not an adaptive test.)
- You can mark an answer or skip an answer and return to it later.

On the paper-and-pencil test, you can leave an answer blank or put a question mark next to an item and return to it later. Be sure to erase all stray marks, however. Otherwise, your answers might be marked incorrectly.

The computer-based test is basically the same as the paper-and-pencil version. By using a special tool that marks answers, you can leave a question blank and return to it later. In addition, you can mark a question you answered and go back to review or change it. A review screen tells you whether a question has been answered, not yet seen, or marked for review.

### Paper-and-Pencil Format

If you have taken the PPST previously, you will notice that the number of items and skills have changed, as ETS has revised the exam. At this time, the number of test items and time allocated for the paper-and-pencil version of the PPST are as follows:

| Test | Number of Test Items | Time |
| --- | --- | --- |
| PPST in Reading | 40 | 60 minutes |
| PPST in Mathematics (Code 0730) | 40 | 60 minutes |
| PPST in Writing (Code 0720) | 38 multiple-choice items<br>1 essay | 30 minutes<br>30 minutes<br>(60 minutes total) |

Here is the specific breakdown of test items:

**PPST in Reading**

| Specific Content Area | Number of Test Items (May vary slightly from test to test) | Percentage of Test Items (May vary slightly from test to test) |
| --- | --- | --- |
| Literal understanding | 18 | 45% |
| Inferential and critical understanding | 22 | 55% |

**PPST in Mathematics**

| Specific Content Area | Number of Test Items (May vary slightly from test to test) | Percentage of Test Items (May vary slightly from test to test) |
| --- | --- | --- |
| Operations and numbers | 13 | 32% |
| Algebra | 8 | 20% |
| Geometry and measurement | 9 | 22% |
| Probability, data analysis | 10 | 25% |

**PPST in Writing**

| Specific Content Area | Number of Test Items (May vary slightly from test to test) | Percentage of Test Items (May vary slightly from test to test) |
| --- | --- | --- |
| Grammar and usage | 13 | 17% |
| Sentence structure | 14 | 18.5% |
| Mechanics (punctuation, capitalization) Diction (word choice) | 11 | 14.5% |
| Essay | 1 | 50% |

## Computerized Format

At this time, the number of test items and time allocated for the computerized version of the PPST are as follows:

| Test | Number of Test Items | Time |
|------|---------------------|------|
| PPST in Reading (Code 5710) | 46 | 75 minutes |
| PPST in Mathematics (Code 5730) | 46 | 75 minutes |
| PPST in Writing (Code 5720) | 44 multiple-choice items 1 essay | 38 minutes 30 minutes (68 minutes total) |

Here is the specific breakdown of test items:

### PPST in Reading

| Specific Content Area | Number of Test Items (May vary slightly from test to test) | Percentage of Test Items (May vary slightly from test to test) |
|------|------|------|
| Literal understanding | 21 | 45% |
| Inferential and critical understanding | 25 | 55% |

### PPST in Mathematics

| Specific Content Area | Number of Test Items (May vary slightly from test to test) | Percentage of Test Items (May vary slightly from test to test) |
|------|------|------|
| Operations and numbers | 15 | 32% |
| Algebra | 9 | 20% |
| Geometry and measurement | 10 | 22% |
| Probability, data analysis | 12 | 25% |

**PPST in Writing**

| Specific Content Area | Number of Test Items (May vary slightly from test to test) | Percentage of Test Items (May vary slightly from test to test) |
|---|---|---|
| Grammar and usage | 15 | 17% |
| Sentence structure | 16 | 18.5% |
| Mechanics (punctuation, capitalization) Diction (word choice) | 13 | 14.5% |
| Essay | 1 | 50% |

Each part of the computer-based test is really two hours long. This means you will spend four and a half hours at the testing site. However, the actual test time for each section is the same as the individual tests. ETS uses the extra time for tutorials and to collect background information from you.

The Computerized PPST in Reading, Mathematics, and Writing is also offered as a combined test that you can take at a single testing session. The combined test has four separately timed sections: Reading, Mathematics, Multiple-Choice Writing, and Essay Writing. There is an optional 15-minute break between the Mathematics and Writing sections. The ETS score report that you receive will have individual scores for Reading, Mathematics, and Writing.

# HOW THE TESTS ARE SCORED

For the paper-and-pencil version, you complete the test, the proctor collects it, and it is scored by ETS or an agency that ETS has hired for that purpose. You must wait for the score to be posted online. You must wait even longer to receive your official score by mail. The scoring usually takes several weeks, at a minimum.

For the computer-based version, you receive your unofficial score when you complete the test. You still have to wait for the official score to arrive by mail, however.

A great deal of confusion has arisen over the computerized scoring. On both the paper-and-pencil and computer-based versions, each test item has a different value. For example, item 1 might be worth 2 points, item 2 might be worth 4 points, item 3 might be worth 1.5 points, and so on. The point value varies with each version of the test.

When you take the computer-based version, the test will end when/if you reach the passing score for your state. The number of questions you must answer to pass depends on the point value for each question and the passing rate for your state. For instance, you might be finished when you answer 26 questions correctly, 30 questions correctly, or 42 questions correctly. Or you might have to complete the entire test. You have no way of knowing this, because you don't know how much each question is weighted.

On the paper-and-pencil test, however, you have to complete the entire test, even if you have already achieved the passing score. That's because you have no way of knowing if you have passed.

## Neither Format Is Computer-Adaptive

This confusion has led some people to believe that the computer-based version of the PPST is a computer-adaptive test. This means that the questions get easier or more difficult depending on your level of skill. *The PPST is not and never has been a computer-adaptive test. ETS has no plans to make it one.* The computer-based test and the paper-and-pencil test are the same linear tests. They are simply offered in different formats.

## No Penalty for Guessing

In either type of test, your score is based on the number of questions you answer correctly. There is no penalty for answering a question incorrectly. Thus, it's a good idea to write down an answer for every question. Don't leave any blanks.

*Take the paper-and-pencil version if . . .*
- You are not comfortable working on computers or with this technology.
- You think it will unnerve you if the test suddenly stops (meaning you passed).
- You think you will earn a higher score this way.

*Take the computer-based version if . . .*
- You are comfortable working on computers.
- You want your unofficial score immediately.
- You can't wait for the next paper-and-pencil test date.
- You think you will earn a higher score this way.

# HOW OFTEN THE TESTS ARE OFFERED

The paper-and-pencil test is offered five times a year, as of publication date. These dates are in November, January, March, April, and July. You choose the time and place when you register.

The computer-based test is offered much more frequently. You make an appointment through Prometric Testing Centers. To arrange an appointment, call Prometric candidate services at 1-800-853-6773.

**Important!** As far as ETS is concerned, a year runs from September to July, *not* from January to January. Thus, if you intend to take the Praxis more than once in a "year," do your best to take it within ETS's year to avoid paying the registration fee twice.

# FREQUENTLY ASKED QUESTIONS (FAQS)

**Q: Which test(s) should I take?**

**A:** The test(s) you take depends entirely on your state and college requirements. ETS has a link to each state's requirements. Check with your college teacher certification office to determine its requirements. Remember: each state and each college has its own requirements.

**Q: How do I register for the test?**

**A:** You can obtain registration forms in several ways.

1. Contact the Educational Testing Service online at its website: www.ets.org/praxis. (The e-mail address is praxis@ets.org.) You cannot register online if . . .

   - You need services for students with disabilities.
   - You are registering the first time for Sunday testing.
   - You are testing in certain countries (including Taiwan, Nigeria, Benin, Togo, Ghana, and Kenya).

2. Write to the Educational Testing Service at this address:

   ETS—The Praxis Series
   P.O. Box 6051
   Princeton, NJ 08541-6051

3. Obtain an application from your college department of education.

   - ETS will reduce fees for students who can demonstrate financial need. Do not send money to ETS.
   - Your university's department of education or financial aid office will have this information.

**Q: Where should I take the test?**

**A:** As with all ETS tests, the paper-and-pencil version of the Praxis is administered at colleges, universities, high schools, and civic centers. As mentioned earlier, the computer-based test is given at Prometric Testing Centers as well as select colleges and universities.

Register for a convenient location close to your home. This will help you reduce test anxiety. If you have to go to an inconvenient site, try to visit it prior to the test to get your bearings. If you don't meet the registration deadline, don't despair. If they have space, most test centers accept walk-in test takers. You'll pay an extra fee for this service, but at least you'll be able to take the test on the day you wish.

**Q: What do I have to bring with me on test day?**

**A:** You will need the following items to take the test:

- If you register by phone or mail, your admission ticket. ETS will send this to you. But if you registered for a paper-based Praxis test by mail or phone and don't receive your admission ticket at least one week before the test date, contact ETS to confirm your test appointment.

- If you register online, your e-ticket. ETS has taken a page from the airlines and gone to ticketless travel: candidates who register online will no longer receive a printed paper ticket in the mail. Instead, you must print out an e-ticket from the online registration system.
- A photo ID. The following documents are acceptable:

    Passport
    Driver's license
    State ID
    National identification
    Military identification

- Sharpened number 2 pencils and an eraser
- A calculator, if you are allowed to use one on the test you are taking. Be sure to check this ahead of time, as not all of the Praxis mathematical tests allow you to use a calculator at this time.
- A watch. Do *not* assume that you will be able to use your cell phone as a watch or that the test room will have a clock on the wall. Test takers are not allowed to bring their cell phones into the test rooms because of the possibility of downloading information that can be used to obtain answers. In addition, many test rooms do not have clocks—and if they do, you can't assume they work!

**Q: What types of questions will I have to answer on the PPST?**

**A:** Remember that the PPST is designed to measure basic skills in reading, writing, and mathematics. Expect questions similar to those on the SAT.

**Q: What can I expect on the PPST in Reading?**

**A:** Fortunately, there are no surprises here because this is a standard ETS reading test: a series of reading passages followed by multiple-choice questions with five answer choices each. Reading passages range from just a few sentences to about 500 words. As you learned earlier in this book, the reading skills tested can be divided as follows:

- Finding literal details: about 45%
- Making inferences: about 55%

This means that about half the questions require you to go back into the passage to find the answers. The information you need will be stated directly. The other questions will require you to read between the lines to find the answers. You'll combine information in the passage to infer the answers.

**Q: What can I expect on the PPST in Mathematics?**

**A:** Again, you'll be dealing with multiple-choice questions with five answer choices. You'll be tested on a wide variety of mathematical concepts. The breakdown of the mathematical skills was explained earlier in this chapter. Naturally, you'll want to allocate your study time accordingly, spending more time not only on your weakest areas but also on the areas that will get the most emphasis on the test.

**Q: Can I use a calculator on the PPST in Mathematics?**

**A:** Alas, no. The calculator has to stay home.

**Q: What can I expect on the PPST in Writing?**

**A:** Remember that this test has two parts: multiple-choice questions and an essay. (The number of multiple-choice questions is different on the paper-and-pencil and the computerized versions of the test, but the breakdown of the skills is the same.) Each part of the test counts as 50 percent of your final score.

The multiple-choice part of the test has usage questions and sentence correction questions. Each type of question has a different format.

*Usage Questions*

These questions have four answer choices consisting of underlined words or groups of words. The fifth choice is always "No error." Here is a sample question:

The <u>top three winners</u> in the <u>state competition</u> <u>goes</u> to the national finals
             A                              B                    C
<u>to be held</u> this year in San Francisco, California. <u>No error</u>
     D                                                         E

**Answer:** C. The underlined word in choice C, <u>goes</u>, should be <u>go</u>, since the plural subject <u>winners</u> requires the plural verb <u>go</u>.

*Sentence Correction Questions*

These questions have some or all of the words underlined. Each sentence is followed by five choices: the first is the same as the underlined part, and the others are revisions. You must decide whether the original or one of the rewrites is best. Here is a sample question:

Dr. Seuss, one of the world's most famous children's book <u>authors, he has written</u> books for adults and advertising copy as well.

(A)  authors, he has written

(B)  authors, written by him has been

(C)  authors him has written

(D)  authors written

(E)  authors, has written

**Answer:** E. As written, the sentence is incorrect because there is no reason to include the pronoun *he*. As you approach these questions, always start by looking for the easiest and least convoluted way of revising the sentence. The easiest way here is to delete the pronoun *he*. The other choices create wordy, awkward, and incorrect sentences. The correct sentence reads: *Dr. Seuss, one of the world's most famous children's book authors, has written books for adults and advertising copy as well.*

*The Essay Part of the Test*

You will be given a topic (the "writing prompt") to write on. You do not have a choice: there is one prompt and one prompt only. *Never* make up your own writing prompt. If you do, you won't receive any credit on this part of the test. Respond directly to the prompt the test gives you.

**Q: What can I expect if I decide to take the computer-based version of the PPST?**

**A:** As explained earlier, this form of the test is the same as the pencil-and-paper test. It's just transferred to a computer version.

**Q: If I don't know the answer, should I guess?**

**A:** On many of the other ETS tests, such as the SAT, you are penalized for guessing. This is not the case on the Praxis. Only questions answered correctly count toward the reported score. Therefore, it is better to guess than to leave an answer blank. If you do have to guess, always try to eliminate as many incorrect answers as possible first.

**Q: How do I get my score?**

**A:** Your official scores will be available online at the ETS site 45 days after you take the test. You can also call to get your score, but this costs extra. In addition, you can request your score by mail. Further information is available on the ETS website.

ETS will send your score to as many as three certification agencies, colleges, or other agencies without charge. You designate these agencies when you register for the test. For more than three reports, you have to pay an extra fee.

# FOR ADDITIONAL INFORMATION

For additional information about the Praxis tests, you can contact ETS.

| | |
|---|---|
| E-mail: | praxis@ets.org |
| Website: | www.ets.org/praxis |
| Phone: | United States, U.S. Territories, and Canada   1-800-772-9476 |
| | All other locations                                            1-609-771-7395 |
| | TTY 1-609-771-7714 |
| Mail: | ETS—The Praxis Series, P.O. Box 6051, Princeton, NJ 08541-6051 |
| Fax: | 1-609-771-7906; 1-609-530-0581 |

# CHAPTER 2

# Coping with Test Anxiety

President Franklin Delano Roosevelt said, "The only thing we have to fear is fear itself." He was right, but try telling that to all the butterflies in your stomach the night before the Praxis. You *can* deal with nerves, though. Here's how.

Start by building your self-confidence. Getting yourself all upset before the test will make you feel more nervous. It can also rob you of the confidence you need to succeed. Remind yourself that you have prepared well, so you will do well. A positive attitude yields great results.

## TECHNIQUES FOR REDUCING TEST ANXIETY

Fortunately, there are many effective ways to deal with test jitters. Here are some of my most effective techniques.

1. **Downplay the test.** It's natural to feel nervous before a high-pressure situation; in fact, some scientists think we're hardwired to get an adrenaline rush when we're in tight spots. These scientists theorize that tension under pressure comes from ancient times when we faced bison and other gigantic creatures. The adrenaline gave us the power we needed to run away. Now, however, we can't run away; we have to stay and face the pressure.

    So how can you deal with this flood of tension? Start by downplaying the test. Instead of referring to the Praxis as "The Worst Day of My Life" (or "Doomsday," "The Kiss of Death," "My Personal Waterloo," and so on), think about it as one more hurdle to overcome. Be casual when you talk about it, and don't let your classmates, parents, partner, or instructors push your panic button.

2. **Don't dismiss your fears.** In your attempt to downplay the test, don't go to the opposite extreme of saying, "Oh, this old Praxis doesn't mean a thing. I can still become a teacher if I bomb the test." Recognize that the Praxis *does* matter. Nonetheless, even in the most high-pressure test situations, the test will never be the sole measure of your qualifications. And the Praxis certainly has nothing to do with your worth as a human being.

3. **Learn (and use) relaxation techniques.** Use visualization and breathing techniques to overcome your fear of failure. Visualize or imagine yourself doing well, filling in the blanks or writing the essays with confidence. Imagine receiving a high score on the Praxis. Visualizing success puts you in control.

Breathing techniques can also help you relax during the test. If you feel yourself losing control, take slow, deep breaths to calm yourself. If you have time before the test, try to get in some exercise. It's a great way to reduce tension. Even 10 minutes of jogging can take the edge off.

4. **Be optimistic.** We can't all be little rays of sunshine, especially when faced with a big, important test like the Praxis. Nonetheless, studies have clearly shown that people who approach tense situations with an upbeat attitude do better than those who trudge in, already defeated. Imagine achieving success rather than automatically dooming yourself to failure.

**Test Hint:** Right before a big test, stay away from people who bring you down by preying on your stress and anxiety. You don't need them pulling you down with their doom-and-gloom scripts.

# DEALING WITH PANIC

What if none of my suggestions work for you and panic strikes during the Praxis? Start by recognizing that panic is a natural reaction to a high-pressure situation. Nonetheless, it can prevent you from doing your best, so let's reduce or banish it. Here are some techniques that can help you deal with panic:

- **Don't panic if . . .** some questions seem much harder than others. They probably are. That's the way the test was designed. Accept this and do the best you can. Remember that you don't have to answer each question to do well. That's because you're not being marked against yourself; rather, you're being judged against all other test takers. Furthermore, they're feeling the same way you are.
- **Don't panic if . . .** you can't get an answer. Just skip the question and move on. If you have enough time, you can return to the question later. If you run out of time before you can return to it, you were still better off answering more questions than wasting time on one you didn't know.
- **Don't panic if . . .** you freeze and just can't go on. If this happens, remind yourself that you have studied and are well prepared. Remember that every question you have answered is worth points.

Reassure yourself that you're doing just fine. After all, you are. Stop working and close your eyes. Take two or three deep breaths. Breathe in and out to the count of five. Then go on with the test.

**Test Hint:** Take comfort from this: A minor case of nerves can actually help you do well in a test—especially a standardized test like the Praxis—because it keeps you alert and focused on the task at hand.

# CHAPTER 3

# Your Individualized Praxis Prep Plan

*Myth: You can't study for a standardized test.*
*Reality: Oh, yes you can.*

Many people still believe that you can't improve your score on a standardized test because these tests are designed to assess the knowledge you have gained during many years of education. While it is undeniably true that *cramming* for a Praxis or any other standardized test won't have a noticeable effect on your score, you most certainly can significantly improve your score by *studying*.

Your Individualized Praxis Prep Plan provides guidelines for what to do in the months leading up to the test and the day of the test. Following this plan can help you earn your highest possible score on the Praxis. Here's how to do it.

## STEP 1: EXPAND YOUR READING SKILLS

Half of the American people have never read a newspaper. Half have never voted for President. One hopes it is the same half.

—GORE VIDAL, AUTHOR

Since 1982, the reading of literary works (novels, short stories, and so on) has fallen in all demographic groups and segments. College-age people (18–24) have had the sharpest drop in reading, around 40 percent compared to the nearly 60 percent who were reading 20 years ago. Young adults (25–34) weren't immune to the decline in reading either, as their rate dropped more than 15 percent during the same time frame.

According to the National Endowment for the Arts, recreational reading is way down. "We've got a public culture which is almost entirely commercial- and novelty-driven," says NEA chairman Dana Gioia. The following sobering statistics bear out Gioia's claim:

- Twenty-seven percent of adults did not read a single book for pleasure last year.
- Sixty-five percent of college freshmen said they read little or nothing for pleasure.
- Seventy percent of Americans haven't visited a bookstore in five years.
- Only 32 percent of the U.S. population has ever been in a bookstore.

The easiest and most enjoyable way to pump up your score on the Praxis is to read, read, and read some more. Reading increases your vocabulary, reading speed, and overall comprehension. It helps you on the PPST in Mathematics too, as that assessment contains a great deal of text. You can't read just anything, however. *What* you read matters a lot, because all reading is not the same.

---

**Test Hint:** To get the maximum effect from your reading, choose novels and nonfiction works of recognized literary value, not trashy bestsellers.

---

# STEP 2: CREATE A STUDY CENTER

You need a place devoted to study. It doesn't have to be a suite at the Ritz, but it does have to be a quiet place supplied with all the materials you need to study. Here's what you need:

- This book
- Scratch paper
- Pencils or pens
- A watch
- A good light
- A desk and chair

You can set up your study center at a desk in your bedroom, basement, attic, or spare room. If you don't have the space at home, consider a carrel at the library. Most libraries have spaces set aside for quiet reading, and these spaces work very well for studying.

Avoid studying at the dining room or kitchen table, as you're likely to be disturbed by people walking by. You'll also have to remove all your papers and notes every time people want to use the room for a meal. Don't study on your bed; it's too comfortable. As a result, you're more likely to doze off.

# STEP 3: LEARN THE PRAXIS SCORING AND TEST DIRECTIONS

Obviously, studying this book helps you save time on the day of the test. As you work your way through the chapters, not only will you review your skills, but you will also become thoroughly familiar with the test directions and format. This way, you won't waste valuable time puzzling over the directions and orienting yourself to the test content. You'll be able to sit down and get right to work. Here are two areas to concentrate on to get you started:

- **Understand the scoring:** As explained earlier, you are not penalized for guessing on the Praxis. Therefore, you should always try to eliminate answers you know to be wrong and then guess from the remaining choices. Never leave an answer blank.
- **Learn the test directions:** Any time that you can save during the test is that much more time you'll have to answer questions. If you learn the test directions for each section, you will save the time you would otherwise have spent reading them during the actual test. This extra time will certainly help you earn a better score and could even make a crucial difference in your results.

# STEP 4: CHOOSE A TEST STRATEGY

Approach the Praxis as you would any other large project: get a strategy. In this instance, you want to choose a test strategy, and there are three ways you can approach the Praxis:

1. **Work in chronological order.** Work from beginning to end, answering every question in order. Answer every single question, even if you have to guess. This is the most common test strategy. It has several advantages; chief among them is that it's easy. Furthermore, this strategy helps you keep your place in the test so you don't run the risk of mismarking the answers. However, you also run the risk of spending too much time on a difficult question and not answering some easy ones.

2. **Go from easy to difficult.** With this technique, you answer the easy questions first and then go back and work on the harder ones. This approach has many advantages. First, it helps you use your time well by getting the most correct answers down fast. Also, you build confidence as you write down the correct answers. You may think of clues that help you answer the more difficult questions. You may even find the correct answer to a hard question revealed in another test question. You build momentum, which gets your mind into the test mode. You must be sure to leave time to return to the harder questions, though.

3. **Go from difficult to easy.** Here, you answer the difficult questions first and then go back and answer the rest. This strategy helps you get the most difficult questions out of the way first, but you run the risk of spending too much time on them and not being able to finish the test. Thus, you sacrifice the chance of getting some easy points.

None of these test-taking methods is right or wrong, but for most people, strategy 2 works best. If you decide to use this method, answer the easy questions first and then go back to figure out the more difficult ones.

As you work from the beginning to the end of the test, put a check mark next to any question you skip. Write in pencil so you can erase the check marks. When you get to the end of the test, go back to the beginning and start answering the questions you skipped.

Keep moving so you stay within your time limit. Never let yourself get bogged down on one or two questions, especially if they are not worth many points.

**Test Hint:** As you work through the sample Praxis exams in this book, try each of the three test strategies. Based on your scores, choose the test approach that works best for you.

Regardless of the strategy you adopt, follow these suggestions to get the highest score:

• **Work carefully:** Imagine that you come to question 3 on the PPST: Writing test. It's a multiple-choice question with five choices—A, B, C, D, E. You read the test item and choice A. "Ah ha!" you think. "The correct choice is clearly A." Should you mark A on your answer sheet? No.

Even if you think you have spotted the correct answer immediately, read every answer to make sure you are correct. You might have misread the question, a common mistake. People tend to see what they expect, not what is really on the page.

- **Don't second-guess yourself:** "The short-answer pattern really matters," some people say. "You can never have two Cs (or As, Bs, and so on) in a row." Not true. The pattern of letters on the answer sheet doesn't matter at all. You may have an ABCDE, ABCDE pattern, an AABBCCDDEE pattern, another pattern, or no pattern at all. It never matters.

  If you do see a pattern, don't be fooled into changing your answers. Your grade will always be higher if you answer questions based on what you know rather than on the way the answers look on the page. If you start to think that you've chosen the incorrect answer, analyze the question rather than the answer pattern. If you can't think of a good reason to change the answer, leave it alone. Studies show that your first analysis is more often the correct one.

# STEP 5: SET UP A STUDY ROUTINE

To make the most of your study time, get into a study routine. Consider these Five Fast Facts:

1. **We are creatures of habit.** Study at the same time every day in the same place. Sit at your desk in your study center to get into the study habit. Try to study for at least 30 minutes at a time. Any less, and you're not apt to get much done. Any more, and your mind is apt to wander from fatigue.

2. **Start with the hardest information.** Study your most difficult material first, when you are the least tired. You get a lot more done and retain more when you're rested.

3. **Ambience matters.** If your study center has a radio, television, video game system, stereo, or any other distraction—turn it off. "I study better with some noise in the background," you protest. No, you don't. No one does. Turn off the television, radio, or CD when you study. You will always study better without distractions. You'll get a lot more done if you devote yourself to studying for the Praxis in a quiet place. Why waste your time?

4. **Go for the points.** Concentrate on the areas of the test that carry the most credit, such as the essay.

5. **Take a break, and give yourself a treat.** As you study, give yourself a break. Stretch every 15 minutes or so. Even if you want to soldier through, resting briefly a few times every hour helps recharge your batteries. And since you're working hard to succeed on the Praxis, give yourself a treat. It doesn't have to be a designer watch or vacation in the south of France: breakfast with a buddy or an hour in front of the TV gives a lot of pleasure for a lot less money.

# STEP 6: FOLLOW YOUR STUDY SCHEDULE

A full-day conference at work. A holiday celebration. A pile of laundry. Help! You're pressed for time. Why not leave all your studying to the last minute and cram it all in? Here's why not—cramming doesn't work. It also tends to make you panic when you realize there's no way you can learn everything you need for the Praxis in a week. Instead of wasting your time cramming, follow this study schedule to earn your highest score:

*Six Months Before the Test*
- Preview this book to get an overview of the Praxis.
- Determine which test(s) to take, when you have to register, at which location you want to take the test(s), and to which schools or colleges to send your scores.

*Five Months Before the Test*
- Concentrate on one of the three tests, such as the PPST in Reading.
- Complete the first two practice Reading tests to assess your strengths and weaknesses.
- Target your weakest areas that will get you the most points on the Praxis.

*Four Months Before the Test*
- Concentrate on one of the three tests, such as the PPST in Writing.
- Complete the first two practice Writing tests to assess your strengths and weaknesses.
- Target your weakest areas that will get you the most points on the Praxis.

*Three Months Before the Test*
- Concentrate on one of the three tests, such as the PPST in Mathematics.
- Complete the first two practice Mathematics tests to assess your strengths and weaknesses.
- Target your weakest areas that will get you the most points on the Praxis.

*Two Months Before the Test*
- Take the last practice test for all three subjects—Reading, Writing, and Mathematics—under test conditions. Use only the amount of time you would be allocated on the real Praxis.
- Score yourself.
- Use this information to decide which areas to review.

*The Month Before the Test*
- Skim the first six tests that you have already taken, reading the questions, answers, and explanations.
- Review the material.

*The Day Before the Test*
- Check the directions to the test site.
- Relax.

*The Night Before the Test*
- Lay out your clothing, pens or pencils, watch, lunch, and other test supplies. You don't want to be rushing around in the morning. Choose comfortable clothing. Avoid itchy sweaters or starchy pants. Your clothes should be loose enough so you're comfortable.

- Get a good night's sleep. Yes, I know you've heard it before, but it really works. A solid eight hours of sleep can recharge your batteries and give you the winning edge on any test.

*The Day of the Test*
- Be sure to eat breakfast, and make sure it's nourishing. You may want to have yogurt and fruit, eggs, French toast, or pancakes. Don't make do with a toaster pastry or a doughnut. Too much caffeine can give you the jitters, so avoid caffeinated colas or too many cups of coffee.
- Leave yourself enough time in the morning. This is not the day to be rushing around.

# STEP 7: DEAL WITH SPECIAL NEEDS

The Americans with Disabilities Act (ADA) forbids discrimination on the basis of disability in employment, state and local government, public accommodations, commercial facilities, transportation, and telecommunications. This is the law.

To be protected by the ADA, you must have a disability. The ADA defines a person with a disability "as a person who has a physical or mental impairment that substantially limits one or more major life activities, a person who has a history or record of such an impairment, or a person who is perceived by others as having such an impairment." The ADA does not specifically name all of the impairments that are covered.

Under the ADA, "privately operated entities offering certain types of courses and examinations must provide specific accommodations with persons classified as have a disability. . . . Courses and examinations related to professional, educational, or trade-related applications, licensing, certifications, or credentialing must be provided in a place and manner accessible to people with disabilities, or alternative accessible arrangements must be offered." ETS cooperates fully with these federal regulations.

As a result, ETS offers a wide variety of accommodations for people who qualify under the ADA. Accommodations available for the Praxis include the following:

**Praxis Test Accommodations for People with Disabilities**

| | | |
|---|---|---|
| Additional rest breaks | Large-print answer sheet | Printed copy of spoken directions |
| Audio test | Large-print test book (16 pt.) | Sign language interpreter for spoken directions only |
| Braille slate and stylus | Listening section omitted | Test reader |
| Braille test | Oral interpreter | Writer/recorder of answers |
| Extended testing time | Perkins Brailler | |

In addition, ETS offers Monday testing for military or religious reasons. You can also get extended test time if English is not your main language.

For further information:

Phone:     1-609-771-7780
Mail:      ETS Disability Services, P.O. Box 6054, Princeton, NJ 08541-6054
Website:   www.ets.org/praxis

---

**Test Hint:** If you qualify for test accommodations because you have a special need, it is your responsibility to contact ETS with sufficient time to schedule the accommodation. *Do not wait until the test day to arrange for accommodations.*

---

Being an international student also presents some special needs. ETS makes sure that the Praxis is not biased against international test takers. The test makers pretest all questions by including them in "experimental" test sections given to both U.S. and international test takers. If statistics prove that any of the new questions put the internationals at a disadvantage, those items never appear on the test. Still, international test takers face certain challenges.

## Improving Your English

The biggest and most obvious difficulty for non-native English speakers and international test takers is the language barrier. The entire test, including instructions and questions, is in English. Your writing, reading comprehension, and grammar skills are directly tested on the Praxis.

Most experts advise non-native English speakers to read as much in English as they can in the months leading up to the test. Other activities that might help you are creating and using flash cards with difficult English words on them and practicing your English by communicating with others who speak the language. To improve your understanding of spoken English, you can watch American TV shows, often available online as well as on television. Keep a journal and express your thoughts about what you have read and seen in writing. Your goal should be to practice presenting evidence in a cohesive and interesting way to support your arguments in the PPST: Writing exam. When you read items from American publications, pay particular attention to how the writers gather evidence and present it, because there are often subtle cultural differences at play. Remember that the quantitative part of the Praxis is also in English, so it is a good idea to review math formulas and glossaries in English.

## Becoming Familiar with Standardized Tests

Getting acquainted with standardized tests is another must-do for international test takers. This type of exam is a part of the average American's educational experience but is not necessarily a cultural norm in other parts of the world. Some people from outside the United States may be unfamiliar with multiple-choice questions. These are questions in which you are given several choices from which to choose the correct answer. There are strategies for choosing the best one when you're not sure. For example, you can eliminate answers that you know are incorrect and then choose from among the remaining answers. This is called "taking an educated guess," and it can improve your chances of picking the correct answer.

Timing is a very important part of standardized tests. Keeping calm is the first step to overcoming the pressure. Taking practice tests is key to learning how to pace yourself to maximize your performance in a limited time period. Taking practice tests will also help you become familiar with the test format. Further, understanding the instructions for each part of the test in advance can save you time during the exam, because you won't have to spend time on the instructions in addition to the other reading you have to do.

## STEP 8: THINK ABOUT STUDYING WITH PEERS

Studying with other people who will be taking the Praxis, usually classmates, can help you in many ways. For instance, group members can take turns summarizing the material aloud or quizzing each other on important topics. Some group members ask questions to help clarify confusing points, while others provide the answers. Study groups are a staple of MBA and law school programs, but should you form a study group for the Praxis? Use the following chart to help you decide.

| Study on your own if you . . . | Study with others if you . . . |
|---|---|
| Can't concentrate if others are talking | Absorb material better if you hear people talking about it |
| Talk to yourself as you study | Find you learn better when you explain information to other people |
| Don't enjoy working with others | Enjoy working with others and have classmates who are serious about the test and can stay on task |
| Feel relatively confident of your abilities in all the subject areas tested on the Praxis | Feel weak in certain subject areas (such as mathematics or writing) and have classmates who are strong in those areas |
| Believe your way of studying is the best way (or even the only way!) to approach the test | Are not strong on organization and may be missing important notes |
| Can set a schedule and stick with it; get annoyed when people don't follow a set schedule | Have difficulty sitting down to work and find your mind wandering when you study alone |

## STEP 9: USE THE PRACTICE TESTS EFFECTIVELY

Follow this five-step plan to get the most from the practice tests:

1. Take the practice tests one at a time.
2. After each practice test, carefully analyze the questions you missed.

3. Use the minilessons and detailed explanations in the answer key to learn the topics you missed before moving on to another practice test.
4. Always focus on the topics that will gain you the most points.
5. Strictly observe the test time limits.

# STEP 10: PUT YOUR BEST FOOT FORWARD ON TEST DAY

The following strategies can help you ace the Praxis.

1. **Follow the directions.** On the day of the test, pay close attention to all directions: Even though you'll be completely familiar with the test format, the proctor may say something very important, such as outlining safety procedures in the event of a fire drill or an actual fire. As a result, it is important to listen closely.
2. **Jot down notes and key facts.** During the test, write down any important details and facts while they are still fresh in your memory. These notes will very likely help you answer questions later on. In addition, having some notes reduces test anxiety because it reminds you that you have learned a lot. Write your notes on scrap paper, inside the test booklet, or in the test margins.
3. **Be creative, but don't overthink.** Sometimes the answer isn't obvious, so you have to think outside the box by analyzing the question from different angles. You have to use creative thinking skills by inferring, analyzing, and drawing conclusions.

   However, when you think creatively, be sure not to overthink. When you do, you analyze your answers so deeply that you create relationships that don't really exist. You might get hopelessly lost too.

   When in doubt, go for the most logical and obvious answer. If that doesn't fit, look more deeply into the question and see if you can find an answer that matches your line of thought.
4. **Pace yourself to avoid making careless errors.** The PPST is both a sprint and a marathon. You have less than a minute, on average, for each question, so it is essential to develop the ability to work through these questions quickly and efficiently. Speed is not enough; Praxis I requires that you have mental stamina so you can stay focused throughout the test. The best way to prepare yourself is to take the practice tests in this book while following the time limits strictly.

   During the Praxis, make sure you are wearing a watch or can see a clock. This will help you keep working at the right pace. You want to work quickly but not so quickly that you throw away points by being careless. It's an awful feeling to lose points on questions that you really can answer. You will get the wrong answer if you:

   - Misread a question
   - Miscalculate a math problem
   - Mark the wrong spot on your answer sheet (such as meaning to mark C but marking B instead because you're working too fast)

   To prevent these careless errors, try to save a few minutes at the end of the test to check the answer sheet against the choices on the test. Read the answer and the letter to yourself. Say the letter in your head.

When you are working on math problems, check that your answers make sense. Are they logical? For example, if you are figuring a discount, make sure that it's not more than the original price.

5. **Check your work.** When you finish the test, always check your work. Even if you have just a minute or two, use the time to look over your papers. Ask yourself these questions as you check the essay part of the Praxis:

   - Have I included all necessary words? People often omit words when they are in a hurry.
   - Have I spelled all the words correctly? Check easy words as well as more difficult ones.
   - Is my punctuation correct?
   - Have I checked my grammar and usage?
   - Can my writing be read easily?

   Ask yourself these questions as you check the multiple-choice part of the Praxis:

   - Have I filled in my responses at the correct places on the answer sheet?
   - Since I am not being penalized for guessing, did I fill in each answer?
   - Did I erase stray marks that might be misread?

   Losing your place on an answer sheet is a major disaster that should never occur. Here's how it happens: You're working from the beginning to the end of the test. You get stuck on a few test items, so you skip them and keep on working. You focus on the next question and forget to skip a space on the answer sheet. As a result, you mark the correct answer in the wrong spot.

   When you get to the last spot on the answer sheet, you have two spaces left. You suddenly realize that when you skipped questions, you forgot to skip the appropriate spaces on the answer sheet—even though you put check marks next to the questions!

   You can avoid this disaster by checking your answer sheet each time you skip a question. Keeping your answer sheet next to the test booklet can help you remember to keep checking.

6. **Be neat.** If your writing is difficult to read, consider printing. Don't use all block capitals, however. Instead, use the accepted mix of uppercase and lowercase letters.

7. **Use all your allotted time.** *Never* turn your test booklet in early and leave. Be sure to use all the time you have been given—every single minute. Check your work over and think about your answers. If you are sure you're completely done, set your test aside and take a brief break. A few minutes later, look back at the test and your answers. Errors often become apparent when you've stepped away from the test. You don't want to be out the door and suddenly realize you've finished so early because you forgot to complete one part of the test.

8. **Deal with test anxiety.** This is covered in detail in Chapter 2.

# PART 2

## Praxis I PPST Practice Tests

# READING PRACTICE TEST 1

## Answer sheet

| | | |
|---|---|---|
| 1 Ⓐ Ⓑ Ⓒ Ⓓ Ⓔ | 8 Ⓐ Ⓑ Ⓒ Ⓓ Ⓔ | 15 Ⓐ Ⓑ Ⓒ Ⓓ Ⓔ |
| 2 Ⓐ Ⓑ Ⓒ Ⓓ Ⓔ | 9 Ⓐ Ⓑ Ⓒ Ⓓ Ⓔ | 16 Ⓐ Ⓑ Ⓒ Ⓓ Ⓔ |
| 3 Ⓐ Ⓑ Ⓒ Ⓓ Ⓔ | 10 Ⓐ Ⓑ Ⓒ Ⓓ Ⓔ | 17 Ⓐ Ⓑ Ⓒ Ⓓ Ⓔ |
| 4 Ⓐ Ⓑ Ⓒ Ⓓ Ⓔ | 11 Ⓐ Ⓑ Ⓒ Ⓓ Ⓔ | 18 Ⓐ Ⓑ Ⓒ Ⓓ Ⓔ |
| 5 Ⓐ Ⓑ Ⓒ Ⓓ Ⓔ | 12 Ⓐ Ⓑ Ⓒ Ⓓ Ⓔ | 19 Ⓐ Ⓑ Ⓒ Ⓓ Ⓔ |
| 6 Ⓐ Ⓑ Ⓒ Ⓓ Ⓔ | 13 Ⓐ Ⓑ Ⓒ Ⓓ Ⓔ | 20 Ⓐ Ⓑ Ⓒ Ⓓ Ⓔ |
| 7 Ⓐ Ⓑ Ⓒ Ⓓ Ⓔ | 14 Ⓐ Ⓑ Ⓒ Ⓓ Ⓔ | 21 Ⓐ Ⓑ Ⓒ Ⓓ Ⓔ |
| | | |
| 22 Ⓐ Ⓑ Ⓒ Ⓓ Ⓔ | 29 Ⓐ Ⓑ Ⓒ Ⓓ Ⓔ | 36 Ⓐ Ⓑ Ⓒ Ⓓ Ⓔ |
| 23 Ⓐ Ⓑ Ⓒ Ⓓ Ⓔ | 30 Ⓐ Ⓑ Ⓒ Ⓓ Ⓔ | 37 Ⓐ Ⓑ Ⓒ Ⓓ Ⓔ |
| 24 Ⓐ Ⓑ Ⓒ Ⓓ Ⓔ | 31 Ⓐ Ⓑ Ⓒ Ⓓ Ⓔ | 38 Ⓐ Ⓑ Ⓒ Ⓓ Ⓔ |
| 25 Ⓐ Ⓑ Ⓒ Ⓓ Ⓔ | 32 Ⓐ Ⓑ Ⓒ Ⓓ Ⓔ | 39 Ⓐ Ⓑ Ⓒ Ⓓ Ⓔ |
| 26 Ⓐ Ⓑ Ⓒ Ⓓ Ⓔ | 33 Ⓐ Ⓑ Ⓒ Ⓓ Ⓔ | 40 Ⓐ Ⓑ Ⓒ Ⓓ Ⓔ |
| 27 Ⓐ Ⓑ Ⓒ Ⓓ Ⓔ | 34 Ⓐ Ⓑ Ⓒ Ⓓ Ⓔ | |
| 28 Ⓐ Ⓑ Ⓒ Ⓓ Ⓔ | 35 Ⓐ Ⓑ Ⓒ Ⓓ Ⓔ | |

# READING PRACTICE TEST 1

## 40 questions, 60 minutes

*Directions:* Each of the following passages is followed by a question and five answer choices. Answer every question based on what is stated directly or suggested in the preceding passage. You are not expected to have any prior knowledge of the information in the passages.

*Questions 1–3*

Invasive plants turn into landscape thugs by outcompeting the surrounding natives. In the mid-Atlantic region, they tend to put their leaves out earlier in the spring and lose them later in the fall than their native counterparts. This extended growth period gives them a significant advantage over the native species. In addition, these plants have no
(5)  natural enemy—neither insect nor disease—and quickly produce abundant offspring. Many invasive plants are unpalatable to deer and quickly take over where deer are abundant.

Before choosing a native plant alternative, first think about the characteristics of the invasive plant you are replacing. For example, with Japanese honeysuckle, you may
(10)  like the sweet fragrance or vining habit. So get rid of the honeysuckle and replant with fragrant summer bloomers like sweetbay magnolia (*Magnolia virginiana*), a tree, and add the summer-blooming leatherflower vine (*Clematis viorna*) if you like the vine habit. The new combination gives you everything you liked about the honeysuckle without its devastating weediness.

**1.** Which of the following BEST describes the organization of this passage?

(A) A series of organically linked events are arranged chronologically by season.
(B) A divisive scientific issue is explained and then shown to be invalid.
(C) A localized botanical problem is explicated, and its results are described.
(D) An important theory is described, and several examples are given.
(E) A challenging issue is explained, and a logical solution is suggested.

**2.** The BEST statement of the main idea of the first paragraph is

(A) each plant has a different use, so gardeners must make careful, informed choices before planting

(B) invasive plants have a foul taste because they are likely poisonous, so they are not attractive food for many insects

(C) invasive plants reproduce more quickly than many other types of plants, so they crowd out indigenous plants

(D) invasive plants that flourish in the mid-Atlantic area have longer growing seasons than many native plants

(E) some fast-growing plants, like early maturing people, can become bullies if left unchecked

**3.** *Invasive plants turn into landscape thugs by outcompeting the surrounding natives.* What assumption does the writer make in this statement?

(A) Invasive plants are inherently undesirable.

(B) Invasive plants usually cost far less than native plants.

(C) Some people are more like invasive plants than we realize.

(D) People can easily tell the difference between invasive plants and native plants.

(E) Attractive and easy-to-maintain landscaping improves the value of a home.

*Questions 4–5*

Many factors are associated with school success, persistence, and progress toward high school graduation or a college degree. These include student motivation and effort, the expectations and encouragement of others, learning opportunities, and financial assistance. Monitoring these factors in relation to the progress of different groups of
(5) students through the educational system and tracking their educational attainment are important to knowing how well we are doing as a nation in education.

4. According to this article, all of the following contribute to achievement in school EXCEPT

   (A) how much individual effort a student puts forth
   (B) a student's socioeconomic status and the funding available to him or her
   (C) how strongly others believe in the student's potential to succeed
   (D) how closely educational theorists scrutinize our students' achievement
   (E) what classes, field trips, and other educational experiences students are offered

5. This passage is primarily concerned with

   (A) promoting the critical importance of higher education to success in life
   (B) discussing different groups of students—both high and low achievers—in our great nation
   (C) criticizing ineffective administrators who do not track student progress sufficiently
   (D) analyzing why America has fallen behind other nations in educational achievement
   (E) arguing the importance of recording and analyzing many factors to determine educational progress

*Question 6*

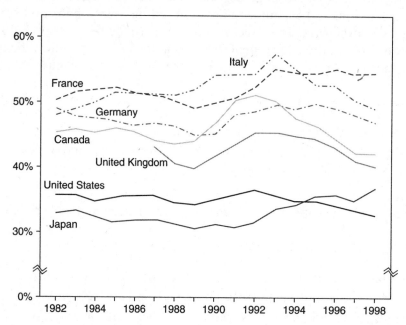

**Total Government Outlays as a Percentage of GDP**

Source: Organisation for Economic Co-operation and Development, calendar year data.

**6.** What does this chart show?

(A) All countries spend far more on their governments than is necessary to be efficient, thus governmental spending should be reduced.

(B) Canada and Germany have consistently spent a larger share of their gross domestic product (GDP) than France and Italy.

(C) The amount of GDP an industrialized country allocates depends on a wide variety of factors that remain relatively constant.

(D) Compared to six other industrialized nations, the United States allocated the largest share of its GDP to government spending in 1996–1998.

(E) Compared to six other industrialized nations, the United States allocated the smallest share of its GDP to government spending in 1996–1998.

*Questions 7–8*

Thirty-eight percent of U.S. voting-age citizens who had not completed high school voted in 2010, compared with 77 percent of those with a bachelor's degree or higher. Fifty percent of U.S. students in grade nine participated in a community-related volunteer organization in 2011, a higher percentage than in any of the 27 other
(5)   countries participating in the Civic Education Study.

7. Which of the following conclusions can you draw from this passage?

   (A) Voting in presidential elections is one of our most precious constitutional rights, so everyone should vote, especially in presidential elections.
   (B) Few children younger than grade nine participated in a community-related volunteer organization in 2011.
   (C) People who vote are more likely to volunteer for organizations in their local neighborhood.
   (D) The more education people have, the more likely they are to vote in presidential and congressional elections.
   (E) The less education people have, the more likely they are to vote in presidential and congressional elections.

8. This excerpt would most likely be published in a

   (A) pamphlet on voting given out at the polls
   (B) government web page for educators
   (C) math textbook for high school students
   (D) private blog published by a writer
   (E) newspaper editorial on the importance of voting

*Questions 9–11*

Spring is the time of year when many things change—including the weather. Temperatures can swing back and forth between balmy and frigid. Sunny days may be followed by a week of stormy weather. Sometimes extreme weather changes can occur even within the same day. Mark Twain once said, "In the spring I have counted 136 kinds
(5)   of weather inside of four and twenty hours."

Thunderstorms cause most of the severe spring weather. They can bring lightning, tornadoes, and flooding. Whenever warm, moist air collides with cool, dry air, thunderstorms can occur. For much of the world, this happens in spring and summer. Every thunderstorm produces lightning; in the United States, an average of 300 people are
(10)   injured and 80 people are killed each year by lightning.

Because spring weather is so unpredictable, you may be unprepared when severe conditions hit. This is especially important if you live in a region that does not often experience thunderstorms, tornadoes, or flooding. And when severe weather occurs unexpectedly, the risk of injury and death increases. So planning ahead makes sense;
(15)   prepare for storms, floods, and tornadoes as if you know in advance they are coming, because in the spring, they very likely will.

**9.** Why are people most likely to be caught unaware by severe weather in the spring?

(A) The weather often changes without warning.
(B) People rarely plan ahead, especially when the weather is nice.
(C) People don't read Mark Twain and other classic authors.
(D) People are too busy having fun to pay attention to the weather.
(E) Some locales rarely experience dramatic weather fluctuations.

**10.** Which sentence BEST states the main idea of the second paragraph?

(A) Thunderstorms cause most of the severe spring weather.
(B) They can bring lightning, tornadoes, and flooding.
(C) Whenever warm, moist air collides with cool, dry air, thunderstorms can occur.
(D) For much of the world, this happens in spring and summer.
(E) Every thunderstorm produces lightning; in the United States, an average of 300 people are injured and 80 people are killed each year by lightning.

**11.** Which of the following words, if substituted for the word *frigid* in line 2, would introduce the LEAST change in the meaning of the sentence?

(A) distant
(B) reserved
(C) glacial
(D) aloof
(E) repressed

*Questions 12–13*

The National Highway Traffic Safety Administration and the U.S. Environmental Protection Agency have jointly issued a final rule establishing new requirements for a fuel economy and environment label that will be posted on the window sticker of all new automobiles sold in the United States. The redesigned label provides expanded
(5)   information to American consumers about new vehicle fuel economy and consumption, greenhouse gas and smog-forming emissions, and projected fuel costs and savings; it also includes a smartphone interactive code that permits direct access to additional web resources.

**12.** The passage states that the new fuel labels

   (A)  require drivers to have a smartphone to operate the vehicle
   (B)  provide details about fuel usage and environmental concerns
   (C)  will make cars more affordable to the average person
   (D)  are more attractive and easier to use than the old labels
   (E)  will soon be used in Europe as well as in America

**13.** Which of the following is an unstated assumption made by the author of the passage?

   (A)  Consumers are familiar with the labels affixed to new cars.
   (B)  New automobiles are a better value than previously owned automobiles.
   (C)  Fuel cost and emissions are consumers' primary concerns when buying a car.
   (D)  It is easier to get around when you have a car and don't have to rely on public transportation.
   (E)  The National Highway Traffic Safety Administration and U.S. Environmental Protection Agency are the best groups to do this work.

*Questions 14–16*

A place created and planned as the seat of government; a young city that powerfully evokes the past; treasury of a nation's heritage; home to hundreds of thousands of people. The Mall's formal structures, ceremonial spaces, and carefully planned vistas have their roots in earlier European capitals designed to showcase autocratic regimes.

(5) But these are, in Walt Whitman's words, democratic vistas, where the American people can freely assemble to play, attend cultural events, or petition the government for change. In 1933, stewardship of the Mall area passed to the National Park Service, whose rangers will help you get the most out of your visit, whether you see the president's home, ascend the Washington Monument, or just relax and enjoy the beauty of our

(10) national green.

**14.** Which is the most logical conclusion you can draw from this passage?

(A) There is so much to see in Washington, DC, that visitors should allow at least a week to appreciate the city in all its splendor.

(B) Washington, DC, is the most beautiful capital of any nation because it was so carefully planned and designed.

(C) One of the highlights of spending time in the nation's capital is the fact that all of the sites are free and beautifully maintained by the National Park Service.

(D) The nation's capital can be seen from a number of perspectives, all of which are better understood after a visit to the National Mall area.

(E) More people travel to Washington, DC, than to any other national capital.

**15.** To evaluate the validity of the author's claim regarding the Mall's design (lines 3–4), it would be most helpful to know which of the following?

(A) How much it cost in today's dollars to design the Mall originally

(B) The European cities used as the basis for the design of Washington, DC

(C) Who ruled Europe when Washington, DC, was designed and built

(D) How many buildings are set on the Mall and in what order they were built

(E) The provenance of the stones and other materials used in the buildings

**16.** According to the passage, all of the following are elements of the Mall EXCEPT

(A) the Washington Monument

(B) beautiful lawns and other public spaces

(C) the seat of government

(D) autocratic regimes

(E) the White House

*Questions 17–19*

The territory is home to 21 missions, built during different epochs: San Diego, the first, was built in 1769; its distance from the Presidio, an army post of the same name, is two leagues. The rest were built successively, according to circumstances and necessity. Among the latter are San Juan Capistrano (1776), which is among the most famous; San

(5)  Miguel Arcangel (1797); and Santa Ines (1804). The last one was founded in 1822 under the name of San Francisco Dolores and is the most northern of all.

The edifices in some of these missions are more extensive than in others, but they are all nearly equal in form. They are all fabricated from mud bricks, and the divisions are according to necessity. In all of them may be found commodious habitations for

(10)  the ministers and storehouses to keep their goods in; proportional granaries; offices for soap-makers, weavers, and blacksmiths; large parterres and horse and cattle pens; independent apartments for Indian youths of each sex; and all such offices as were necessary at the time of its institution. Contiguous to and communicating with the former is a church, forming a part of the edifice of each mission; they are all very proportional and

(15)  are adorned with profusion.

17. Which of the following words, if substituted for the word *leagues* in line 3, would introduce the LEAST change to the meaning of the sentence?

(A) miles
(B) years
(C) leaders
(D) compacts
(E) associations

18. Which mission was built first?

(A) San Francisco Dolores
(B) The Presidio
(C) San Diego
(D) San Juan Capistrano
(E) San Miguel Arcangel

19. The missions are similar in all of the following ways EXCEPT they

(A) are all lavishly and richly decorated
(B) all have large rooms for holy men
(C) were all built of the same material
(D) were all erected around the same time
(E) all feature places for tradesmen to work

*Question 20*

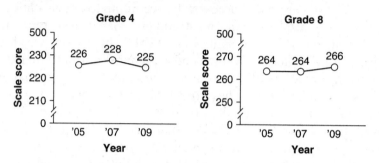

**Trend in Average Scores for Fourth- and Eighth-Grade AI/AN Students in NAEP Mathematics**

Source: U.S. Department of Education, Institute of Education Sciences, National Center for Education Statistics, National Assessment of Educational Progress (NAEP), 2005, 2007, and 2009 National Indian Education Studies.

20. Which conclusion about student performance is BEST supported by the data on the graphs shown?

(A) While the percentage of fourth-graders at or above the Proficient level of 220 in 2009 was not significantly different from the percentages in earlier assessments, the percentage of eighth-graders was higher in 2009 than in 2005.

(B) While the percentage of eighth-graders at or above the Proficient level of 260 in 2009 was not significantly different from the percentages in earlier assessments, the percentage of fourth-graders was higher in 2009 than in 2005.

(C) The percentage of fourth-graders at or above the Proficient level of 220 in 2009 was significantly different from the percentages in earlier assessments.

(D) Both charts show essentially the same information but in different formats, suggesting the assessment was not statistically valid.

(E) Students need greater support from their teachers to reach their full potential, so teacher salaries should increase.

*Questions 21–23*

According to legend, in 1776, George Washington commissioned Philadelphia seam-stress Betsy Ross to create a flag for the new nation. Historical scholars debate this legend but agree that Mrs. Ross most likely knew Washington and sewed flags. To date, there have been 27 official versions of the flag, but the arrangement of the stars varied
(5) according to the flag-makers' preferences until 1912, when President Taft standardized the then-new flag's 48 stars into six rows of eight. The 49-star flag (1959–1960), as well as the 50-star flag, also have standardized star patterns. The current version of the flag dates to July 4, 1960, after Hawaii became the fiftieth state on August 21, 1959.

**21.** Which is the most logical conclusion you can draw from this passage?

(A) Scholars agree that Betsy Ross, a Philadelphia seamstress, sewed our first flag.
(B) All countries need a flag to embody their values and help them achieve their goals.
(C) The United States has had 27 official versions of its flag.
(D) It was difficult to create the American flag because it carries such significance.
(E) No one is absolutely certain who created the first American flag.

**22.** How were the stars arranged on the American flag prior to 1912?

(A) The stars were arrayed in 27 specific patterns.
(B) Their arrangement was both arbitrary and random.
(C) The 48 stars were lined up in six rows of eight.
(D) They were arrayed in a star pattern.
(E) The stars were lined up in eight rows of six.

**23.** The next paragraph of this passage will most likely

(A) trace Betsy Ross's lineage, focusing on her relationship to George Washington
(B) predict how America's flag will change in the coming decades
(C) compare and contrast America's flag to the flags of other countries
(D) discuss the creation of other American symbols, such as the Liberty Bell
(E) argue that the flag we have today is a direct result of bipartisan collaboration

*Questions 24–26*

Not long after Jupiter formed, it got pulled slowly toward the sun, carried on currents of swirling gas. Saturn also got pulled in, and when the two giant planets came close enough to each other, their fates became linked. Their sun-bound death spiral came to a halt when Jupiter was about where Mars is now, then the pair turned and moved away
(5)  from the sun. The researchers who developed this model of the early solar system call it the Grand Tack, a reference to a sailing maneuver. Over the aeons, the giant planet roamed toward the center of the solar system and back out again. Jupiter's travels profoundly influenced the solar system, changing the nature of the asteroid belt and making Mars smaller than it should have been.

24. Which is the BEST statement of the main idea of this passage?

(A) The sun affects the paths of different planets, which is why the sun is the center of our solar system.
(B) The death struggles of large planets, such as Jupiter and Saturn, are highly dramatic events in the Grand Tack.
(C) The arrangement of the planets was significantly affected by Jupiter's movements early in the formation of the solar system.
(D) Scientists have hypothesized that, because of the way the solar system was formed, Mars is not as large as it should have been.
(E) When the solar system was formed, Jupiter was pulled toward the sun on waves of spinning gases.

25. Which of the following, if substituted for the word *Tack* in line 6, would introduce the LEAST change in the meaning of the sentence?

(A) turn
(B) fastener
(C) nail
(D) boat
(E) tactic

26. To evaluate the validity of the author's description of the solar system, it would be helpful to know which of the following?

(A) what Jupiter and Saturn look like today as compared to their appearances in the past
(B) whether other planets followed the same pattern as Jupiter and Saturn
(C) who postulated the Grand Tack theory and the academic credentials of these people
(D) the specific link between sailing and the formation of the solar system
(E) how all of the planets were formed

*Questions 27–30*

Like a bolt of lightning out of a darkening sky, war burst upon the American landscape in the spring of 1861, climaxing decades of bitter wrangling and pitting two vast sections of a young and vigorous nation against each other. Northerners called it the War of the Rebellion; Southerners, the War between the States. We know it simply as the Civil
(5) War.

In the east, beginning in the spring of 1861, the cry from Union headquarters was "On to Richmond!" For the next four years, a succession of Northern commanders struggled desperately to do just that—get to Richmond. One well-designed effort in 1862
(10) used the mammoth naval might of the Union to reach the vicinity of the Confederate capital by water routes. The other attempts stubbornly slogged across a narrow central Virginia corridor and sought to disperse tenacious Southern defenders who seemed always to be athwart the path. Confederate successes offered occasional opportunities to take the war north into Maryland and Pennsylvania and to threaten Washington.
(15) Both sides came to see the enemy army as the proper goal, and both recognized the obligation of the enemy army to defend its respective capital city against military threats. The consequence was four years of war fought to the death, mostly in a relatively small strip of Virginia countryside between Washington and Richmond.

When the guns were finally silenced in the spring and early summer of 1865 and the authority of the federal government was once again restored, the Union had been per-
(20) manently scarred. As Mark Twain put it, the war had "uprooted institutions that were centuries old, . . . transformed the social life of half the country, and wrought so profoundly upon the entire national character that the influence cannot be measured short of two or three generations."

**27.** *Northerners called it the War of the Rebellion; Southerners, the War between the States. We know it simply as the Civil War.* What conclusion can you draw from these two sentences from the passage?

(A) It is important to have a consistent name for key historical events so people do not get confused.

(B) Northerners and Southerners viewed the Civil War in a very different light.

(C) The Civil War had many different causes and effects, including economic differences between the North and South.

(D) The Southerners rebelled by seceding from the Union, and many states were involved in the brutal war.

(E) Wars may have different names while they are still being fought, reflecting the confusion of battles.

28. Based on this passage, the writer would be LEAST likely to agree with which of the following statements about the Civil War?

    (A) The South likely could have triumphed over the North had they been willing to fight outside their comfort zone between Washington and Richmond.
    (B) Despite many forewarnings of war, people were still taken by surprise when the Civil War erupted in 1861.
    (C) From the start of the war, the Union was determined to seize Richmond because it was the Confederate capital; thus its seizure would be a major blow to the South.
    (D) Although divided by their beliefs, the Confederate and Union sides were similar in their military strategy.
    (E) The Civil War was a grueling conflict that took many lives and left lasting wounds on the American psyche.

29. The word *mammoth* in line 10 most nearly means

    (A) successful
    (B) animalistic
    (C) mammoth
    (D) wooly
    (E) colossal

30. According to the passage, the Civil War changed America in all of the following ways EXCEPT

    (A) overturning social customs that had spanned many years
    (B) changing the way people interacted in their leisure time
    (C) leading to the invention of successful new weapons
    (D) altering America's identity in a way that would not be understood for decades
    (E) leaving the country with damage that would never heal

*Questions 31–34*

"Slamming" occurs when a phone company illegally switches your phone service without your permission. If you notice a different company name on your bill or see phone charges that are higher than normal, take action:

(5)
- Contact the company that slammed you and ask to be switched back to your original company. Tell the company that you are exercising your right to refuse to pay any charges.
- Report the problem to your original company and ask to be enrolled in your previous calling plan. If you are unable to resolve your complaint, contact the Federal Communications Commission (FCC).

(10)    "Cramming" occurs when companies add charges to your telephone bill without your permission. These charges may be for services such as voice mail, ringtones, or club memberships. You may not notice these monthly charges because they are relatively small—$5 to $30—and look like your regular phone charges.

1. **Block changes to your phone service.** Ask your telephone service provider if it
(15)    offers a blocking service, which usually requires the company to notify you before making any changes to your service.
2. **Read the fine print on contest entry forms and coupons.** You could be agreeing to switch your phone service or buy optional services.
3. **Watch out for impostors.** Companies could falsely claim to be your regular phone
(20)    company and offer some type of discount plan or change in billing. They might also say they are taking a survey or pretend to be a government agency.
4. **Beware of "negative option notices."** You can be switched or signed up for optional services unless you say no to telemarketers.
5. **Examine your telephone bill carefully.** Check the pages that show the details, and
(25)    look for suspicious charges.

**31.** This passage is primarily concerned with

(A) instructing consumers about how to report problems with their phone companies
(B) educating consumers about unethical and illegal phone charges
(C) persuading readers to use telephone blocking services
(D) making sure that consumers pay careful attention to contest forms
(E) being sure that consumers watch for optional service tricks

**32.** Which would be the BEST subtitle for the numbered list?

(A) Find Out About Special Services
(B) Beware of Tricks!
(C) Read All Bills Carefully and Completely
(D) Problems with Internet and Phone Providers
(E) Take These Steps to Avoid Slammers and Crammers

**33.** Which of the following unstated assumptions does the author make?

(A) Savvy and assertive consumers can solve problems with telephone scams on their own.

(B) If consumers do not examine their phone bills, they are certain to be victims of scams.

(C) Other service providers, such as utility companies, also engage in unethical practices.

(D) Telephone scams are a relatively new problem, so consumers are unaware of them.

(E) Telephone companies are inadequately regulated and require more government intervention.

**34.** Which of the following phrases, if substituted for the word *impostors* in line 19, would introduce the LEAST change in the meaning of the sentence?

(A) survey organizations

(B) frauds and thieves

(C) government agencies

(D) discount plans

(E) your usual phone company

*Questions 35–36*

Consider a couple looking to purchase their first home. Let's say they want a 30-year mortgage loan and their FICO credit scores are 720. They could qualify for a mortgage with a low 5.5 percent interest rate.* But if their scores are 580, they would probably pay 8.5 percent* or more—that's at least 3 full percentage points more in interest. On

(5)  a $100,000 mortgage loan, that 3-point difference will cost them $2,400 dollars a year, adding up to $72,000 dollars more over the loan's 30-year lifetime.

35. What is the most logical conclusion you can draw from this passage?

(A)  Your credit scores can have a significant influence on your buying power.
(B)  People should buy homes because they are wise economic investments.
(C)  The total cost of a mortgage involves points as well as the actual interest rate.
(D)  People with a poor credit score are usually unable to secure a mortgage.
(E)  The credit scoring agency FICO is a powerful governmental entity.

36. Which of the following BEST describes the organization of this passage?

(A)  A problematic issue is raised, and a partial solution is provided.
(B)  A series of interrelated events are arranged in chronological order.
(C)  A common problem is described, and two examples are provided.
(D)  A thesis is advanced and then supported by a specific example.
(E)  A significant issue is explained, and a logical solution is suggested.

---

*Interest rates are subject to change. These rates were offered by lenders in 2011.

*Questions 37–40*

The following table illustrates total fat, saturated fat, trans fat, and cholesterol content per serving for selected food products.

**Total Fat, Saturated Fat, Trans Fat, and Cholesterol Content Per Serving**

| Product | Common Serving Size | Total Fat (g) | Sat. Fat (g) | DV for Sat. Fat | Trans Fat (g) | Combined Sat. and Trans Fat (g) | Chol. (mg) | DV for Chol. |
|---|---|---|---|---|---|---|---|---|
| French fried potatoes (fast food) | Medium (147 g) | 27 | 7 | 35% | 8 | 15 | 0 | 0% |
| Butter | 1 tbsp | 11 | 7 | 35% | 0 | 7 | 30 | 10% |
| Margarine, stick | 1 tbsp | 11 | 2 | 10% | 3 | 5 | 0 | 0% |
| Margarine, tub | 1 tbsp | 7 | 1 | 5% | 0.5 | 1.5 | 0 | 0% |
| Mayonnaise (soybean oil) | 1 tbsp | 11 | 1.5 | 8% | 0 | 1.5 | 5 | 2% |
| Shortening | 1 tbsp | 13 | 3.5 | 18% | 4 | 7.5 | 0 | 0% |
| Potato chips | Small bag (42.5 g) | 11 | 2 | 10% | 3 | 5 | 0 | 0% |
| Milk, whole | 1 cup | 7 | 4.5 | 23% | 0 | 4.5 | 35 | 12% |
| Milk, skim | 1 cup | 0 | 0 | 0% | 0 | 0 | 5 | 2% |
| Doughnut | 1 | 18 | 4.5 | 23% | 5 | 9.5 | 25 | 8% |
| Cookies (cream filled) | 3 (30 g) | 6 | 1 | 5% | 2 | 3 | 0 | 0% |
| Candy bar | 1 (40 g) | 10 | 4 | 20% | 3 | 7 | < 5 | 1% |
| Cake, pound | 1 slice (80 g) | 16 | 3.5 | 18% | 4.5 | 8 | 0 | 0% |

Sat. = saturated; DV = daily value; Chol. = cholesterol.

**37.** Which two foods have the same amount of saturated and trans fat per serving?

(A) shortening and a slice of pound cake
(B) butter and margarine
(C) a candy bar and butter
(D) mayonnaise and potato chips
(E) whole milk and a donut

**38.** Which food has the greatest amount of fat per serving?

(A) shortening
(B) potato chips
(C) butter
(D) a donut
(E) French fries

**39.** What is the most valid assumption you can make, based on the information in this chart?

(A) Most people eat far too many fattening foods, which can be very deleterious to their long-term health outlook.
(B) It is not always obvious which foods contain trans fat, since most people would expect butter, mayonnaise, and milk to contain it.
(C) Scientific evidence shows that consumption of saturated fat, trans fat, and dietary cholesterol raises low-density lipoprotein (LDL), or "bad" cholesterol levels, which increases the risk of coronary heart disease (CHD).
(D) There is no way to avoid trans fat, since it is in virtually everything we eat.
(E) Don't assume similar products are the same. Be sure to check the nutrition facts panel on packaged food, because even similar foods can vary in calories, ingredients, nutrients, and the size and number of servings in a package.

**40.** This chart is primarily concerned with

(A) educating consumers about dietary choices
(B) arguing for cheaper and more healthful natural foods
(C) criticizing consumers for making poor food choices
(D) condemning processed food manufacturers
(E) analyzing American food habits

# STOP. This is the end of Reading Practice Test 1.

# READING PRACTICE TEST 1: ANSWERS

**1. E** The author states a challenging issue, the problems posed by invasive plants that crowd out all competition in a garden or other outdoor setting. The issue is stated in the first sentence of the first paragraph: *Invasive plants turn into landscape thugs by outcompeting the surrounding natives.* Then the author proposes a solution: first analyze the invasive plant and then choose replacement plants that have its positive but not its negative qualities. The solution is stated in the first sentence of the second paragraph: *Before choosing a native plant alternative, first think about the characteristics of the invasive plant you are replacing.*

Choice A is incorrect because the passage is not arranged in time order; do not be misled because planting occurs in seasons. Choice B is incorrect because the author does not discuss a "divisive scientific issue"; this discussion of invasive plants has only one side, and no one is arguing in favor of these plants. Choice C is wrong because it is only partly correct. The first paragraph states the problem and results, but the second paragraph proposes a solution. Finally, choice D is incorrect because the author's thesis is fact, not theory. Again, this answer disregards the information in the second paragraph.

> **Test Hint:** To find the organization in a passage quickly in a timed test, look for the topic sentences, as illustrated in this explanation. The topic sentence will most often be the first sentence in each paragraph. Since the topic sentences state the main ideas, they will help you identify the organization.

**2. C** The answer is directly stated in this sentence: *Invasive plants turn into landscape thugs by outcompeting the surrounding natives.* Choice A is wrong because it concerns information in the second paragraph, not the first. Choice B indicates a misreading, as the last sentence of the first paragraph states, *Many invasive plants are unpalatable to deer and quickly take over where deer are abundant.* Deer are not insects. Choice D is a detail, not the main idea. Choice E also indicates a misreading of the information; the author is comparing invasive plants to thugs to show that these plants crowd out others, but this has nothing to do with people bullying others.

> **Test Hint:** The main idea may be stated outright or implied in a passage. If it is implied, you will need to figure it out from clues in the passage. To save time, always start by looking for a stated main idea. In many cases, the first sentence will state the main idea of the entire passage. If you cannot find the main idea in the first sentence, check the last one, as the conclusion often restates it.

**3. A**    By comparing the plants to thugs (bullies), the author conveys the assumption or opinion that these plants are less valuable than many other native plants. The information in choice B is true, but it is not based on the statement provided, so it cannot be the correct answer. The same is true of choice E. Choice C takes the analogy too far and thus is not valid. The information in choice D cannot be determined by the information in the statement, as native plants and invasive plants may not be easily distinguished from each other.

**4. D**    The word *except* in the question stem tells you that you are looking for the exception, a factor that is *not* listed in the passage. Every choice but D can be found in the passage. Choice D, the last sentence in the passage, is not a factor in student success. Rather, it states the importance of tracking students' progress so we know how well we are doing as a nation to educate our students.

**Test Hint:** When you see the words *except, but,* or *not including* in the question stem, you can tell that the item requires you to find the exception to the rule, the one choice that is not included in the set. In these instances, use the process of elimination. Skim the passage and the answer choices. Find each choice in the passage. The one you cannot find will be the correct answer.

**5. E**    The main idea is directly stated in the last line of the passage: *Monitoring these factors in relation to the progress of different groups of students through the educational system and tracking their educational attainment are important to knowing how well we are doing as a nation in education.* Choice A is likely a true statement, but it is not primarily concerned with the content of the passage. Actually, it is not even in the passage! Choice B is too vague, as it presents empty political rhetoric rather than meaningful content that links to the passage. Choice C takes the last line too far, as the author does not criticize anyone. Choice D is wrong because the author is not making a comparison—no other nation is mentioned in the passage.

**Test Hint:** The phrase "primarily concerned with" tells you that this is a main idea question. These questions can also be phrased as "The main idea of this passage is. . . ."

**6. E**    The dip in the line from 1996 to 1998 shows that choice E is true: compared to six other industrialized nations, the United States allocated the smallest share of its GDP to government spending during that time. Choice A is incorrect because it is an opinion not shown by the data in the chart. Choices B and D state the opposite of what the data show. Choice C may be true but cannot be determined from the data in this chart.

**Test Hint:** If you are not a visual learner, summarize the information you see on a chart or other visual representation in a sentence. This will help you make sure that you understand what the chart shows.

**7. D** You can draw this conclusion from the information in the first sentence: *Thirty-eight percent of U.S. voting-age citizens who had not completed high school voted in 2010, compared with 77 percent of those with a bachelor's degree or higher.* Choice A is an opinion not supported by the information in the passage, although many people will agree with it. Be sure to base your answers *only* on the information in the passage, not on your personal beliefs or prevailing wisdom. Choice B cannot be determined by the information in the passage. Choice C links unrelated information: the two sets of facts are presented together in the passage, but they are not related to each other. Choice E reverses the information given.

**8. B** Choice A is incorrect because voters would not need this information, nor would they be likely to read it at the polls. Choice C is unlikely because the passage does not contain a math problem to be solved. Choice D is vague and has insufficient information to enable you to draw a conclusion. Choice E is wrong because it misses the main point. The article doesn't argue that people should vote; rather, it presents the link between voting and education.

**9. A** This information is directly stated in the following sentence: *Because spring weather is so unpredictable, you may be unprepared when severe conditions hit.* None of the other choices is related to the information in the passage.

**Test Hint:** Base your answer on the information in the passage. Even if an answer choice contains valid information, if the information cannot be found in the passage, the answer is wrong.

**10. A** Only choice A states the main idea. Remember that the main idea is the overarching thesis, the author's primary point. Details are small pieces of information that support the main idea. All the other choices are details, not the main idea.

**11. C** *Frigid* has several meanings, so it is important to examine context clues as you make your choice. If the temperature is swinging "back and forth between balmy and frigid" as the passage states, you are looking for a word that is the opposite of *balmy*, which means "warm and mild." Only choice C, *glacial*, fits the context.

**Test Hint:** When a vocabulary word has multiple meanings, plug each choice into the sentence to see if it makes sense. Remember to choose the meaning that makes the most logical sense in context.

**12. B**   This is a recall question, so you can look back at the passage to find the information you need. Indeed, the answer is directly stated in the first sentence: *The National Highway Traffic Safety Administration and the U.S. Environmental Protection Agency have jointly issued a final rule establishing new requirements for a fuel economy and environment label that will be posted on the window sticker of all new automobiles sold in the United States.*

Choice A is wrong because a smartphone is not required; rather, having one allows the consumer to access additional information. Choice C is incorrect because it takes the information in the passage too far: the new labels *do* have more information, but that does not make the cars cost less. Indeed, the opposite might be true, as the new labels may raise the price of the cars if the manufacturers pass on the cost of the new design to the consumer. Choice D is wrong because the passage does not describe the label's appearance, only its content. There is no support in the passage for choice E.

**13. A**   This choice is the most logical conclusion because the author does not describe the labels, assuming that readers know what they look like. Choices B and C are not supported by the information in the passage. Choice D may be true but has nothing to do with the passage. There is no information in the passage that would point to choice E.

**14. D**   When you reach a conclusion, you combine all the details the author provides to make an inference or unstated summary. Here, you would combine all the details about the Washington, DC, Mall area provided in the passage. Choices A and C contain valid information but not as presented in the passage. Do not be misled by the word *freely*. Remember to base your answers only on the information in the passage. Choices B and E are not valid conclusions based on the passage, as other capitals are not described.

**15. B**   Knowing what the European cities looked like would best help you assess the author's claim: *The Mall's formal structures, ceremonial spaces, and carefully planned vistas have their roots in earlier European capitals designed to showcase autocratic regimes.* The cost (choice A) is irrelevant, as we are dealing with appearance. Knowing the rulers (choice C) could help you assess their tastes, but this leads to choice B, which is an easier and more effective method. The number of buildings (choice D) and where the stones came from (choice E) are irrelevant to the author's claim.

**16. D**   Remember that here, you are looking for the exception, a factor that is *not* listed in the passage. Every choice but D can be found in the passage. Choices A and C are stated directly. Choice B is a restatement of "carefully planned vistas." Choice E is stated in the passage as "the president's home." Thus, using the process of elimination, only choice D is valid.

**17. A**   *League* has several different meanings: it can refer to a group, an agreement between people to further common interests or to help each other, or a measurement of distance. The context clue *distance* in the first sentence helps you figure out that *leagues* has the last meaning in this passage. Here is the clue: *. . . the first, was built in 1769; its distance from the Presidio, an army post of the same name, is two leagues.*

**18. C**  This is a recall question, and the answer can be found in the opening sentence: *The territory is home to 21 missions, built during different epochs: San Diego, the first, was built in 1769. . . .* You can immediately eliminate choice B, the Presidio, because it is a fort, not a mission.

> **Test Hint:** If one answer choice is clearly and obviously wrong, eliminate it first. Any answer choice that you can eliminate dramatically increases your chances of getting the question right.

**19. D**  This is also a recall question; the answers are directly stated in the second paragraph. Here, you are looking for the exception, a factor that is *not* listed in the passage. Every choice but D can be found in the passage.

**20. A**  You can conclude that choice A is correct because the data for grade four varied little from 2005 to 2009, from 226 to 228 to 225. However, the data for eighth-graders shows an increase in 2009, from 264 to 266. Choice B reverses the information shown on the chart. Choice C is wrong because the percentage of fourth-graders at or above the Proficient level of 220 in 2009 was *not* significantly different from the percentages in earlier assessments. Choice D is wrong because both charts do not show the same information. Further, the validity of the assessment cannot be determined from the charts: the first chart shows the results of testing fourth-graders while the second chart shows the results of testing eighth-graders. Finally, choice E cannot be deduced from the information on the charts, even though some people may believe it is true. Remember to base your conclusions on the information in the passage or on the visuals, not on your prior knowledge.

**21. E**  You can reach this conclusion from the phrases "According to legend" and "scholars debate this legend." According to the passage, most historical scholars believe that Betsy Ross was acquainted with George Washington and that she sewed flags, but the repeated word *legend* emphasizes that no one is completely certain that she was actually the first flag's seamstress. This negates choice A. Choice B extends the information too far, as the passage discusses only America's flag. Choice C is wrong because it is a direct statement, not a conclusion. To draw conclusions, "read between the lines" by using clues in a passage to make inferences. Choice D is not supported by the information in the passage, as no information is given about the difficulty of designing or sewing the flag.

> **Test Hint:** As you draw conclusions, look for key words that state important information. These will most often be nouns and verbs rather than adjectives, adverbs, prepositions, and so on. Look especially for repeated words, as authors include these to emphasize key points in the passage.

**22. B**    This is a recall question, as the information is directly stated in the following sentence from the passage: *To date, there have been 27 official versions of the flag, but the arrangement of the stars varied according to the flag-makers' preferences until 1912, when President Taft standardized the then-new flag's 48 stars into six rows of eight.* Choice A is a misreading of the line *To date, there have been 27 official versions of the flag*, as this does not refer to the way the stars were arranged before 1912. Choice C refers to their arrangement after 1912, not before. Choice D is a misreading of the passage. Choice E switches the numbers, using the post-1912 arrangement.

**23. D**    Since the entire paragraph discusses one of our most powerful national symbols, we can assume that the next paragraph will explore another national symbol, such as the Liberty Bell. Choice A is wrong because Betsy Ross is mentioned only briefly. Since she is not the focus of the passage, it would not make sense to focus on her history in the subsequent paragraph. Choice B seems unlikely because the passage does not include any mention of the flag continuing to evolve. Choice C is not logical because the passage describes only America's flag. Finally, choice E doesn't make sense because the author does not bring political allegiance into the discussion.

**24. C**    This is the best statement of the main idea because it most closely reiterates the author's main point as stated in the following sentence from the passage: *Jupiter's travels profoundly influenced the solar system, changing the nature of the asteroid belt and making Mars smaller than it should have been.* Choices A and B are misstatements of ideas in the passage; choices D and E are minor details, not main ideas.

> **Test Hint:** While the topic sentence usually appears as the first or last sentence in a passage, it can appear anyplace.

**25. A**    *Tack* has more than one meaning, so you have to use context clues to see how it is used here. You can figure out that *tack* must be used to mean "turn" from the clue *the pair turned and moved away from the sun.*

> **Test Hint:** Don't be intimidated by long, difficult words in a passage. Identify the story's critical terms, the words that are necessary to figure out the author's message. You can often ignore other large words that have little impact on meaning.

**26. C**    This question requires you to make an evaluation, or a judgment. Since the theory in this passage is radical, it would be most useful to know who created it and what specific credentials they have. The other information would not help you judge the truthfulness of the author's hypothesis.

**27. B** As stated in the prompt, this question requires you to draw a conclusion, so you can use the process of elimination to cross out answers that are not conclusions. Start by eliminating choice A, which is not a conclusion; rather, it is an opinion. In the same way, choices C and D are not conclusions. Both are statements of historically valid information that have nothing to do with the statements that people on opposing sides called the war by different names. This leaves choices B and E. Choice B is correct because the difference in names reveals how each side viewed the conflict, showing their bias. Choice E is a conclusion, but it is incorrect because it does not address this specific war and the difference in viewpoints the names reveal.

**28. A** Choice A is the correct answer since the writer would be least likely to agree with it, as there is no textual proof in the passage to support it. You can deduce that the author would agree with choice B from the first sentence: *Like a bolt of lightning out of a darkening sky, war burst upon the American landscape in the spring of 1861, climaxing decades of bitter wrangling and pitting two vast sections of a young and vigorous nation against each other.* The phrases "darkening sky" and "climaxing decades of bitter wrangling" foreshadow the war; the "bolt of lightning" suggests that people were still shocked when active hostilities broke out. Similarly, you can conclude that the author would agree with choice C from the clues *. . . beginning in the spring of 1861 . . . 'On to Richmond!'* and *. . . a succession of Northern commanders struggled desperately to do just that—get to Richmond . . . the Confederate capital.* You can deduce that the author would agree with choice D from the sentence: *Both sides came to see the enemy army as the proper goal, and both recognized the obligation of the enemy army to defend its respective capital city against military threats.* Likewise, the author would agree with choice E because of the phrase "four years of war fought to the death."

**29. E** Since *mammoth* has multiple meanings, you must use context clues to determine how the word is used here. You can deduce that, in this sentence, it means "colossal" from the clue "naval might."

**30. C** The passage does *not* say that the Civil War resulted in the invention of successful new weapons, although this may be true. Remember to base your answers on the information in the passage only. The final sentence shows that choices A, B, D, and E resulted from the war. The sentence reads: *As Mark Twain put it, the war had "uprooted institutions that were centuries old, . . . transformed the social life of half the country, and wrought so profoundly upon the entire national character that the influence cannot be measured short of two or three generations."*

**31. B** This is a main-idea question. You can figure this out from the phrase "primarily concerned with" in the question stem. The main idea is directly stated in the first sentence of the first paragraph (*"Slamming" occurs when a phone company illegally switches your phone service without your permission.*) and the first sentence of the second paragraph (*"Cramming" occurs when companies add charges to your telephone bill without your permission.*). The other choices are all details.

**32. E** This is a drawing-a-conclusion question. You can reach this conclusion by combining all the details in this part of the passage. Choices A, B, and C omit the main ideas. Choice D is off the topic.

**33. E**    This is a drawing-a-conclusion question, which you can tell from the phrase "unstated assumptions" in the question stem. You can reach this conclusion based on the fact that the entire passage provides suggestions for avoiding illegal and unethical telephone scams. If the industry were more vigorously regulated, the author would not have to provide these warnings. Choice A cannot be correct because the author tells readers, *If you are unable to resolve your complaint, contact the Federal Communications Commission (FCC).* Choice B overstates the case, because its tone is too extreme for the author's professional approach to the topic. Choice C is only a minor detail in the numbered list, so it is too slight to function as the title of the entire list. Finally, choice D is incorrect because the list doesn't describe problems with Internet and phone providers. Rather, it lists ways to deal with these problems.

**Test Hint:** Finding the title of an entire passage or the subtitle of one paragraph in a passage is simply a main idea question in another form. To answer this type of question, combine all the details in the passage to write your own topic sentence. Then find the choice that best matches what you've written.

**34. B**    You can figure this out from the clues "falsely claim" and "pretend to be a government agency."

**35. A**    You can reach this conclusion from the examples cited, as the lower credit score results in significantly higher interest rates. Choice B may or may not be true, but the passage offers no proof of its validity. Choice C is directly stated, so it is not a conclusion. Choice D is wrong because the passage shows that people with a poor credit rating can often secure a mortgage, but they pay more for it. Finally, choice E is incorrect because the passage does not say that FICO is a government agency. Base your responses only on the information in the passage.

**36. D**    The author begins with the unstated thesis that a FICO score has a significant influence on a person's mortgage rates and then develops the thesis with a specific example that shows how a low credit rating results in a higher mortgage interest rate. There is no support for any of the other choices.

**37. C**    This is a recall question, so return to the passage (a chart, in this instance) to find the information. Both a candy bar and butter have 7 grams of saturated and trans fat per serving. This information can be found in the seventh column. None of the sets of food items in the other choices have the same amount of saturated and trans fat per serving.

**38. E**    As with the previous question, this one involves recall of the information given in the chart. French fries have 27 grams of fat. Every other food on the chart has less.

**Test Hint:** There is no penalty for guessing on the Praxis. Try not to guess randomly, but don't leave any answer choice blank.

**39. B** This is the most logical assumption you can make because butter, mayonnaise, and milk all contain fat, but not trans fat, according to the chart. Putting this information together, you can conclude that many people would expect these foods to contain trans fat. Choice A cannot be supported by the information given in the chart, although it may be true. The same is true of choices C and E. Finally, choice D is not logical, because the chart shows that people *can* avoid trans fat if they eat carefully. Remember to base your response on the information given in the passage or the visual, not on information you may already know.

**40. A** The chart shows consumers the amount of different fats in their foods, so it serves to educate them. Choices B, C, and D overstate the case. Choice E is too general and thus not correct; the chart focuses on only one type of nutrient.

## Skills Spread

| | Item Numbers |
|---|---|
| Literal (18) | 2, 4, 6, 9, 10, 12, 16, 18, 19, 20, 22, 24, 25, 29, 30, 31, 37, 38 |
| Inferential (22) | 1, 3, 5, 7, 8, 11, 13, 14, 15, 17, 21, 23, 26, 27, 28, 32, 33, 34, 35, 36, 39, 40 |

# WRITING PRACTICE TEST 1

## Answer sheet

1 (A) (B) (C) (D) (E)
2 (A) (B) (C) (D) (E)
3 (A) (B) (C) (D) (E)
4 (A) (B) (C) (D) (E)
5 (A) (B) (C) (D) (E)
6 (A) (B) (C) (D) (E)
7 (A) (B) (C) (D) (E)

8 (A) (B) (C) (D) (E)
9 (A) (B) (C) (D) (E)
10 (A) (B) (C) (D) (E)
11 (A) (B) (C) (D) (E)
12 (A) (B) (C) (D) (E)
13 (A) (B) (C) (D) (E)
14 (A) (B) (C) (D) (E)

15 (A) (B) (C) (D) (E)
16 (A) (B) (C) (D) (E)
17 (A) (B) (C) (D) (E)
18 (A) (B) (C) (D) (E)
19 (A) (B) (C) (D) (E)
20 (A) (B) (C) (D) (E)
21 (A) (B) (C) (D) (E)

22 (A) (B) (C) (D) (E)
23 (A) (B) (C) (D) (E)
24 (A) (B) (C) (D) (E)
25 (A) (B) (C) (D) (E)
26 (A) (B) (C) (D) (E)
27 (A) (B) (C) (D) (E)
28 (A) (B) (C) (D) (E)

29 (A) (B) (C) (D) (E)
30 (A) (B) (C) (D) (E)
31 (A) (B) (C) (D) (E)
32 (A) (B) (C) (D) (E)
33 (A) (B) (C) (D) (E)
34 (A) (B) (C) (D) (E)
35 (A) (B) (C) (D) (E)

36 (A) (B) (C) (D) (E)
37 (A) (B) (C) (D) (E)
38 (A) (B) (C) (D) (E)

# WRITING PRACTICE TEST 1

## SECTION 1: MULTIPLE-CHOICE QUESTIONS

## 38 questions, 30 minutes

*Directions:* The following sentences require you to identify errors in grammar, usage, punctuation, and capitalization. Not every sentence has an error, and no sentence will have more than one. Every sentence error, if there is one, is underlined and lettered. If the sentence does have an error, select the one underlined part that must be changed to make the sentence correct and blacken the corresponding circle on your answer sheet. If the sentence does not have an error, blacken circle E. Elements of the sentence that are not underlined are not to be changed.

*Part A*
*21 questions*

Suggested time: 10 minutes

1. As a special treat, my uncle served waffles to the guests on a silver platter. No error.
   A          B                    C              D              E

2. A core curriculum helps prepare college students to become better-functioning
                        A
   adults, as classes such as Introduction to Psychology and Economics I provide students
        B                              C
   with some basic tools for dealing with people and to resolve financial matters. No error.
                                                         D                      E

3. Just as parents teaching their children to protect themselves outside the home by not
                    A                      B
   speaking to strangers and so on, parents should teach their children how to protect
                              C
   themselves online by avoiding chat rooms and never giving out personal information
                       D
   on social networking sites. No error.
                              E

4. Through the Fair Labor Standards Act, the U.S. Department of Labor establishes the
           A                                                              B
   minimum wage that private and governmental employers can pay their workers, this is
                                                                              C
   the lowest legal wage that employers can pay their workers. No error.
           D                                                    E

**5.** The <u>delicious desserts</u> of AnneMarie Proto <u>has earned</u> high praise, <u>not only</u> from
          A                                 B              C
well-respected food reviewers, <u>but also from</u> people who appreciate fine food the world
                                    D
over. <u>No error.</u>
        E

**6.** In Michigan, driving without a seat belt is a primary offense, which means <u>if you're</u>
        A                                                                         B
seen without a seat belt on, <u>one</u> can be <u>pulled over and fined.</u> <u>No error.</u>
                                  C                      D            E

**7.** <u>After documenting</u> the significant <u>advantages of decreased employee turnover,</u>
             A                                     B
absenteeism, and lateness, <u>on-site child care</u> is being provided more frequently as a
                                    C
bonus <u>for working parents.</u> <u>No error.</u>
                D             E

**8.** The toddlers are fond of apple slices and <u>eating cookies</u> , but their babysitters
                                            A   B
<u>are</u> unwilling to give the children snacks <u>between meals.</u> <u>No error.</u>
    C                                          D            E

**9.** On the morning of <u>December 7, 1941,</u> one of the <u>more tragic</u> and famous of all
                         A                                B
wartime offensives <u>occurred, the</u> Japanese attack on the U.S. Pacific Fleet in
                           C
<u>Pearl Harbor, Hawaii.</u> <u>No error.</u>
          D          E

**10.** After Taylor <u>shattered</u> her arm in <u>a skiing accident</u>, she <u>is absent</u> from school
                   A                    B            C
<u>for a full</u> month. <u>No error.</u>
      D            E

**11.** If <u>you</u> are angry about <u>an offense or a slur</u>—even if it <u>occurred on purpose</u> and
        A                  B                          C
maliciously—<u>one</u> should try not to seek revenge. <u>No error.</u>
              D                            E

**12.** <u>If the reason for promoting such a law</u> was to <u>look out for</u> the well-being of
                     A                        B
<u>citizens, the</u> state police would pull people over, suggest they put their seat belts on,
      C
and <u>making them</u> turn their cell phones off. <u>No error.</u>
            D                            E

**13.** <u>Now, it</u> appears there is an initiative to ban cell phone use while <u>driving if you</u> have
      A                                                        B
your cell phone out and you text the local police department about an accident on the
<u>highway, you</u> may soon be <u>receiving</u> a fine for breaking the law. <u>No error.</u>
          C                   D                             E

**14.** The party supply store in town has <u>scarcely no</u> costumes left in stock because
                                           A

<u>Halloween</u> occurred on a Saturday this <u>year; as a result,</u> far more people
    B                                   C

<u>decided to have</u> elaborate celebrations and parties. <u>No error.</u>
     D                                         E

**15.** One <u>cause</u> of the increase in new students in <u>our state colleges</u> and universities
       A                                      B

<u>is</u> enthusiastic recruiters <u>who travel great distances</u> to meet with prospective
C                          D

candidates. <u>No error.</u>
           E

**16.** Two gourmet chefs, <u>Edward and him,</u> <u>were given</u> very large raises because
                      A         B

<u>their restaurants</u> had performed <u>unusually well.</u> <u>No error.</u>
     C                       D       E

**17.** The <u>surprise birthday party</u> was a catastrophe, <u>not having realized</u> that
          A                             B

<u>Jimmy's birthday</u> had been the <u>previous month.</u> <u>No error.</u>
    C                     D      E

**18.** The new <u>employee's clothing</u> was <u>out of line to</u> the <u>company's unspoken</u> dress
              A            B           C

code, which was very conservative. <u>No error.</u>
 D                        E

**19.** <u>With the sharp increase in medical costs and the concurrent decline in employment and</u>
                                          A

<u>subsequent loss of medical insurance,</u> many individuals <u>falsely believe</u> that medical
                                                  B

practitioners should provide free medical services to the <u>indigent, much</u> as lawyers
                                                   C

provide pro bono assistance to people accused of crimes <u>who</u> cannot afford to pay for
                                             D

legal representation. <u>No error.</u>
                 E

**20.** <u>When Dorothy stood in the doorway and looked around she</u> could see nothing but the
                                 A

<u>great gray</u> prairie on every side—not a tree nor a house <u>broke</u> the broad sweep of flat
   B                                          C

country <u>that reached to the edge of the sky</u> in all directions. <u>No error.</u>
               D                           E

**21.** <u>Freezing in the ice-cream maker,</u> Sunita could <u>almost taste</u> the <u>creamy</u> chocolate-chip
              A                         B       C

ice cream, <u>which</u> she planned to serve that evening. <u>No error.</u>
        D                            E

*Part B*
*17 questions*

Suggested time: 20 minutes
*Directions:* Choose the best version of the underlined portion of each sentence. Choice A is the same as the underlined portion of the original sentence. If you think that the original sentence is better than any of the suggested revisions, choose A. Otherwise, choose the revision you think is best. Answers and explanations follow the questions.

22. Not only did Edgar Allan Poe popularize <u>the Short story</u> as a respected literary form, but he also argued that this genre deserves the same status as other time-honored literary forms.

    (A) the Short story
    (B) the short story
    (C) The Short Story
    (D) The short Story
    (E) The Short story

23. <u>The dictates of his conscience were acted out by Thoreau</u> with a determination unsettling to those living more cautious and conventional lives.

    (A) The dictates of his conscience were acted out by Thoreau
    (B) The dictates of his conscience by Thoreau were acted out
    (C) By Thoreau, the dictates of his conscience had been acted out
    (D) Acting out the dictates of his conscience were done by Thoreau
    (E) Thoreau acted out the dictates of his conscience

24. <u>Due to the fact that</u> the college has the authority to tow any motor vehicle that is not registered as required or is parked in violation of any of the campus traffic regulations, it is critical that all students purchase parking decals before the first day of classes.

    (A) Due to the fact that
    (B) Because
    (C) As a result of the situation that
    (D) In the event that
    (E) At the present time

25. Life coaching, the process of helping individuals discover their talents and reach their potential, <u>have increased</u> significantly in the past decade.

    (A) have increased
    (B) has increased
    (C) has increase
    (D) have been increasing
    (E) have increase

26. Before thermometers were invented, brewers would dip a thumb into the mix to find the right temperature for adding <u>yeast too</u> cold and the yeast wouldn't grow, but too hot and the yeast would die.

    (A) yeast too
    (B) yeast, too
    (C) yeast: too
    (D) yeast: two
    (E) yeast, to

27. Hawthorne's first <u>American ancestor, William Hathorne</u>, was a magistrate who once had a Quaker woman publicly whipped in the streets.

    (A) American ancestor, William Hathorne,
    (B) American Ancestor, William Hathorne,
    (C) American ancestor, william Hathorne,
    (D) American ancestor William Hathorne,
    (E) american ancestor William Hathorne,

28. A Frenchman who spent more than half of <u>his' life</u> in the New World, Crevecoeur contributed two key concepts to the American consciousness.

    (A) his' life
    (B) his's life
    (C) he's life
    (D) his life
    (E) he life

29. Formal assessment indicates that students are captivated by the more engaged learning <u>experiences: have formed communities have established bonds with each other often meet outside of class</u> and are more involved in campus activities.

    (A) experiences: have formed communities have established bonds with each other often meet outside of class
    (B) experiences: have formed communities: have established bonds with each other often meet outside of class
    (C) experiences have formed communities, have established bonds with each other, often meet outside of class,
    (D) experiences have formed, communities, have established bonds, with each other, often meet outside of class
    (E) experiences have formed communities have established bonds with each other often meet outside of class,

**30.** In 1934, reviewing Agatha Christie's novel *Why Didn't They Ask Evans?*, the critic <u>said, Mrs. Christie describes the risks (Bobby Jones and Frankie Derwent) ran in her lightest and most sympathetic manner. She plays with her characters as a kitten will play with a ball of wool.</u>

(A) said, Mrs. Christie describes the risks (Bobby Jones and Frankie Derwent) ran in her lightest and most sympathetic manner. She plays with her characters as a kitten will play with a ball of wool.

(B) said, "Mrs. Christie describes the risks (Bobby Jones and Frankie Derwent) ran in her lightest and most sympathetic manner." She plays with her characters as a kitten will play with a ball of wool.

(C) said, "Mrs. Christie describes the risks (Bobby Jones and Frankie Derwent) ran in her lightest and most sympathetic manner." "She plays with her characters as a kitten will play with a ball of wool."

(D) said, "Mrs. Christie describes the risks (Bobby Jones and Frankie Derwent) ran in her lightest and most sympathetic manner. She plays with her characters as a kitten will play with a ball of wool".

(E) said, "Mrs. Christie describes the risks (Bobby Jones and Frankie Derwent) ran in her lightest and most sympathetic manner. She plays with her characters as a kitten will play with a ball of wool."

**31.** At the pound, Isabel and Julia had narrowed their choice to four kittens, and now they had to decide which of the adorable little balls of fur they would take home <u>from among</u> those four.

(A) from among

(B) from within

(C) from between

(D) from inside

(E) to among

**32.** <u>William Shakespeare couldn't figure out a standard way to spell his own name</u>, several variations on "Shakespeare" appear in his plays and in his last will and testament—even on his tombstone.

(A) William Shakespeare couldn't figure out a standard way to spell his own name,

(B) Even William Shakespeare couldn't figure out a standard way to spell his own name:

(C) Figuring out how to spell his name a standard way should have been done by William Shakespeare:

(D) Before William Shakespeare couldn't figure out a standard way to spell his own name,

(E) While William Shakespeare couldn't figure out a standard way to spell his own name,

**33.** It was raining so fiercely that the wom<u>ens</u>' feet were soaked in the seconds it took them to dash from the bus to the office.

    (A) womens'
    (B) womens
    (C) women's
    (D) woman's
    (E) woman

**34.** While the world expected one definition of success, <u>Thoreau lived quite a different one his writing</u> won for itself a permanence that belied the scorn of his contemporaries.

    (A) Thoreau lived quite a different one his writing
    (B) Thoreau lived quite a different one, his writing
    (C) Thoreau lived quite a different one, or his writing
    (D) a different one was lived by Thoreau, since his writing
    (E) Thoreau lived quite a different one, and his writing

**35.** <u>Because students</u> must be provided with the opportunity to demonstrate the capability and willingness to take initiative and responsibility for sustained academic involvement.

    (A) Because students
    (B) Since students
    (C) In spite of the fact that students
    (D) Students
    (E) If students

**36.** <u>At the same time Vachel</u> Lindsay immortalized such figures on the American landscape as Abraham Lincoln ("Abraham Lincoln Walks at Midnight") and John Chapman ("Johnny Appleseed"), often blending facts with myth.

    (A) At the same time Vachel
    (B) At the same time: Vachel
    (C) At the same time, Vachel
    (D) At the same time—Vachel
    (E) At the same time; Vachel

**37.** The firm's management argued that the company would save significant funds annually if all employees looked <u>more thorough</u> for small ways to economize on a daily basis.

    (A) more thorough

    (B) thorough

    (C) more, thorough

    (D) more thorougher

    (E) more thoroughly

**38.** How many people do you know who annoy you because they are always quoting hackneyed old sayings such <u>as, "A stitch in time saves nine"</u>?

    (A) as, "A stitch in time saves nine"?

    (B) as A stitch in time saves nine?

    (C) as "A stitch in time saves nine?"?

    (D) as, "A stitch in time saves nine.?"?

    (E) as, "A stitch in time saves nine?"

# STOP. This is the end of Section 1: Multiple-Choice Questions.

# SECTION 2: ESSAY

## 30 minutes

*Directions:* Write an essay on the following topic. You will not receive any credit for writing on a topic other than the one given here. Plan your essay carefully and be sure to include specific examples and details that illustrate your point. Write your essay on your own paper. (On the real Praxis PPST test, paper for writing your essay will be provided.)

**You will not receive credit if you write on any other topic. For your response to be scored, you must write in English. You cannot write in a foreign language.**

Read the quotation that follows:

> Television is more interesting than people. If it were not, we would have people standing in the corners of our rooms.
>
> —ALAN CORENK

In an essay, agree or disagree with this statement. Be sure to support your opinion with specific examples from readings, your experiences, your observations, or the media.

The space below is for your notes.

**Test Hint:** Stay on topic. You must address the specific subject, not a subject of your choice. No matter how well written your essay may be, you will not receive any credit if it is off topic.

# WRITING PRACTICE TEST 1: ANSWERS

## SECTION 1: MULTIPLE-CHOICE QUESTIONS

*Part A*

> **Note: This part of the test does *not* require you to correct the sentence, only to identify the error that it may or may not contain. However, to help you learn more about grammar and usage to earn a higher score on the entire Praxis Writing Test (including Part B and the essay) and to improve your teaching, all errors are corrected and the relevant grammar and usage rules explained.**

**1. D**  This sentence has a misplaced modifier. A *modifier* is a word or phrase that describes something. The modifiers are underlined in the following examples:

> I wore a <u>red</u> dress.

> As she was walking down the street, Lucia found a man's <u>gold</u> watch.

A *misplaced modifier* is a word, phrase, or clause that is not in the correct place in the sentence. Usually, it is too far from the word that it modifies (describes). Because the modifier is misplaced, the sentence usually sounds awkward, confusing, or even amusing. Here is an example:

> As she was walking down the street, Lucia found a <u>gold man's watch</u>.

Moving the modifier *gold* to the wrong place creates an illogical and amusing sentence.

You can correct a misplaced modifier by moving the modifier to the correct place in the sentence. Here is our test item:

- Misplaced modifier

   *As a special treat, my uncle prepared waffles to the guests served on a silver platter.*

- Corrected sentence:

   *As a special treat, my uncle served waffles on a silver platter to the guests.*

**Test Hint:** To test for a misplaced modifier, read the sentence aloud—but do it quietly! If it sounds illogical or unintentionally funny, it most likely has a misplaced modifier. Then find the describing words that are in the wrong place.

**2. D**  The sentence has an error in parallel structure. *Parallel structure* means using the same grammatical pattern to show that two or more ideas have the same level of importance. You can parallel words, phrases, or clauses (word groups with a subject and a verb).

To correct faulty parallelism, identify the grammatical pattern at the beginning of the sentence. Match all subsequent elements to that pattern. In our test item, the first grammatical pattern is a prepositional phrase: "for dealing with people." The second phrase should match this, changing the infinitive "to resolve" to "for resolving." Thus, the correct sentence reads: *A core curriculum helps prepare college students to become better-functioning adults, as classes such as Introduction to Psychology and Economics I provide students with some basic tools* <u>for dealing with people</u> *and* <u>for resolving financial matters</u>.

**3. A**  This sentence is a fragment because it is missing a complete verb. *Fragments* are incomplete sentences. To be a complete sentence, a word group must fulfill three qualifications: it must have a subject; it must have a verb; and it must express a complete thought. Thus, a fragment will be missing a subject or a verb, or it will not express a complete thought. Here are some examples:

- Missing a subject

  *With the main purpose of all education is to gain knowledge.*

- Missing a verb or a complete verb

  *Trash of all kinds scattered around.*

- Not expressing a complete thought

  *Such as meatballs, spaghetti, and Italian bread every Sunday afternoon.*

Our test item is missing a complete verb. The incomplete verb *teaching* must be replaced by the complete verb *teach*. Here is the corrected sentence: *Just as parents teach their children to protect themselves outside the home by not speaking to strangers and so on, parents should teach their children how to protect themselves online by avoiding chat rooms and never giving out personal information on social networking sites.*

**Test Hint:** Don't be fooled by the length of a sentence. A fragment can be very long, as is the case here. Take the sentence apart and study each piece to make sure the sentence is complete and logical.

**4. C**   This is a run-on sentence, the error occurring between the two independent clauses. *Run-on sentences* are two independent clauses (two complete sentences) that are joined incorrectly. You can correct run-on sentences in one of four ways:

- Join the two independent clauses with one of the coordinating conjunctions (*and, but, for, or, nor, so, yet*), and use a comma before the connecting word.
- Join the two independent clauses with a semicolon.
- Break the two run-together sentences into two sentences.
- Create a subordinate clause and an independent clause.

Here's how it looks with our test item:

- Join the two independent clauses with a coordinating conjunction

   *Through the Fair Labor Standards Act, the U.S. Department of Labor establishes the minimum wage that private and governmental employers can pay their workers, for this is the lowest legal wage that employers can pay their workers.*

- Join the two independent clauses with a semicolon

   *Through the Fair Labor Standards Act, the U.S. Department of Labor establishes the minimum wage that private and governmental employers can pay their workers; this is the lowest legal wage that employers can pay their workers.*

- Break the run-together sentence into two sentences

   *Through the Fair Labor Standards Act, the U.S. Department of Labor establishes the minimum wage that private and governmental employers can pay their workers. This is the lowest legal wage that employers can pay their workers.*

- Create a subordinate clause and an independent clause

   *Through the Fair Labor Standards Act, the U.S. Department of Labor establishes the minimum wage that private and governmental employers can pay their workers, because this is the lowest legal wage that employers can pay their workers.*

---

**Test Hint:** Just as a sentence fragment can be very long, a run-on sentence can be very short. Here is an example: *We ate we took a nap.* Look for the subjects and verbs in the sentences to determine whether they are complete and not run-ons.

**5. B**    This question tests your knowledge of subject-verb agreement. The subject—*desserts*—is plural. Thus, it requires a plural verb. The correct sentence reads: *The delicious desserts of AnneMarie Proto <u>have</u> earned high praise, not only from well-respected food reviewers, but also from people who appreciate fine food the world over.*

Here is a quick review of subject-verb agreement.

- A subject must agree with its verb in number. A singular subject takes a singular verb; a plural subject takes a plural verb.
- If the subject is made up of two or more nouns or pronouns connected by *or, nor, not only,* or *but also,* the verb agrees with the noun closest to the pronoun.
- Collective nouns (nouns that name groups of people or things) are singular, even if they end in -*s*. Don't be fooled by plural-looking subjects like *measles, news, mathematics,* and *social studies*. They're still singular, even though they end in -*s*.
- Ignore words or phrases that come between the subject and the verb because they don't affect agreement. For example:

The <u>captain</u> of the guards <u>stands</u> at attention.
    singular                 singular

**Test Hint:**

**Singular and Plural Verbs in the Present Tense**

| 1st and 2nd Person Singular | 3rd Person Singular | 1st, 2nd, and 3rd Person Plural |
|---|---|---|
| (I, you) start | (he, she, it) starts | (we, you, they) start |
| (I, you) do | (he, she, it) does | (we, you, they) do |

**6. C**    This question tests consistency of pronoun use. Don't switch point of view in the middle of a sentence or passage. Since the sentence first uses the word *you* (*you're* or *you are*), the writer cannot switch to the pronoun *one* in the middle of the sentence. The correct sentence reads: *In Michigan, driving without a seat belt is a primary offense, which means if you're seen without a seat belt on, <u>you</u> can be pulled over and fined.*

**7. C** This sentence has a dangling modifier. A *dangling modifier* is a word or phrase that describes something that has been left out of the sentence. A modifier is said to dangle when the word it modifies (describes) is not actually in the sentence.

Correct a dangling modifier by adding a noun or pronoun to which the dangling construction can be attached. Here are two examples:

- Dangling modifier

  Flying over the countryside, the houses looked like toys. (states that the houses were flying)

- Corrected sentence

  As they were flying over the countryside, the houses looked like toys. (added the pronoun *they* and the helping verb *were*)

Dangling:  After studying hard, the test was easy. (states that the test was doing the studying)

Corrected:  After Samara studied hard, the test was easy. (added the noun *Samara* and changed the form of *studying* to match)

With our test item, on-site child care is not seeing the benefits of decreased employee turnover, absenteeism, and lateness. Rather, companies are seeing the results. The correct sentence should read: *After documenting the significant advantages of decreased employee turnover, absenteeism, and lateness, more and more companies are providing on-site child care more frequently as a bonus for working parents.*

**8. A** This sentence has an error in parallel structure. To correct it, the sentence should read: *The toddlers are fond of apple slices and cookies, . . .*

**9. B**  This sentence has an error in comparison. Use the superlative degree (*most*) to show the comparison is among three or more objects or instances, which is the case here.

Adjectives and adverbs have different forms to show the degree of comparison: positive, comparative, and superlative:

- **Positive degree:** the base form of the adjective or adverb. It does not show comparison.
- **Comparative degree:** the form an adjective or adverb takes to compare two things.
- **Superlative degree:** the form an adjective or adverb takes to compare three or more things.

The following chart shows the three degrees of comparison with some sample adjectives and adverbs.

|  | **Positive** | **Comparative** | **Superlative** |
|---|---|---|---|
| **Adjectives** | tall | taller | tallest |
|  | good | better | best |
| **Adverbs** | slowly | more slowly | most slowly |
|  | well | better | best |

Let's review the rules for forming the comparative and superlative degrees.

- To form the comparative degree, add *-er* or *more* (never both!) to most one- and two-syllable adjectives and adverbs. To form the superlative degree, add *-est* or *most* (never both!) to most one- and two-syllable adjectives and adverbs. For example:

| weak | weaker | weakest |
|---|---|---|
| strong | stronger | strongest |
| frail | more frail | most frail |
| honest | more honest | most honest |

- Use *more* or *most* to form the comparative and superlative degrees of all adjectives and adverbs that have three or more syllables. For example:

| extensive | more extensive | most extensive |
|---|---|---|
| prevalent | more prevalent | most prevalent |

- Use *more* and *most* with all adverbs that end in *-ly*. For example:

| easily | more easily | most easily |
|---|---|---|
| rudely | more rudely | most rudely |
| nicely | more nicely | most nicely |

**10. C** This sentence has an error in tense consistency. The verb tense must be consistent within the sentence so the writing makes sense. The past tense *shattered* requires the past tense *was* rather than the present tense *is*.

**11. D** As you learned with test item 6, use consistent pronouns. Since the sentence first uses the pronoun *you*, do not switch to the pronoun *one*. Rather, stay with *you*.

**12. D** This sentence has an error in parallel structure. *Parallel structure* means that all elements in a sentence have to be in the same grammatical form. <u>*Make*</u> *them turn their cell phones off*—not <u>*making*</u> *them turn their cell phones off*—parallels *pull people over* and *suggest they put their seat belts on*.

**13. B** This is a run-on sentence, meaning two sentences joined incorrectly. Here are several correct versions of this sentence:

- Sentences joined with a coordinating conjunction

  *Now, it appears there is an initiative to ban cell phone use while driving, so if you have your cell phone out and you text the local police department about an accident on the highway, you may soon be receiving a fine for breaking the law.*

- Sentences joined with a semicolon

  *Now, it appears there is an initiative to ban cell phone use while driving; if you have your cell phone out and you text the local police department about an accident on the highway, you may soon be receiving a fine for breaking the law.*

- Two separate sentences

  *Now, it appears there is an initiative to ban cell phone use while driving. If you have your cell phone out and you text the local police department about an accident on the highway, you may soon be receiving a fine for breaking the law.*

**14. A** The error is a double negative. Use *scarcely any* or *no*, but not *scarcely no* together in the same sentence.

**15. C** This sentence has an error in agreement. The plural subject *recruiters* agrees with the plural verb *are*, not the singular verb *is*. Do not be misled by the singular predicate nominative *cause*.

**16. A** This sentence has an error in case. A pronoun used in apposition to a noun must be in the same case as the noun. An *appositive* is a noun or pronoun placed after another noun or pronoun to identify or explain it. Here, the pronoun *he* must be in the nominative case because it is in apposition with the noun *gourmet chefs*, which is also in the nominative case.

**17. B**   This sentence has a dangling modifier, so it does not explain who did the realizing. As a result, the sentence does not make sense. It should read: *The surprise birthday party was a catastrophe because we did not realize that Jimmy's birthday had been the previous month.*

**18. B**   This sentence has an error in usage: idioms. An *idiom* is a group of words that are always used together or a group of words that has a figurative meaning based on common use or that is understood as meaning something apart from the literal meanings of the individual words. English has lots of idioms and they are often misused, especially because they are rarely logical.

   Here are some examples:

- Back down: stop defending your side in a debate or argument
- Back away: get out of a previous commitment
- Back out, back out of: renege on a promise or deal
- Back up: provide support or move in reverse
- Back into: hit something while moving backward
- Back off: escape or run away from something
- Shut off: close
- Shut down: close permanently
- Shut in: confine
- Shut up: stop talking
- Shut out: prevent participation

   In our test item, the correct idiom is *out of line with*, not *out of line to*. The correct sentence reads: *The new employee's clothing was out of line with the company's unspoken dress code, which was very conservative.*

---

**Test Hint:** You can often identify idioms because the sentence will sound awkward. Isolate the words that don't sound right.

---

**19. E**   The sentence is correct as written.

**20. A**   This sentence has an error in punctuation. Use a comma after any introductory word, phrase, or clause. In this test item, a comma must be used after the introductory subordinate clause *When Dorothy stood in the doorway and looked around.*
Here are some examples to review:

- Use a comma after an introductory word

   *Yes, I'd be delighted to stay for dinner.*

   *No, I didn't know that you were serving snails and tofu soufflé.*

- Use a comma after an introductory phrase:

   *Over the rainbow, we saw a pot of gold.*

   *In a perfect world, pro baseball players would complain about teachers being paid contracts worth millions of dollars.*

- Use a comma after an introductory clause:

   *If at first you don't succeed, try, try again.*

   *After you read the report, you will probably agree that we all deserve a vacation.*

**21. A**   This sentence has a misplaced modifier. As written, the sentence states that Sunita is freezing in the ice-cream maker. Here is a correct revision: *Sunita could almost taste the creamy chocolate-chip ice cream freezing in the ice-cream maker, and she planned to serve the ice cream that evening.*

### Part B

**22. B**   This sentence has an error in punctuation. The term "the short story" is not being used here as a proper noun. Rather, it is a common noun, and common nouns are not capitalized.

---

**Test Hint:** Capitalize all proper nouns and proper adjectives. Capitalize a compass point when it identifies a specific area of the country, as in this example: *Cowboys live in the West.* Don't capitalize a compass point when it refers to direction: *The airplane comes from the east.*

---

**23. E**    This sentence has an error in voice. Only choice E recasts the sentence in the active voice, which is more concise and vigorous than the passive voice.

As you consider the structure of your sentences, you need to decide whether to have the subject perform the action or receive the action. Here are two examples:

- Harry found my bracelet. (subject performs the action)
- My bracelet was found by Harry. (subject receives the action)

This is called voice. English has two voices: active and passive. In the *active voice*, the subject performs the action. In the *passive voice*, the subject receives the action. For instance:

- Active voice

  My dog ate the toothpaste. He had minty fresh breath. We bought fresh toothpaste.

- Passive voice

  The toothpaste was eaten by my dog. Minty fresh breath was had by him. Fresh toothpaste was bought. (Notice that the subject is not named here.)

As a general rule, use the active instead of the passive voice. The former is more direct and concise, which makes it clearer.

**Test Hint:** There are two instances where the passive voice is preferable. First, use the passive voice when you don't want to assign blame or emphasize who or what performed an action:

*A mistake was made.*

*The windows were left open over the weekend.*

Second, use the passive voice when you don't know who performed an action:

*The package was shipped at 10:02 A.M.*

*All the cookies were eaten.*

**24. B**    This sentence's error is its wordiness; every one of the phrases listed is verbose. The sentence is best stated without any of the redundant openings. Good writing is concise, direct, and to the point. As Winston Churchill once said, "Old words are best, and short words best of all."

The following chart shows some wordy phrases and their concise alternatives. Notice how well the concise versions communicate meaning without unnecessary wordiness:

| Wordy | Concise |
| --- | --- |
| covered over | covered |
| true facts | facts |
| sum total; end result | result |
| most unique | unique |
| proceed ahead | proceed |

**25. B**   This sentence has an error in agreement. Use the singular verb *has* to agree with the singular subject *life coaching*.

**26. C**   This sentence has an error in structure. As written, it is a run-on, meaning two sentences run together without the correct punctuation. Since the second independent clause defines the first, use a colon. If the second independent clause is a complete sentence, it is capitalized. Choice A is incorrect because it lacks any punctuation between the two independent clauses. Choice B uses a comma, which is not sufficient to join two independent clauses. Using a comma creates a specific type of run-on called a *comma splice*. Choices D and E are incorrect because they introduce new errors.

The four rules for using colons:

- Rule #1: Use a colon before part of a sentence that defines what was just stated.

  *"The Tell-Tale Heart" opens this way: "True!—nervous—very, very dreadfully nervous I had been and am; but why will you say that I am mad? The disease had sharpened my senses—not destroyed—not dulled them."*

- Rule #2: Use a colon before a list.

  *Liz plans to visit the following countries: France, Germany, Switzerland, and Ireland.*

- Rule #3: Use a colon before a long quotation of more than five lines.

  *In* Letters from an American Farmer, *Hector St. John de Crèvecoeur wrote: "What, then, is the American, this new man? He is neither a European nor the descendent of a European; hence that strange mixture of blood, which you will find in no other country. I could point out to you a family whose grandfather was an Englishman, whose wife was Dutch, whose son married a French woman, and whose present four sons now have four wives of different nations."*

- Rule #4: Use a colon after the salutation of a business letter.

  *Dear Dr. Greene:      Dear Ms. Chin:*

**27. A**   The sentence is correct as written. Capitalize the names of nationalities and people, as both are proper nouns.

**Test Hint:** As you take this test, look for test items that contain errors in capitalization, especially concerning organizations, languages, and other proper nouns and adjectives. Nearly every Praxis writing test includes one question on capitalization.

**28. D**  This sentence has an error in possession. Since the life belongs to Crevecoeur, a possessive pronoun is needed. This eliminates choice E. Possessive pronouns do not take an apostrophe, eliminating choices A and B. Choice C is wrong because it is a contraction for "he is."

Here is a quick review of the possessive case. *Possession* means ownership. Nouns and pronouns are both used to show possession.

Here are the rules to create possessive nouns using apostrophes:

- Add an apostrophe and an *s* to singular nouns:

| | |
|---|---|
| frog | frog's tongue |
| William Shatner | William Shatner's singing |
| Girl Scout | Girl Scout's cookies |

- Add an apostrophe after the *s* with plural nouns ending in *s*.

| | |
|---|---|
| frogs | frogs' tongues |
| Trekkies | Trekkies' songs |
| Girl Scouts | Girl Scouts' cookies |

- Add an apostrophe and an *s* with plural nouns not ending in *s*.

| | |
|---|---|
| men | men's socks |
| mice | mice's holes |
| fish | fish's bubbles |

Here are the rules to use pronouns to show possession. Possessive pronouns can be used before nouns or alone. Here are some examples:

- Possessive pronoun before a noun:

  Mark left *his* scarf at the club.

- Possessive pronoun alone

  Do you mind *my* borrowing your other one?

  The car is *mine*, not *yours*.

**Test Hint:** Never confuse possessive pronouns and contractions. Possessive pronouns never take an apostrophe, as these examples show:

| *Possessive Pronoun* | *Contraction* |
|---|---|
| your | you're |
| its | it's |
| their | they're |
| his | he's |

**29. C** This sentence has an error in punctuation: commas. Separate items in a series with commas. Here, the items are phrases rather than individual words. Be sure to set off each complete phrase. You can test the logic of your sentence by reading it aloud.

Here is a quick review:

- Series of words

  *Our pets include a cat, a dog, an iguana, and a hippo.*

- Series of phrases

  *The hippo likes to wallow in the mud, enjoy a massage, and rest on the deck.*

- Series of clauses

  *The children played basketball, the coaches kept score, the grandparents cheered, and the parents read the newspaper.*

**30. E** This sentence has an error in punctuation: quotation marks. All of the speaker's exact words should be surrounded with quotation marks. Thus, the sentences are incorrect as written. Also, choice B is wrong because it does not include everything the speaker said. Choice C is incorrect because there is no reason to break this quotation into two parts. Periods are placed inside the quotation marks, so choice D is also incorrect.

Quotation marks always come in pairs. Here is a quick review:

- Rule #1: Use quotation marks to set off a speaker's exact words.

  *The doctor said to the patient, "Stick your tongue out the window."*

  *"What will that do?" asked the patient.*

  *The doctor replied, "I'm mad at my neighbor."*

- Rule #2: Use quotation marks to set off the titles of short works such as poems, essays, songs, short stories, and magazine articles.

  "The Road Not Taken"

  "America the Beautiful"

  "The Ransom of Red Chief"

  "How to Cook a Perfect Roast"

**31. A** This is a usage question. The sentence is correct as written because *among* is used to show a relationship among three or more people or things. Use *between* to show a relationship between two people or things.

**32. B** This sentence has an error in structure. As written, it is a run-on. Since the second independent clause defines the first, use a colon.

**33. C** This sentence has an error in possession. To show possession in the plural noun *women*, add an apostrophe and an *s*.

**34. E**    This sentence has an error in structure. As written, it is a run-on, meaning two sentences run together without the correct punctuation. Choice B does not correct the error because a comma is used within a sentence, not to join two sentences. The coordinating conjunction *or* is illogical, so you can eliminate choice C. Choice D is in the passive voice, which makes it wordy and awkward. Further, the subordinating conjunction *since* doesn't make sense in context. Only choice E is correct and logical.

**35. D**    This sentence has an error in structure. As written, it is a fragment created by the subordinating conjunction *because*. Choices B, C, and E are all subordinating conjunctions, so they do not correct the error. By eliminating the subordinating conjunction—choice D—the sentence is correct.

**36. C**    This sentence has an error in punctuation: commas. Use a comma after an introductory subordinate clause.

**37. E**    This sentence has a usage error. Use an adverb (*thoroughly*) to modify or describe a verb (*looked*).

**38. A**    The sentence is correct as written. Set off a direct quotation with quotation marks. The question mark goes outside the closing quotation marks because the entire expression—not just the part in quotes—is a question. Finally, the quotation is set off from the rest of the sentence by a comma.

### Skills Spread

| Specific Content Area | Item Numbers |
| --- | --- |
| Grammar and usage (13) | 1, 5, 6, 9, 10, 11, 15, 16, 25, 28, 31, 33, 37 |
| Sentence structure (14) | 2, 3, 4, 7, 8, 12, 13, 17, 21, 23, 26, 32, 34, 35 |
| Mechanics—punctuation, capitalization Diction—word choice (11) | 14, 18, 19, 20, 22, 24, 27, 29, 30, 36, 38 |
| Essay | 1 |

# SECTION 2: ESSAY

The following model essay would receive a 6, the highest score, for its specific details; organization; and style (such as appropriate word choice, sentence structure, and consistent facility in use of language). It is an especially intelligent and insightful response.

sophisticated diction creates clear voice and style

clear argumentative thesis statement

three clear and relevant points, to be developed in the following paragraphs

transition

specific examples prove the thesis

humor creates clear voice and style

transition

specific examples prove the thesis

transition

humor creates clear voice and style

ideas fully developed

specific examples prove the thesis

Alan Corenk quips that, "Television is more interesting than people. If it were not, we would have people standing in the corners of our rooms." Cornek's comment may have been intended in jest, but his statement is accurate nonetheless. Television programming is more entertaining and holds our attention far better than the majority of our personal interactions. That's because television programming is more instantly gratifying, more easily accessible, and generally of higher quality than an individual would be in terms of entertainment.

First, television offers far greater variety than any one person can, particularly in this age of thousands of specialty channels and on-demand content. My cable company provides me with more than 700 channels on every conceivable topic: in addition to network shows, I get programs on arcane sports like curling, classic movies from the 1940s, elaborate cake decorating for weddings, and vegan cooking demonstrations. Whereas it would be rude to interrupt a conversation to change the topic, channel-surfing is expected when television programming fails to entertain. Similarly, a television never gets tired, does not lose interest in your favored topic, and is never required to answer the call of nature.

Next, television requires no input from the viewer to provide entertainment. A conversation, by definition, requires two participants and an exchange of ideas. The television is selfless, existing only to give. Even reading a book requires the reader to imagine the scenes and voices, but a television program requires no work at all. After all, who has to pay attention during *Two and a Half Men* or *America's Got Talent*?

Finally, thanks to the efforts of talented writers, directors, and actors, television characters are smarter, wittier, and more capable than real people. (They are consistently more beautiful, as well.) Television actors speak more clearly and succinctly, never using malapropisms or wandering down verbal garden paths as friends do. Every detail they provide is something that will matter to their character or the overall plot, and there are no pointless tangents. In addition, these television characters can gratify the viewer's ego by being more incompetent (particularly regarding communication with each other), less knowledgeable about common topics, and more likely to blunder into humorously embarrassing situations than we are. This allows us to retain our feeling of superiority, given the characters' stumbles. For instance, Phil Dunphy in *Modern Family*, Al Bundy in *Married with Children*, and Steven Keaton in *Family Ties* are all familiar tropes of the bumbling dad.

insightful, intelligent
conclusion

There should be no question that television is more interesting than people; if it were not, we would not have bothered to invent it. <u>That said, had Corenk commented that television was more *fulfilling* than interacting with people, I would be more inclined to disagree. No television show can substitute for an evening with friends and family.</u>

# MATHEMATICS PRACTICE TEST 1

## Answer sheet

1  Ⓐ Ⓑ Ⓒ Ⓓ Ⓔ
2  Ⓐ Ⓑ Ⓒ Ⓓ Ⓔ
3  Ⓐ Ⓑ Ⓒ Ⓓ Ⓔ
4  Ⓐ Ⓑ Ⓒ Ⓓ Ⓔ
5  Ⓐ Ⓑ Ⓒ Ⓓ Ⓔ
6  Ⓐ Ⓑ Ⓒ Ⓓ Ⓔ
7  Ⓐ Ⓑ Ⓒ Ⓓ Ⓔ

8  Ⓐ Ⓑ Ⓒ Ⓓ Ⓔ
9  Ⓐ Ⓑ Ⓒ Ⓓ Ⓔ
10 Ⓐ Ⓑ Ⓒ Ⓓ Ⓔ
11 Ⓐ Ⓑ Ⓒ Ⓓ Ⓔ
12 Ⓐ Ⓑ Ⓒ Ⓓ Ⓔ
13 Ⓐ Ⓑ Ⓒ Ⓓ Ⓔ
14 Ⓐ Ⓑ Ⓒ Ⓓ Ⓔ

15 Ⓐ Ⓑ Ⓒ Ⓓ Ⓔ
16 Ⓐ Ⓑ Ⓒ Ⓓ Ⓔ
17 Ⓐ Ⓑ Ⓒ Ⓓ Ⓔ
18 Ⓐ Ⓑ Ⓒ Ⓓ Ⓔ
19 Ⓐ Ⓑ Ⓒ Ⓓ Ⓔ
20 Ⓐ Ⓑ Ⓒ Ⓓ Ⓔ
21 Ⓐ Ⓑ Ⓒ Ⓓ Ⓔ

22 Ⓐ Ⓑ Ⓒ Ⓓ Ⓔ
23 Ⓐ Ⓑ Ⓒ Ⓓ Ⓔ
24 Ⓐ Ⓑ Ⓒ Ⓓ Ⓔ
25 Ⓐ Ⓑ Ⓒ Ⓓ Ⓔ
26 Ⓐ Ⓑ Ⓒ Ⓓ Ⓔ
27 Ⓐ Ⓑ Ⓒ Ⓓ Ⓔ
28 Ⓐ Ⓑ Ⓒ Ⓓ Ⓔ

29 Ⓐ Ⓑ Ⓒ Ⓓ Ⓔ
30 Ⓐ Ⓑ Ⓒ Ⓓ Ⓔ
31 Ⓐ Ⓑ Ⓒ Ⓓ Ⓔ
32 Ⓐ Ⓑ Ⓒ Ⓓ Ⓔ
33 Ⓐ Ⓑ Ⓒ Ⓓ Ⓔ
34 Ⓐ Ⓑ Ⓒ Ⓓ Ⓔ
35 Ⓐ Ⓑ Ⓒ Ⓓ Ⓔ

36 Ⓐ Ⓑ Ⓒ Ⓓ Ⓔ
37 Ⓐ Ⓑ Ⓒ Ⓓ Ⓔ
38 Ⓐ Ⓑ Ⓒ Ⓓ Ⓔ
39 Ⓐ Ⓑ Ⓒ Ⓓ Ⓔ
40 Ⓐ Ⓑ Ⓒ Ⓓ Ⓔ

# MATHEMATICS PRACTICE TEST 1

## 40 questions, 60 minutes

*Directions:* Select the best choice for each item and mark the answer on your answer sheet.

1. What are the coordinates of point D?

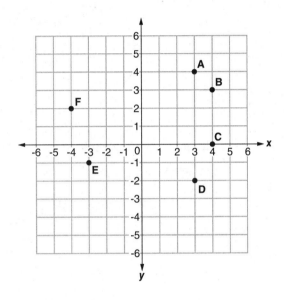

(A) $(2, 3)$
(B) $(3, 2)$
(C) $(3, -2)$
(D) $(-3, 2)$
(E) $(-3, -2)$

2. If $x \div 5 = y$, what is $2x$?

(A) $y$
(B) $y \div 5$
(C) $y \div 10$
(D) $5y$
(E) $10y$

**3.** Elmont is 12 miles due west of Farmingdale. The beach is 5 miles due south of Elmont. What is the approximate straight-line distance from Farmingdale to the beach?

(A)  7 miles
(B)  14.5 miles
(C)  13 miles
(D)  12 miles
(E)  17 miles

**4.** In a deck of 52 cards, there are four equal suits: clubs, hearts, spades, and diamonds. What percentage of the cards is made up of hearts and diamonds?

(A)  4 percent
(B)  50 percent
(C)  25 percent
(D)  13 percent
(E)  52 percent

**5.** On the gas gauge shown, the arrow indicates that the tank is:

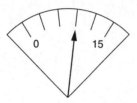

(A)  full
(B)  $\frac{3}{4}$ full
(C)  $\frac{1}{4}$ full
(D)  more than $\frac{1}{2}$ full
(E)  less than $\frac{1}{2}$ full

**6.** In a box of 20 cookies, 8 have vanilla cream and 12 have chocolate cream. What percentage have strawberry cream?

(A)  10%
(B)  50%
(C)  25%
(D)  33.3%
(E)  0%

**7.** If $A = x/2 - 2$, and $A = 6$, then $x =$

(A) 12

(B) 0

(C) 3

(D) 18

(E) 16

**8.** If the scale for a dollhouse is 3 inches = 2 feet, and a shelf is 6 feet high, how high would you make a dollhouse-scale shelf?

(A) 1.5 inches

(B) 2 inches

(C) 12 inches

(D) 9 inches

(E) 3 feet

**9.** The number of sandwiches sold in the deli each weekday is represented by the following chart. What is the approximate mean number of sandwiches sold for the week?

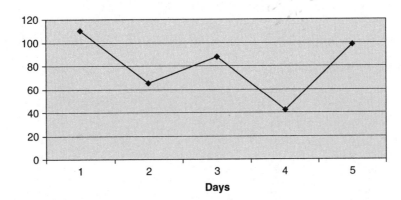

(A) 40

(B) 81

(C) 60

(D) 100

(E) 65

**10.** Which of these problems have the same numerical answer?

    I.  If you need 4 eggs to make a soufflé, and you have 18 eggs, how many soufflés can you make?

    II.  If you need 4 sandwiches to feed everyone at a picnic, how many picnics can you go on if you have 18 sandwiches?

    III.  If you can fit 4 glasses in a box, how many boxes do you need to hold 18 glasses?

(A) I and II

(B) I and III

(C) II and III

(D) I, II, and III

(E) None of the above

**11.** If there are 8 forks, 8 spoons, and 6 knives in a drawer, and you pick one at random, what is the probability of picking a spoon?

(A) $\frac{1}{3}$

(B) $\frac{4}{11}$

(C) $\frac{6}{22}$

(D) $\frac{8}{24}$

(E) $\frac{1}{8}$

**12.** 3,640,000 is how many times 3.64?

(A) 1,000

(B) 10,000

(C) 100,000

(D) 1,000,000

(E) 10,000,000

**13.** Which of the following numbers is a third of a million?

(A) 300,000

(B) $1,000,000 \times 0.3$

(C) 3/1,000,000

(D) 1,000,000/3

(E) 1,000,000/3.3

**14.** Which decimal is least?

(A) 0.0034

(B) 0.0956

(C) 0.000998

(D) 0.00475

(E) 0.0001156

15. The following chart shows the amount of profit a company earns for a given number of employees and customers. If the company has 30 customers, how many employees should it hire to have the greatest profit?

| | | Customers | | | |
|---|---|---|---|---|---|
| | 10 | 20 | 30 | 40 | 50 |
| 1 | 30 | 32 | 34 | 36 | 38 |
| 2 | 25 | 60 | 62 | 64 | 66 |
| 3 | 20 | 55 | 90 | 92 | 94 |
| 4 | 15 | 50 | 85 | 120 | 122 |
| 5 | 10 | 45 | 80 | 115 | 150 |
| 6 | 5 | 40 | 75 | 110 | 145 |

(A) 1
(B) 2
(C) 3
(D) 4
(E) 5

16. The gauge on the oil tank looks like this. Approximately how full is the tank?

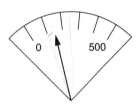

(A) 75 percent
(B) 50 percent
(C) 90 percent
(D) 15 percent
(E) 30 percent

17. If $A = 5x + 5$, and $A = 35$, then $x =$

(A) 6
(B) 5
(C) 35
(D) 10
(E) 200

18. A large group of your friends takes you out to a restaurant for a birthday dinner. When the bill comes, the tax on it is $24.96. If you know the tax rate is 8.75 percent, approximately how much should they leave as an 18 percent tip?

    (A) $25.00
    (B) $40.00
    (C) $45.00
    (D) $50.00
    (E) $87.50

19. If the scale on a dollhouse is 1 inch = 2.5 feet, and a coatrack is 5.5 feet high, how high would you make a dollhouse-scale coatrack?

    (A) 0.45 inch
    (B) 2.20 inches
    (C) 13.75 inches
    (D) 1.15 feet
    (E) 2.20 feet

20. Which pairs of decimals and fractions are equivalent?
    I.   0.125 and $\frac{1}{7}$
    II.  0.25 and $\frac{2}{8}$
    III. 0.61 and $\frac{12}{18}$
    IV.  1.25 and $\frac{5}{4}$

    (A) I and III
    (B) II only
    (C) II and III
    (D) I, II, and IV
    (E) II and IV

21. Which of the following is true?

    (A) $\frac{9}{7} < 1.1$
    (B) $\frac{5}{4} = 1.25$
    (C) $\frac{7}{14} = 7.14$
    (D) $\frac{5}{6} > 78\%$
    (E) $\frac{1}{10} > 0.1$

**22.** Three groups of voters are represented by the chart. If a majority is required for a motion to pass or be defeated, which of the following is not true?

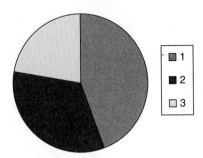

(A) Groups 1 and 3 together could pass a motion.

(B) Groups 2 and 3 together could defeat a motion.

(C) Group 3 cannot defeat a motion.

(D) Group 2 can pass a motion.

(E) Group 1 has the most members.

**23.** If $2x + 4 = 9x - 10$, then $x =$

(A) 2

(B) 6

(C) 10

(D) 12

(E) 18

**24.** The following chart represents five baseball games between the Yankees and the Angels. How many runs did the Angels score in all?

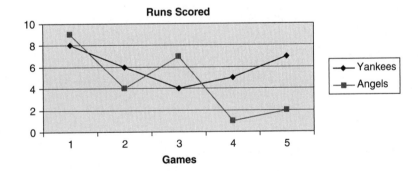

(A) 30

(B) 23

(C) 15

(D) 9

(E) 27

**25.** If the team that scored more runs won the game, how many games did the Yankees win?

(A) 1
(B) 2
(C) 3
(D) 4
(E) 5

**26.** What is the average number of runs the Yankees scored per game?

(A) 4
(B) 5
(C) 6
(D) 7
(E) 8

**27.** Jane is sorting socks in a laundry basket. If there are 60 socks in the laundry basket and half are white, how many pairs of white socks are there?

(A) 20
(B) 15
(C) 25
(D) 30
(E) 10

**28.** Which pairs of decimals and fractions are equivalent?

     I.   $0.2, \frac{1}{4}$
    II.   $0.25, \frac{4}{16}$
   III.   $0.6, \frac{3}{5}$

(A) I only
(B) II only
(C) I and II
(D) II and III
(E) I, II, and III

**29.** Which of these fractions is not equivalent to the others?

(A) $\frac{1}{5}$
(B) $\frac{5}{15}$
(C) $\frac{4}{20}$
(D) $\frac{2}{10}$
(E) $\frac{20}{100}$

**30.** Which answer is closest to $0.0005 \times 8.35$?

(A) 42

(B) 0.42

(C) 0.042

(D) 0.0042

(E) 0.00042

**31.** Mrs. Jones says that the points given for a drama student's performance are broken down as shown in the following pie chart. If dancing should constitute about 33 percent of a student's points, about how much should singing constitute?

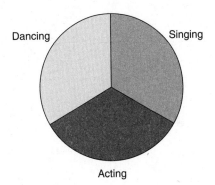

(A) 0 percent

(B) 25 percent

(C) 33 percent

(D) 50 percent

(E) 66 percent

**32.** "Some eggs are brown." Which of the following is true according to this statement?

(A) All eggs are brown.

(B) All limes are green.

(C) Some brown things are eggs.

(D) No limes are brown.

(E) Things that are not brown are not eggs.

**33.** 593,000 is how many times .593?

(A) 100

(B) 1,000

(C) 10,000

(D) 100,000

(E) 1,000,000

**34.** Which answer is closest to $788 \times 3{,}112$?

(A) 2,500,000
(B) 2,000,000
(C) 30,000,000
(D) 25,000,000
(E) 20,000,000

**35.** Which of the designated points on the following graph satisfy the equation $x^2 + y^2 = 4$?

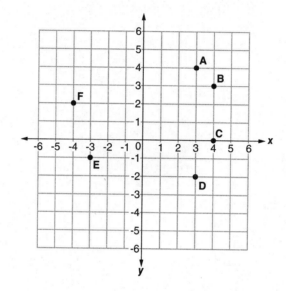

(A) C only
(B) A, C, and F
(C) A and C
(D) C and F
(E) None of them

**36.** Which number falls between $\frac{4}{5}$ and $\frac{8}{9}$?

(A) 80 percent
(B) 0.723
(C) $\frac{9}{10}$
(D) 0.85
(E) $\frac{40}{45}$

**37.** If you roll 2 six-sided dice, what is the probability that the combined total shown will be 4?

(A) $\frac{1}{6}$
(B) $\frac{7}{36}$
(C) $\frac{1}{12}$
(D) $\frac{1}{9}$
(E) 0

**38.** Which of these problems has the same numerical answer?

    I.   If I need 3 eggs to make 1 omelet, how many omelets can I make with 25 eggs?

    II.   If three people share the $25 cost of a gift evenly, how much does each of them pay?

    III.   If three people divide up 25 pizzas to take home, how many pizzas will each person get?

(A) I and II

(B) I and III

(C) II and III

(D) I, II, and III

(E) None of the above

**39.** If carpet must be purchased in rolls that are 9 feet wide, how much carpet will be left over once this room is carpeted?

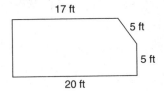

17 ft

5 ft

5 ft

20 ft

(A) 4 square feet

(B) 6 square feet

(C) 20 square feet

(D) 12 square feet

(E) 9 square feet

**40.** Which of the following numbers is half a million?

(A) 200,000

(B) $1,000,000 \times 0.05$

(C) $2/1,000,000$

(D) $1,000,000/0.2$

(E) $1,000,000 \times 0.5$

# STOP. This is the end of Mathematics Practice Test 1.

# MATHEMATICS PRACTICE TEST 1: ANSWERS

**1. C**  (3, –2) means 3 to the right, then 2 down.

**2. E**  $x = 5y$, so $2x = 10y$.

**3. C**  The trip is a right triangle, so use the Pythagorean equation. $12^2 = 144$. $5^2 = 25$. $144 + 25 = 169$. The square root of 169 is 13.

> **Test Hint:** When you start the PPST in Mathematics, write down the important formulas you have memorized. Even if you don't use the formulas, having them written down will give you confidence.

**4. B**  There are 13 cards in each suit, so two suits is 26 cards. 26 is 50 percent of 52.

**5. D**  Each line on the gauge represents 3, so the arrow is at 9 gallons. This is more than $\frac{1}{2}$, but less than $\frac{3}{4}$, so there is only one correct answer.

**6. E**  None of the cookies have strawberry cream, which equals 0 percent.

**7. E**  $16/2 = 8$. $8 - 2 + 6$.

**8. D**  2 feet = 3 inches, so 6 feet = 9 inches.

**9. B**  $110 + 65 + 90 + 40 + 100 = 405$. $405/5 = 81$.

**10. A**  This is a remainder interpretation problem. I is 4 soufflés; II is 4 picnics; and III is 5 boxes.

> **Test Hint:** As you work through the test, put a check mark next to any question you skip. Write in pencil so you can erase the check marks at the end of the test. When you get to the end, go back and answer any questions you left blank.

**11. B**  Eight chances out of a possible 22 (8 + 8 + 6), reduced to lowest terms.

**12. D**  $1,000,000 \times 3.64$.

**13. D**  One-third of a million is 1,000,000 divided by 3.

**14. E**  Find the number with the most leading zeroes; if two are tied, compare the first nonzero place.

**15. C**  Three employees give a profit of 90, which is higher than any of the other possibilities.

**16. E**  Each line on the gauge represents 100, so the tank contains about 150 gallons of oil. 150/500 = 30%.

---

**Test Hint:** Never let yourself get bogged down on one or two questions. Keep working so that you stay within your time limit.

---

**17. A**  $35 = 5x + 5$, so subtract 5 from both sides to get $30 = 5x$; then divide both sides to get $6 = x$.

**18. D**  Estimate: $25 is about 9 percent of the bill, so 18 percent of the bill would be twice as much.

**19. B**  Use equivalent fractions: $1/2.5 = x/5.5$, so $2.5x = 5.5$, and $x = 2.2$.

**20. E**  $\frac{1}{7} = 0.143$, $\frac{12}{18} = 0.667$.

**21. B**  Convert fractions to decimals by dividing.

**22. D**  None of the groups has a majority.

**23. A**  $2x + 4 = 9x - 10$, subtract $2x$ from both sides so $4 = 7x - 10$, add 10 to both sides so $14 = 7x$, and then divide both sides by 7. $x = 2$.

---

**Test Hint:** Be sure to check your work, even if you have just a minute or two. Use the time to look over your calculations.

---

**24. B**  $9 + 4 + 7 + 1 + 2$.

**25. C**  3.

**26. C**  $(8 + 6 + 4 + 5 + 7)/5$.

**27. B**  Thirty socks are white, so there are 15 pairs.

**28. D**  Change fractions to decimals and compare.

**29. B**  $\frac{5}{15} = \frac{3}{5}$. All the others equal $\frac{1}{5}$.

**30. D** Estimate, then count spaces past the decimal point.

**31. C** The chart is divided into thirds, so each portion is 33 percent.

---

**Test Hint:** When you are working on the PPST in Mathematics, check that your answers make sense and are logical.

---

**32. C** If some eggs are brown, then some eggs are not brown and some brown things are eggs. You don't know anything about limes or what other things might be brown or not brown.

**33. E** $1,000,000 \times 0.593 = 593,000$.

**34. A** Estimate by rounding to the nearest 100 ($800 \times 3,100 = 2,480,000$).

**35. E** Points that satisfy the equation fall within a circle of radius 2. None of the designated points falls within that circle.

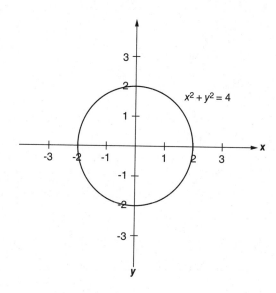

**36. D** Convert the fractions to decimals (0.80 and 0.8889) and determine which answer falls between them.

**37. D** Four combinations out of 36 add up to 4, so $\frac{1}{9}$ is the answer.

**38. C**    This is a remainder interpretation problem. I is 8 omelets, II is \$8.33, III is $8\frac{1}{3}$ pizzas.

---

**Test Hint:** To prevent careless errors, save a few minutes at the end to check the answer sheet against the choices on the test. Read each answer and the letter to yourself. Say the letter in your head.

---

**39. B**    The triangular cutout space is a right triangle with one side 3 feet long (20 feet – 17 feet) and a hypotenuse of 5 feet. Therefore, the remaining side is 4 feet long. A 3 × 4 rectangle would be 12 square feet; half of 12 square feet is 6.

**40. E**    $1,000,000 \times 0.5$.

# READING PRACTICE TEST 2

## Answer sheet

1 Ⓐ Ⓑ Ⓒ Ⓓ Ⓔ
2 Ⓐ Ⓑ Ⓒ Ⓓ Ⓔ
3 Ⓐ Ⓑ Ⓒ Ⓓ Ⓔ
4 Ⓐ Ⓑ Ⓒ Ⓓ Ⓔ
5 Ⓐ Ⓑ Ⓒ Ⓓ Ⓔ
6 Ⓐ Ⓑ Ⓒ Ⓓ Ⓔ
7 Ⓐ Ⓑ Ⓒ Ⓓ Ⓔ

8 Ⓐ Ⓑ Ⓒ Ⓓ Ⓔ
9 Ⓐ Ⓑ Ⓒ Ⓓ Ⓔ
10 Ⓐ Ⓑ Ⓒ Ⓓ Ⓔ
11 Ⓐ Ⓑ Ⓒ Ⓓ Ⓔ
12 Ⓐ Ⓑ Ⓒ Ⓓ Ⓔ
13 Ⓐ Ⓑ Ⓒ Ⓓ Ⓔ
14 Ⓐ Ⓑ Ⓒ Ⓓ Ⓔ

15 Ⓐ Ⓑ Ⓒ Ⓓ Ⓔ
16 Ⓐ Ⓑ Ⓒ Ⓓ Ⓔ
17 Ⓐ Ⓑ Ⓒ Ⓓ Ⓔ
18 Ⓐ Ⓑ Ⓒ Ⓓ Ⓔ
19 Ⓐ Ⓑ Ⓒ Ⓓ Ⓔ
20 Ⓐ Ⓑ Ⓒ Ⓓ Ⓔ
21 Ⓐ Ⓑ Ⓒ Ⓓ Ⓔ

22 Ⓐ Ⓑ Ⓒ Ⓓ Ⓔ
23 Ⓐ Ⓑ Ⓒ Ⓓ Ⓔ
24 Ⓐ Ⓑ Ⓒ Ⓓ Ⓔ
25 Ⓐ Ⓑ Ⓒ Ⓓ Ⓔ
26 Ⓐ Ⓑ Ⓒ Ⓓ Ⓔ
27 Ⓐ Ⓑ Ⓒ Ⓓ Ⓔ
28 Ⓐ Ⓑ Ⓒ Ⓓ Ⓔ

29 Ⓐ Ⓑ Ⓒ Ⓓ Ⓔ
30 Ⓐ Ⓑ Ⓒ Ⓓ Ⓔ
31 Ⓐ Ⓑ Ⓒ Ⓓ Ⓔ
32 Ⓐ Ⓑ Ⓒ Ⓓ Ⓔ
33 Ⓐ Ⓑ Ⓒ Ⓓ Ⓔ
34 Ⓐ Ⓑ Ⓒ Ⓓ Ⓔ
35 Ⓐ Ⓑ Ⓒ Ⓓ Ⓔ

36 Ⓐ Ⓑ Ⓒ Ⓓ Ⓔ
37 Ⓐ Ⓑ Ⓒ Ⓓ Ⓔ
38 Ⓐ Ⓑ Ⓒ Ⓓ Ⓔ
39 Ⓐ Ⓑ Ⓒ Ⓓ Ⓔ
40 Ⓐ Ⓑ Ⓒ Ⓓ Ⓔ

# READING PRACTICE TEST 2

## 40 questions, 60 minutes

*Directions:* Each of the following passages is followed by a question and five answer choices. Answer every question based on what is stated directly or suggested in each passage. You are not expected to have any prior knowledge of the information in the passages.

### Questions 1–3

"Organically grown" food is food grown and processed using no synthetic fertilizers or pesticides. Pesticides derived from natural sources (such as biological pesticides) may also be used in producing organic food. Increasingly, some consumers are purchasing this type of food as a way to reduce their exposure to pesticides and fertilizers. Many
(5)  supermarkets now stock organic products for their customers. Ask your grocer about organic food and its availability.

*USDA Issues National Organic Standards*
Beginning on October 21, 2002, producers and handlers must be certified by an agent accredited by the U.S. Department of Agriculture (USDA) to sell, label, or represent
(10)  their products as "100 percent organic," "organic," or "made with organic [specified ingredients or food group(s)]." For more information on the National Organic Program, visit the USDA's website.

1. Which of the following words, if substituted for the word *synthetic* in line 1 would introduce the LEAST change in the meaning of the sentence?

(A) artificial
(B) harmful
(C) insincere
(D) unhealthy
(E) costly

2. Which would be the BEST subtitle for the first paragraph?

   (A) The Mission of the USDA
   (B) New Labels on Foods
   (C) What "Organically Grown" Means
   (D) Many Ways to Designate "Organic"
   (E) Visit the Website

3. Why are some people buying organic food?

   (A) They believe it tastes better than nonorganic food.
   (B) It is easier to find in supermarkets today than it was in the past.
   (C) Organic food is increasingly popular and trendy.
   (D) The labels are easier to read and understand.
   (E) They are trying to consume fewer chemicals.

*Question 4*

  Among students from low socioeconomic backgrounds, those who took the most demanding and rigorous science and mathematics classes in high school—especially calculus—were about 10 times more likely than those who did not to have completed a bachelor's degree or higher by 2010. In contrast, among students from high socioeco-

(5) nomic backgrounds, those who completed calculus were 1.7 times more likely as those who did not to have completed a bachelor's degree or higher.

4. Which of the following is the most logical conclusion you can draw from this passage?

 (A) Taking a rigorous class, such as calculus, in high school is the single best way to compensate for a disadvantaged socioeconomic background and ensure college success.

 (B) If you want to succeed in your postsecondary education, you should take demanding high school mathematics classes, especially calculus.

 (C) Without postsecondary education, disadvantaged students cannot succeed, because today everyone needs a bachelor's degree or higher in order to attain lucrative employment.

 (D) Postsecondary attainment rates vary with students' socioeconomic status, but rigorous academic preparation and achievement in high school can partially compensate for disadvantaged backgrounds.

 (E) Students from low socioeconomic backgrounds are often disenfranchised by being shut out of the most demanding high school classes, such as calculus, due to low expectations.

*Questions 5–7*

The principal mountains west of the eastern boundary of California (the Rocky Mountains) are the Bear River, Wasatch, Utah, the Sierra Nevada, and the Coast Ranges. The Wasatch Range forms the eastern rim of the "great interior basin." There are numerous ranges in this desert basin, all of which run north and south, and they are

(5) separated from each other by spacious and barren valleys and plains. The Sierra Nevada range has greater elevations than the Rocky Mountains. The highest summits are covered with perpetual snow that shrouds the peaks year-round. This and the Coast Ranges run nearly parallel with the Pacific shoreline. The former is from 100 to 200 miles from the ocean, and the latter from 40 to 60 miles. The valley between them is the most fertile portion of California.

5. According to this article, all of the following are west of the Rocky Mountains EXCEPT

(A) the Appalachians
(B) the Coast Ranges
(C) the Wasatch Range
(D) the Sierra Nevada
(E) the Utah Mountains

6. This passage is primarily concerned with

(A) promoting tourism in California
(B) analyzing the most fertile portion of California
(C) describing a geographic area in California
(D) comparing mountain ranges in California
(E) helping travelers successfully navigate through California

7. The word *perpetual* in line 7 most nearly means

(A) deep
(B) frozen
(C) beautiful
(D) long-lasting
(E) treacherous

*Questions 8–10*

| Contact Lens Quick Guide | | |
|---|---|---|
| **What Kind of Lens Is It?** | **How Long Can I Wear Them?** | **When Do I Clean Them?** |
| *Disposable lenses*: lenses you throw away. | You can wear the lenses for one day. | You don't need to clean them; you use new lenses each day. |
| *Daily wear lenses*: lenses you use again and again. | You can wear them for one day. Take them out when you go to bed or even take a nap. | Clean and rinse the lenses every time you take them out. Also clean them if you have not worn them in a long time. |
| *Extended wear lenses*: lenses you can leave in for up to 30 days, even while you sleep. | The U.S. Food and Drug Administration (FDA) has only approved these lenses to be worn continuously for up to 30 days. | After 30 days, you need to take the lenses out and clean them. They can increase your chances of getting small sores on your eyes. *See your doctor right away if:* • your sight changes • your eyes get red • your eyes hurt or feel itchy • your eyes water |

8. Which of the following is true about disposable contact lenses?

   (A) They can be left in your eyes for a month.
   (B) You can leave these lenses in your eyes when you sleep.
   (C) If they are not kept clean, you can get sores on your eyes.
   (D) They are likely to cause sore, itchy eyes.
   (E) They are designed to be worn for a day and then discarded.

9. Based on this chart, you can infer that the FDA is most likely

   (A) selling a variety of contact lenses
   (B) regulating the manufacture of glasses
   (C) protecting and promoting public health
   (D) manufacturing contact lenses for sale at home and abroad
   (E) dealing solely with eye care, especially as it pertains to contact lenses

10. Which conclusion about contact lenses is BEST supported by the data in the chart?

   (A) Everyone should try wearing contact lenses.
   (B) Different types of contact lenses suit different wearers.
   (C) Contact lenses cost less now than they did years ago.
   (D) It can often take a long time to get used to wearing contact lenses.
   (E) Contact lenses are apt to cause eye irritation if not worn and handled properly.

*Questions 11–14*

State agriculture departments are concerned with many aspects of everyday life. These agencies promote their individual state's agricultural products; encourage production; and ensure consumer, livestock, and plant safety. Visitors to state agriculture websites may find information on food safety and disease alerts, product recalls, licensing and
(5) permits for producers, market news, trade and consumption marketing initiatives, grant programs, fairs and expositions, members and proceedings of advisory committees, agricultural statistics, regulations, irrigation, alternative energy technologies, environmental and pesticide programs, and inspections and measurement standards. Some sites have online resource directories, lists of licensed vendors, satellite maps, geographic informa-
(10) tion system (GIS) data, rural economic development services, agriculture-in-the-classroom programs, and notices of professional workshops.

**11.** All of the following information may appear on a state agriculture department website EXCEPT

(A) trade marketing initiatives and news about clinical trials
(B) alternative energy technologies and grant programs
(C) agricultural statistics, market news, and product recalls
(D) regulations, irrigation information, and satellite maps
(E) environmental and pesticide programs and food safety alerts

**12.** Which of the following words, if substituted for the word *expositions* in line 6 would introduce the LEAST change in the meaning of the sentence?

(A) vacations
(B) meetings
(C) descriptions
(D) explanations
(E) festivals

**13.** The author would be LEAST likely to agree with which of the following statements about state agricultural departments?

(A) State agricultural departments offer a rich and useful variety of materials and services.

(B) Even people not actively involved in agriculture should peruse state agricultural department websites to become familiar with their contents.

(C) The government established state agricultural departments to help all Americans lead better lives.

(D) Your state's agricultural department has a profound influence on your life in ways that you cannot imagine.

(E) Funding to state agricultural departments should be reduced to reflect the current economic downturn.

**14.** Which of the following BEST describes the organization of this passage?

(A) A series of organically linked events are arranged chronologically by theme.

(B) A general statement is followed by specific examples.

(C) A divisive theory is postulated and then logically supported.

(D) A governmental issue is stated and then fully and fairly debated.

(E) A challenging issue is explained, and a logical solution is suggested.

## Question 15

When you want to attract a particular species of bird and keep it returning to your backyard, your actions will be determined by where you live and the time of year. For example, on any winter day, you are likely to see a cardinal at a sunflower feeder in Virginia, a goldfinch at a thistle feeder in Massachusetts, and hummingbirds at a nectar
(5)   feeder in Southern California.

A bird field identification book has pictures of different birds and will help you find the names for those you're likely to see and during what season you're most likely to see them. So first determine what birds are likely to live in your area.

**15.** This passage is primarily concerned with

(A) discussing the advantages and disadvantages of feeding wildlife
(B) analyzing the different birds that live in various parts of America
(C) helping readers learn how to get started with backyard bird feeding
(D) educating readers about the importance of wildlife conservation
(E) explicating the problems that can arise when humans interfere with nature

*Questions 16–18*

If a product is meant to keep you from getting sick, make you well, or change the way your body works, it is a drug. For example, products that treat dandruff and pimples are drugs. The law treats them differently from cosmetics, and they have different rules for how ingredients are listed. Some products are both cosmetics and drugs. For example, a
(5) shampoo that is just for washing your hair is a cosmetic; one for stopping dandruff is a drug. A shampoo that is used for washing your hair and stopping dandruff is both a cosmetic and a drug. It must follow the rules for both cosmetics and drugs.

**16.** According to this passage, drugs are products that do all of the following EXCEPT

(A) treat illnesses
(B) help cure an illness
(C) help prevent an illness
(D) enhance the body's appearance or odor
(E) alter the mechanics of the body

**17.** Which would be the BEST title for this passage?

(A) How Prescription Medication Works
(B) Different Products You Need to Know
(C) Cosmetics and Drugs for Consumers
(D) Which Are Better: Cosmetics or Drugs?
(E) How Do I Know If It's a Cosmetic or a Drug?

**18.** According to the passage, which of the following would be classified as a cosmetic?

(A) cortisone
(B) antibiotics
(C) aspirin
(D) hair dye
(E) acetaminophen

***Questions 19–20***

Whether you call it by its colloquial names—"sawing logs" and "blowing z's"—or its medical name (*stertor*), snoring is common. You snore when something blocks the flow of air through your mouth and nose. The sound is caused by tissues at the top of your airway that strike each other and vibrate. Many adults, especially men, snore, and the
(5) condition may increase with age.

However, snoring can also be a sign of a grave sleep disorder called sleep apnea. This means you stop breathing for periods of more than 10 seconds at a time while you sleep. Sleep apnea is serious, but there are treatments that can help. Both children and adults can have sleep apnea. If your child snores frequently, have your health care pro-
(10) vider check for sleep apnea.

Here are some tips for reducing snoring:

- Lose weight if you are heavy.
- Cut down on or eliminate alcohol and other sedatives at bedtime.
- Avoid sleeping flat on your back.

**19.** The word *grave* in line 6 most nearly means

(A) tomb
(B) forbidding
(C) medical
(D) serious
(E) mausoleum

**20.** What is the BEST statement of the main idea of the first paragraph?

(A) Snoring, caused by blocked breathing, is commonplace.
(B) There are several amusing names for snoring, including "sawing logs" and "blowing z's."
(C) Men are more likely to snore than women.
(D) As people get older, they are more likely to snore.
(E) Doctors study many medical conditions such as snoring.

*Questions 21–25*

Tattoo removal should be done in a clinic by a doctor and not in a tattoo parlor. There are several ways to remove a tattoo, but they don't always work. Removing a tattoo is often a costly venture, especially because repeated treatment is usually required. Here are some choices:

(5)
- **Laser treatment:** This is the most common way to remove a tattoo. Light from the laser breaks up the ink, and the body itself gets rid of the treated areas over the next few weeks. Most tattoos need more than one laser treatment to be removed completely, and some inks cannot be removed in this manner
- **Dermabrasion:** Sanding down to lower layers of skin is another way to remove a
(10)   tattoo. The area to be sanded is numbed first to lessen the pain, and this procedure may leave a scar.
- **Salabrasion:** A salt solution is used to remove the color. This process must be used with dermabrasion. However, it is not a popular method.
- **Scarification:** In this procedure, the tattoo is eradicated with acid, which leaves a scar
(15)   in its place. Patients can later have surgery to get rid of the scar.

**21.** Which of the following BEST describes the organization of this passage?

(A) A number of theories are summarized, evaluated, and then accepted or rejected.
(B) A problematic issue is discussed, and several possible solutions are suggested.
(C) A serious medical condition is described, and a series of treatments are provided.
(D) A surprising problem is explored, and different theories are proposed.
(E) A challenging issue is explained, and a logical solution is suggested

**22.** Why is salabrasion likely not used very often?

(A) It is costly, and the cost is not covered by insurance.
(B) It must be used with dermabrasion.
(C) It is ineffectual, leaving poor results.
(D) Once it is done, a new tattoo cannot be put in the same place.
(E) Not many health care professionals are familiar with the procedure.

**23.** How does laser treatment work?

(A) The layers of skin around the tattoo are sanded down.
(B) Acid is used to remove the ink on the tattoo.
(C) The tattoo is covered in bandages until it fades.
(D) The ink on the tattoo is broken down by light.
(E) A salt solution is used to take the color off the skin.

**24.** A tattoo can be removed by all of the following methods EXCEPT

(A) dermabrasion
(B) salabrasion
(C) secretion
(D) laser treatment
(E) scarification

**25.** Which of the following is an unstated opinion made by the author of this passage?

(A) People often regret getting a tattoo.
(B) It is usually difficult to remove a tattoo.
(C) Only qualified physicians should attempt to remove tattoos.
(D) Tattoos become increasingly faded as the wearer ages.
(E) Some tattoos are more pleasing and popular than others.

*Questions 26–27*

> An institution like this has often been recommended on merely mercantile consider-
> ations. But an academy founded on such principles can never effect even its own narrow
> purposes. If it has no higher origin, no taste can ever be formed in it which can be useful
> even in manufacturing; but if the higher arts of design flourish, these inferior ends will
> (5) be naturally answered.

**26.** Which of the following words, if substituted for the word *mercantile* in line 1, would introduce the LEAST change in the meaning of the sentence?

(A) artistic
(B) immediate
(C) educational
(D) commercial
(E) ethical

**27.** Which is the most logical conclusion you can draw from this passage?

(A) The author, an eminent artist, is starting his own gallery amid great controversy.
(B) A renowned art college has fallen on hard times because of lack of enrollment.
(C) The speaker is arguing in favor of establishing a college of art.
(D) The board of trustees of a museum wants to expand by adding an upper level.
(E) The author, an art critic, argues that businesses should design more aesthetically pleasing structures.

*Questions 28–30*

Every nation requires its own readily accepted currency. So in 1792, Congress called for the establishment of a national mint. Because Philadelphia was then the nation's capital, it was built there. Congress's next decision concerned the money itself. Legislators decided that American coins would be made of gold, silver, and copper, with $10.00,
(5) $5.00, $2.50, half-dime, and half-cent pieces, in addition to the coin denominations we have now. Unlike today's nickels, the half-dimes were made of silver.

The first mint was erected at 7th and Arch Streets, and by March 1793, it delivered its first circulating coins: 11,178 copper cents. Their production was overseen by David Rittenhouse, a leading American scientist and the first director of the U.S. mint. As the
(10) United States and its economy grew, the nation required more coins and larger minting facilities. The mint expanded accordingly and moved three times. Its current facility, Philadelphia's fourth, opened in 1969.

**28.** When the mint was established, coins were minted in all of the following denominations EXCEPT

(A) half-cents
(B) pennies
(C) half-dimes
(D) $2.50 coins
(E) $15.00 coins

**29.** The passage states that

(A) Congress established the mint and determined which coins would be made
(B) Washington, DC, not Philadelphia, is currently the capital of the United States
(C) scientists such as David Rittenhouse, the first director of the mint, make excellent administrators
(D) since every nation requires it own currency, every nation has a mint to strike coins
(E) our first coins were made of gold, silver, and copper, but today's coins also contain base such as copper-plated zinc

**30.** Which is the BEST title for this passage?

(A) Historical Background: Half-Cents and Five-Dollar Pieces
(B) The Origins of America's Currency
(C) The First Mint in the United States
(D) Currency: Coins and Bills in American Life
(E) The Economic Basis of Contemporary Civilization

*Questions 31–35*

Small turtles may look cute and harmless, but they can make people very ill because they commonly carry bacteria called *Salmonella* on their outer skin and shell surfaces. *Salmonella*, transmitted when people come in contact with turtles in their habitat, causes a serious or even life-threatening infection in people, although the bacteria do
(5)  not make turtles sick. Most people recover without treatment, but some get so sick that they need to be treated in a hospital.

"All reptiles (turtles, lizards, snakes) and amphibians (frogs, salamanders) are commonly contaminated with *Salmonella*," says Joseph C. Paige, DVM, a consumer safety officer in the Food and Drug Administration's (FDA's) Center for Veterinary
(10)  Medicine. "But it is the small turtles that are most often put in contact with young children, where the consequences of infection are likely to be severe." Because of this health risk, since 1975, the FDA has banned the sale of small turtles with a shell less than four inches long.

"Young children are ingenious in constructing ways to infect themselves," explains
(15)  Paige. "They put the small turtles in their mouths or, more often, touch the turtles or dangle their fingers in the turtle tank water and then put their hands in their mouths. Also, sometimes the tanks and reptile paraphernalia are cleaned in the kitchen sink, and food and eating utensils get cross-contaminated." Surfaces such as countertops, tabletops, bare floors, and carpeting can also become contaminated with the bacteria
(20)  if the turtle is allowed to roam on them. Bacteria may survive for a long period of time on these surfaces.

**31.** To evaluate the validity of the author's claim regarding the danger posed by *Salmonella* (lines 3–5), it would be helpful to know which of the following?

(A) what other pets can transmit *Salmonella*
(B) how *Salmonella* is treated in hospitals
(C) the death rates from *Salmonella*
(D) why people would want turtles as pets
(E) why turtles themselves don't get ill from *Salmonella*

**32.** Which of the following BEST describes the organization of this passage?

(A) A problem concerning reptiles and children is arranged in order of importance.
(B) A controversial medical situation is posited and then shown to be legitimate.
(C) An age-related consumer issue is set forth, and the dangers are described.
(D) A warning is issued and supported by expert opinions.
(E) A challenging issue is explained, and a valid solution is presented.

**33.** The word *ingenious* in line 14 most nearly means

    (A) relentless
    (B) sincere
    (C) clumsy
    (D) devious
    (E) clever

**34.** The primary purpose of this passage is to

    (A) instruct consumers about how to care properly for small turtles and other reptiles
    (B) convince readers that no reptile makes a suitable pet for small children
    (C) persuade readers that small turtles are not suitable pets, especially for young children
    (D) make sure that all pets are cared for properly, safely, and humanely
    (E) advocate that mammals such as cats and dogs, rather than reptiles, be adopted as pets

**35.** Why are children most likely to contract *Salmonella* from small turtles?

    (A) Turtles are the most popular pets that carry the bacteria, and they are especially popular with kids.
    (B) Small turtles are the only pets that carry *Salmonella*, so they are especially dangerous to kids.
    (C) The turtles carry a more virulent form of the bacteria than other popular pets.
    (D) The turtles carry a significant health risk for young children because of the bacteria.
    (E) Few consumers recognize the danger that turtles pose to small children.

*Questions 36–37*

A major consideration in approving pesticides for use is whether they pose an unreasonable risk to humans. The Environmental Protection Agency (EPA) assesses risks associated with individual pesticides' active ingredients and with groups of pesticides that have a common toxic effect. The latter assessment is called cumulative risk assessment and is designed to evaluate the risk associated with simultaneous exposure to multiple pesticides that act the same way in the body.

(5)

Part of the EPA's assessment of the health risks of pesticides is a determination of whether there is "reasonable certainty of no harm" posed by pesticide residues that remain on food. Before approving a pesticide, the agency sets limits on how it may be used, how often it may be used, what protective clothing or equipment is required, and so on. These limits are designed to protect public health and the environment.

(10)

36. Which sentence from the passage BEST states the author's overall main idea?

(A) A major consideration in approving pesticides for use is whether they pose an unreasonable risk to humans.

(B) The Environmental Protection Agency [EPA] assesses risks associated with individual pesticides' active ingredients and with groups of pesticides that have a common toxic effect.

(C) The latter assessment is called cumulative risk assessment and is designed to evaluate the risk associated with simultaneous exposure to multiple pesticides that act the same way in the body.

(D) Part of the EPA's assessment of the health risks of pesticides is a determination of whether there is "reasonable certainty of no harm" posed by pesticide residues that remain on food.

(E) Before approving a pesticide, the agency sets limits on how it may be used, how often it may be used, what protective clothing or equipment is required, and so on.

37. Which of the following is an unstated assertion the author of this passage accepts as true?

(A) The EPA is the only organization today that assesses the effects of pesticides.

(B) Pesticides are essential in modern agribusiness.

(C) Today's pesticides are less harmful than those used in the last century.

(D) Cumulative risk assessment is the optimal way to determine the potential effects of pesticides.

(E) Most pesticides do not harm people, only the insects they were designed to eradicate.

*Questions 38–40*

Susan LaFlesche Picotte was born on the Omaha Reservation, which is now Thurston County, in northern Nebraska. She was the daughter of Chief Joseph LaFlesche (Iron Eye) and his wife, Mary (One Woman). Her father was the last recognized chief of his tribe and advocated Indian integration with white society. He raised all of his children
(5) to be independent, educated, and adaptable to a changing Indian society. Susan's decision to attend medical school was highly unusual at a time when formal medical training was rare for women, especially Indian women.

In 1889, Susan graduated (after two years) from the three-year medical program at the Woman's Medical College of Pennsylvania at the top of her class. In 1890, she
(10) accepted a position as physician at the government boarding school on the Omaha Reservation, where she treated children and adults. On becoming the senior physician, she assumed responsibility for the health care of 1,244 tribal members.

In addition to providing health care for her people, she served her tribe in many other ways. She acted as teacher, social worker, and adviser. She also worked as an
(15) advocate for Omaha Indian rights and was a dedicated temperance activist.

Susan Picotte's lifelong dream to have a hospital in which to care for her people became a reality in January 1913. The $8,000 project, funded by a variety of sources, was the first hospital not funded by government money for an Indian reservation. The building contained two general wards, five private wards, a maternity ward, an operat-
(20) ing room, a kitchen, a reception room, and two bathrooms. The facilities served patients until the 1940s. Since then, it has served in numerous capacities. It is presently used as a museum, with exhibits on the history of church missions, the Omaha and Winnebago tribes, and Susan Picotte. The former hospital is also used for various community functions and stands today as a reminder of Susan's important role in the lives of Native
(25) Americans in Nebraska and the nation.

**38.** The former hospital, closed in the 1940s, is used today for all of the following purposes EXCEPT as a

(A) museum with exhibits on the history of church missions
(B) community center
(C) learning center for the Omaha and Winnebago tribes
(D) medical college for Native Americans in the Midwest
(E) way to educate people about the achievements and heritage of Susan Picotte

**39.** You can most logically conclude that Susan LaFlesche Picotte

(A) was the only Native American woman in the late nineteenth century to become a physician
(B) did her most important work as a physician to her people and served as a role model for many
(C) was a brilliant, determined person who was raised to succeed and help her people
(D) wanted to be a physician from childhood because she recognized that her people needed qualified doctors
(E) raised the money necessary to establish the hospital and staffed it herself

**40.** This excerpt would most likely be published in a

    (A) social studies textbook for high school students in the Midwest

    (B) government web page for college history educators

    (C) web page on notable Native American leaders

    (D) private blog published by a Native American writer

    (E) newspaper editorial on the importance of setting goals

# STOP. This is the end of Reading Practice Test 2.

# READING PRACTICE TEST 2: ANSWERS

**1. A** Since *synthetic* does not have a root, suffix, or prefix, you have to use context clues to define it. The passage says that *"Organically grown" food is food grown and processed using no synthetic fertilizers or pesticides*, so *synthetic* must be the opposite of *organic*. Thus, something that is synthetic must be artificial or not natural. This makes choice A the best match.

Something *synthetic* does not have to be harmful (choice B), insincere (choice C), or unhealthy (choice D), so these choices can be eliminated. Finally, choice E doesn't make sense because the passage doesn't have any information about cost.

Let's look more deeply into solving vocabulary questions on the Praxis reading exam. Whenever you can, use context clues to help you deduce the answer. This usually means recognizing signal words—the surrounding words and phrases that act like "road signs" in a sentence, directing the logic and flow of ideas. Here are the most common types of context clues:

- **Definition clues:** The sentence may actually include a definition of the word, often with a word or phrase like *defined as, which means, meaning, also called*, and so on.
- **Similarity clues:** The sentence may include a more familiar synonym of the word or a statement that is equivalent to the one that contains the word, often with a word or phrase like *just as, so, also, like, similarly, in the same way, likewise, another*, and so on.
- **Contrast clues:** The sentence may include a more familiar antonym of the word or a statement that is the opposite of the one that contains the word, often with a word or phrase like *not, but, yet, however, unlike, by contrast, on the contrary, despite, while, although, even though, otherwise, instead*, and so on.
- **Example clues:** The sentence may give one thing as an example of another, often with a word or phrase like *for example, for instance, to illustrate, such as, including, otherwise, else, even*, and so on.
- **Cause-and-effect clues:** The sentence may explain that one thing causes, affects, influences, or changes the other, often with a word or phrase like *because, if, then, since, as a result, consequently, therefore, thus, due to*, and so on.
- **Positivity/negativity clues:** Determine whether the word means something positive or something negative. The correct answer must have the same kind of connotation.
- **Part-of-speech clues:** Determine whether the word is a noun, a verb, an adjective, and so on. The correct answer must be the same part of speech.
- **Grammar clues:** Is the word a noun, and is it singular or plural? If the word is a verb, how is it conjugated, and is it typically used alone or with a specific preposition? The correct answer must fit grammatically.

**Test Hint:** If you think you know the meaning of the word asked about in the test item, think of a synonym for it before you read the answer choices. Then pick the answer that's the best match. For example, let's say you know what *imperfect* means. You might say, "A synonym might be *broken*," and you would look for an answer that's close to that synonym.

**2. C**    Remember that subtitle questions are really asking for the main idea of the passage. Choice C is the best subtitle because it encompasses the entire content. Choices A, B, and E are too general. Choice D is too specific; it is a detail rather than the main idea.

Here are some quick strategies for answering main idea questions:

- To find the main idea, start by skimming the passage and the question(s).
- Next, find the topic, or subject, of the passage. You can find it by deciding what the passage describes as you skim it.
- After you find the topic, look for the sentence that gives the most general information about that topic. This will most likely contain the main idea of the passage. You will know you have chosen the correct sentence if it gives an overview or introduction to the topic by explaining what the entire passage will discuss. The sentence can be anywhere in the passage—the beginning, middle, or end—but it's most often at the beginning and/or the end.
- Check that every other idea in the passage relates to this overarching idea. Remember, you're looking solely for the main idea. If it's not stated directly in the passage—or very strongly implied by the passage as a whole—it can't be the main idea!
- Use the process of elimination. Cross out any choices that focus too much on details (specific pieces of information) from the passage; don't accurately summarize the passage; or misstate, distort, or exaggerate ideas from the passage.
- Choose the answer that is closest to your prediction.
- Finally, quickly double-check the other answer choices to make sure you have chosen the best one.

**3. E**    The answer is directly stated in this sentence: *Increasingly, some consumers are purchasing [organically grown and processed] food as a way to reduce their exposure to pesticides and fertilizers.* Choices A, B, and C may be true, but they are not stated in the passage. The answer must come from information contained in the passage, not outside sources. According to the passage, choice D is not a factor in consumer decisions.

**Test Hint:** When you have to read a passage and answer questions about it on the PPST reading test, first skim the questions for the passage. Ignore the answers for the time being. Then skim the passage itself and mark it up to identify the main points, key names and dates, significant transitions, and so on. Use whatever system you find easiest—underline the relevant points, circle them, draw stars or arrows next to them, number them, and so on. If you don't understand part of the passage, reread that section slowly and carefully.

**4. D** You can reach this conclusion by comparing the quantifiable achievement of high school students who completed calculus to the quantifiable achievement of those who did not. This comparison reveals that taking more demanding classes in high school helps students do well in college. Choice A is too sweeping a generalization, as taking demanding classes may not be the "single best way" to overcome a disadvantaged background. Choice B is also too general to support the information in the passage. Choice C is false, since people in the trades (plumbers, electricians, and so on) who do not have a bachelor's degree can still obtain high-paying jobs in their field. There is no support in the passage for choice E. Even though a choice may contain true information, if that information is not in the passage, the choice is invalid.

**Test Hint:** In general, avoid choices that contain "absolute" words such as *the best, the worst,* and so on. These choices are virtually never correct.

**5. A** This is a recall question, and the answer is directly stated in the first sentence: *The principal mountains west of the eastern boundary of California (the Rocky Mountains) are the Bear River, Wasatch, Utah, the Sierra Nevada, and the Coast Ranges. The Wasatch Range forms the eastern rim of the "great interior basin."* Remember, the word *except* tells you that you are looking for the answer that is the exception.

**6. C** The author's purpose is to describe, shown by the factual tone. Since the author is not arguing a point, choice A cannot be correct. Choice B is too narrow, as the passage only touches on the fertile valley. Conversely, choice D is too broad. Finally, choice E is incorrect because the description is too general to be used as travel directions.

**Test Hint:** A *writer's purpose* is his or her reason for writing. Writers have four main purposes: to persuade (convince), to give information, to entertain, and to describe. A passage can have more than one purpose, but one will be dominant. As you read, always try to identify the writer's purpose so you can understand his or her position on the subject.

**7. D** The context clue is "that shrouds the peaks year-round." This tells you that *perpetual* must mean "long-lasting."

**8. E** This is a recall question. The correct answer is stated in the first row of information, under "Disposable lenses."

9. **C**    Since the FDA has approved extended-wear contact lenses for only 30 days of continuous wear, the FDA must be a public health agency. There is no support for any of the other choices in the passage.

---

**Test Hint:** Always read *all* the answer choices before you make your final decision—even if you are sure you know the correct one!

---

10. **B**    The explanation of each type of lens suggests that individuals must select the kind that suits their lifestyles. Choices A and E are too big a leap, based on the information here. There is no support for choices C and D on the chart, although the statements may be true. Be sure to base your response on the information in the passage, not on information you may already know.

11. **A**    This is a recall question, so you can skim the passage to locate each detail. Choice A is only partly correct: state agriculture websites may contain trade marketing initiatives, but they don't have news about clinical trials. If one part of a response is incorrect, the entire answer is incorrect.

12. **E**    Here, you can use roots and context clues, since *expositions* contains a root and has multiple meanings. The root is *expose*, which means "to present to view, exhibit, display." As used in this passage, *expositions* means a type of show, such as a festival. The context clue is "fairs."

---

**Test Hint:** If you know the meaning of the word but don't know one or more of the answer choices, try first to eliminate any choices you know are definitely wrong, then make an educated guess from the remaining choices. Looking back at test item 12, we can conclude that the answer can't be *descriptions* or *explanations*, so we can cross out choices C and D.

---

13. **E**    The author enthusiastically lists the rich and varied resources that state agricultural departments offer, so it is highly unlikely that he or she would support reducing funding. Further, the phrases "Visitors to state agriculture websites *may* find" and "*Some* sites" suggest that state agricultural departments are already underfunded, since not all of these departments can offer all the services listed here.

14. **B**    The general statement—*State agriculture departments are concerned with many aspects of everyday life*—is then followed by a series of specific examples of ways this is true.

**15. C**   You can make this inference based on the details in the passage; they are all concerned with helping readers learn how to begin the hobby of backyard bird feeding. These details include learning how to attract birds to your yard and learning how to identify the birds you see.

**Test Hint:** If you see two answer choices that mean the *opposite* of each other, you may be tempted to think that one of them must be the right answer. Resist this temptation because they might both be wrong!

**16. D**   This is a recall question, so you can find the answer directly stated in the passage. The first sentence states the definition of a drug. Every choice but D defines a drug.

**17. E**   This is a main idea question. The entire passage explains the differences between cosmetics and drugs, so choice E is the best answer. Choice A is too specific, as it does not include cosmetics. Choice B is too general because it does not name cosmetics or drugs. Choice C is on the topic, but it doesn't show that the passage differentiates between cosmetics and drugs—which is the main idea. Choice D is wrong because the passage doesn't show which is better, cosmetics or drugs.

**Test Hint:** If you see two answer choices that mean much the same thing, eliminate them. If one of them is correct, both of them must be correct—and no question has two correct answers. By the same token, if one of them is wrong, both of them must be wrong.

**18. D**   This is a recall question, so you can find the answer directly stated in the passage. You do not have to make an inference or draw a conclusion. The answer is D; hair dye would be classified as a cosmetic because it is not "meant to keep you from getting sick, make you well, or change the way your body works," the passage's definition of a drug.

**19. D**  *Grave* does not have a root, prefix, or suffix that you can use to figure out its meaning. However, it does have multiple definitions:

- As a noun, it is a hole dug in the earth, or any tomb, in which to bury a corpse.
- As an adjective, it means "solemn or serious, weighty or important, or critical." It can also define a specific accent (`), indicating a low pitch or a syllabic value
- As a verb, it means "to carve, sculpt, or engrave, or to impress deeply."

With a multiple-meaning word such as this, you have to use context clues. The context is shown in the following sentences: *However, snoring can also be a sign of a grave sleep disorder called sleep apnea. This means you stop breathing for periods of more than 10 seconds at a time while you sleep. Sleep apnea is serious. . . .*" The words *disorder*, *stop breathing*, and *serious* tell you that *grave* is used here to mean "serious." Choices A, C, and E are clearly not correct in this context; and choice B (*forbidding*) overstates the case and has the wrong connotation (emotional overtone).

---

**Test Hint:** You should use context clues; word parts (roots, prefixes, and suffixes); and logic to define unfamiliar words on the PPST reading exam. However, to prepare for this exam as well as for your career as a teacher, you will want to improve your vocabulary. Here are some effective and enjoyable ways to do so.

1. First, look words up. Whenever you encounter an unfamiliar word, look up its meaning in the dictionary. This not only lets you discover the correct definition and pronunciation, but it also helps you remember the word better.
2. Play word games, such as Scrabble and Boggle. Do crossword puzzles, acrostics, word scrambles, word finds, and so on.
3. Try to learn one new word each day. You may even want to purchase a "new word a day" calendar and use it.
4. Write the new words down in a notebook or on index cards, one word per card. Take the notebook or cards with you all the time so you can review your new words in spare moments.

---

**20. A**  Remember, to find the main idea, you need to put together the details in the passage to find the "big picture." Write a statement that draws the specifics together and then look at the choices to see which one best matches your conclusion. Here, only choice A states the author's overarching point. Choices B, C, and D are details. Choice E is too general, as it does not include any information on blocked breathing.

**21. B** This is an inference question, as the answer is not directly stated in the passage. The problem explored in this passage is how to get rid of a tattoo. The solutions are various methods, including laser treatment, dermabrasion, and salabrasion. Choice A is wrong because tattoos are not theories. Similarly, choice C is incorrect because tattoos are not a serious medical condition; rather, they are a cosmetic issue. Don't be misled by choice D; getting rid of a tattoo is not a surprising problem. Choice E is partly correct; getting rid of a tattoo is a challenging issue, but the rest of the passage is not a logical solution. The rest of the passage covers possible solutions, not just one.

**22. C** This is also an inference question, as you must draw a conclusion from the information in the passage. Since salabrasion must be used with dermabrasion, you can infer that salabrasion is not very effective. The second part of choice A cannot be deduced from the information in the passage, as cost is not mentioned. There is no support for choices D and E. Choice B is incomplete—ask yourself *why* both processes would have to be used together.

**Test Hint:** An *entire* answer must be correct for the choice to be right. If even a small part of the answer is incorrect, you can eliminate the entire choice.

**23. D** This is a recall question, which means that you can skim the passage to find the information you need. The answer is directly stated in the following sentence: *Light from the laser breaks up the ink.* Choice A describes dermabrasion, choice B describes scarification, and choice E describes salabrasion. Choice C contains information that is not in the passage.

**24. C** This is a recall question, and you are looking for the exception. Every method except C is described in the passage.

**25. A** The phrase "unstated opinion" tells you that you must make an inference. The information will not be stated directly in the passage. You can infer that people often regret getting a tattoo (choice A), because if they didn't experience buyer's remorse, there wouldn't be so many ways to remove one. Choices B and C are facts stated in the passage, not inferences. Choices D and E may be true, but they are not supported by any information in the passage.

**26. D**   The word *mercantile* has a root that you can use to define it: *merchant*. The root refers to "trade." *Mercantile* has only one meaning, so you can use context clues to verify your answer, but you don't have to rely solely on them.

- Using roots, the closest synonym for *mercantile* is choice D (*commercial* contains the root *commerce*, having to do with business).
- Using context clues, the author contrasts the disadvantages of merely commercial organizations to those that have also been designed with attention to aesthetic considerations.

Don't be misled by the word *academy*; choice C is incorrect.

---

**Test Hint:** Sometimes you can find a root in a word to help you define that word. For instance, *terminate* contains the root *term*, which means "end." Therefore, *to terminate* most nearly means "to end."

   If you can't find a root, you can often find a smaller word within the larger one to help you define it. For example, *infinite* contains the smaller word *finite*. You can use this and the prefix (*in-* usually means "not") to figure out that *infinite* means "not ending."

---

**27. C**   The question tells you outright that you have to draw a conclusion, so you know that the answer will not be stated directly in the passage. Thus, you will have to put together clues by studying the details.

   The context clue "an institution like this" in the first sentence shows the establishment of some sort of organization. The clues "has often been recommended on merely mercantile considerations" and "but an academy founded on such principles can never effect even its own narrow purposes" suggest a debate over its founding principles. The tone of the first sentence suggests that the speaker sees more than "mere mercantile" reasons for supporting the endeavor. The clue "higher arts of design flourish" suggests art. Thus, the most logical conclusion is that the speaker is arguing in favor of establishing a college of art.

   Choice A is too big a leap; you cannot conclude from the information in the passage that the author is an eminent artist. The positive tone of the speaker's words suggests that choice B is not valid. Don't be fooled by "no higher" and "higher arts" as pertaining to choice D. There is no support in the passage for choice E.

**28. E**   This is a recall question. You are looking for the exception, as the question stem directs. All of the choices can be found in the passage except choice E. Pay close attention to the phrase "in addition to the coin denominations we have now."

**29. A**  You can tell that this is a recall question from the stem, so look for the answer in the passage and be careful not to bring in outside information. Choices B and E are true, but they are not stated in the passage. Choice C cannot be concluded from the information given. Make sure that the entire choice and not just part of it is correct, as is the case with choice D—the first part is true, but the second part cannot be verified from the information in the passage.

---

**Test Hint:** When you are looking through a passage for a specific detail, mark it up to save time and help ensure that you find the correct answer. Use any method that works for you. For instance, cross out information you don't need and circle information you do.

---

**30. B**  This is a main idea question. Only B includes all relevant detail. Choices A and C are too narrow, while choices D and E are too broad to represent the theme of the passage.

**31. C**  The most useful information for judging the truthfulness of the author's thesis is choice C, because it enables readers to judge the risk factors posed by these pet turtles. Choices A, D, and E are off the topic. Choice B would provide some information, but choice C is a significantly stronger response.

**32. D**  In this passage, the author warns readers about the dangers posed by small pet turtles, supporting the warning by citing a valid expert in the field. Thus, the correct answer is choice D: *A warning is issued and supported by expert opinions.* Choices C and E are partially correct, but choice C is too vague and choice E incorrectly describes the topic as "challenging." People do not need to purchase turtles, so there's nothing challenging here. Choice A is invalid because the passage does not use order of importance. Choice B is wrong because the issue is not controversial.

**33. E**  If you study the word *ingenious*, you might think of the smaller word *genius*, which could help you conclude that someone who is ingenious is clever (choice E). You could also use context clues. The list of ways that children are able to infect themselves with *Salmonella* gives you the clue you need to grasp the author's slightly tongue-in-check tone: children are very clever when it comes to making themselves ill in this way. Regarding choice B, don't confuse *ingenious* (clever) with *ingenuous* (candid, frank, sincere).

---

**Test Hint:** Be sure to read passages and test questions very carefully. This is especially important with vocabulary questions, as many words can easily be confused. In general, the PPST reading test is not designed to trick test takers, but when people are under pressure and working quickly, they do make mistakes, so read carefully.

---

**34. C**    The author is trying to persuade readers that small turtles are not suitable pets, especially for young children. You can conclude this from the following details:

- *Small turtles may look cute and harmless, but they can make people very ill because they commonly carry bacteria called* Salmonella *on their outer skin and shell surfaces.*
- *"But it is the small turtles that are most often put in contact with young children, where the consequences of infection are likely to be severe." Because of this health risk, since 1975, the FDA has banned the sale of small turtles with a shell less than four inches long.*
- *"Young children are ingenious in constructing ways to infect themselves," explains Paige. "They put the small turtles in their mouths or, more often, touch the turtles or dangle their fingers in the turtle tank water and then put their hands in their mouths."*

Choice A misses the point, as you can conclude from the information in the first sentence. Further, the author does not list ways to prevent contamination, just the ways that the contamination occurs. On the other hand, choices B and D go too far, as the passage focuses on small turtles. The passage does not condemn all reptile pets or raise the issue of other types of pets, so choice E is not valid.

**35. A**    This is a recall question, and the information is found in the following sentence: *"But it is the small turtles that are most often put in contact with young children."* Choice B is contradicted by this sentence: *"All reptiles (turtles, lizards, snakes) and amphibians (frogs, salamanders, are commonly contaminated with* Salmonella." The passage does not contain any information to support choices C and E. Choice D, an example of circular reasoning, is too vague.

**36. A**    The first sentence in this passage states the main idea, the broad statement of purpose. The other sentences state details, small pieces of supporting information. Remember, the topic sentence is often first in a passage, although it doesn't have to be.

**37. B**    You can infer that choice B is correct because the phrase "unreasonable risk to humans" tells you that a reasonable risk is acceptable. From this, you can conclude that pesticides, in some form or other, are an inescapable part of the business of modern agriculture. Thus, pesticides are essential in modern agribusiness.

There is insufficient proof for choices A, C, and D. Remember to base your conclusion on the information in the passage. Choice E has no basis in the information given.

**38. D**    The word *except* tells you that you are looking for the one bit of information that is *not* in the passage. Thus, this is a recall question and requires you to go back over the passage to find the answer. The information can be found in the last paragraph: the former hospital is not used as a school. It is used for every other choice given.

**39. C** You can reach this conclusion from the information about Picotte's childhood in the first paragraph and the description of her achievements later on. Choice A overstates the case. The author says that *Susan's decision to attend medical school was highly unusual at a time when formal medical training was rare for women, especially Indian women*. From this, you cannot conclude that she was the *only* Indian woman to become a doctor. Choice B is incorrect because the entire sentence is not true. Remember, the entire answer must be correct for the choice to be valid. In this instance, the second half of the sentence is correct, but the first half is not because it lacks sufficient proof in the passage. Choice D has a problem with logic. Susan LaFlesche Picotte knew that her people needed doctors, but this does not mean that she wanted to be a doctor from childhood. Choice E lacks proof, as we don't even know if she was alive when the hospital was established.

**40. C** Every choice but C is too general and thus could apply to nearly any passage.

## Skills Spread

|  | Item Numbers |
|---|---|
| Literal (18) | 3, 5, 7, 8, 11, 12, 16, 17, 19, 20, 23, 24, 28, 29, 30, 35, 36, 38 |
| Inferential (22) | 1, 2, 4, 6, 9, 10, 13, 14, 15, 18, 21, 22, 25, 26, 27, 31, 32, 33, 34, 37, 39, 40 |

# WRITING PRACTICE TEST 2

## Answer sheet

1 (A) (B) (C) (D) (E)
2 (A) (B) (C) (D) (E)
3 (A) (B) (C) (D) (E)
4 (A) (B) (C) (D) (E)
5 (A) (B) (C) (D) (E)
6 (A) (B) (C) (D) (E)
7 (A) (B) (C) (D) (E)

8 (A) (B) (C) (D) (E)
9 (A) (B) (C) (D) (E)
10 (A) (B) (C) (D) (E)
11 (A) (B) (C) (D) (E)
12 (A) (B) (C) (D) (E)
13 (A) (B) (C) (D) (E)
14 (A) (B) (C) (D) (E)

15 (A) (B) (C) (D) (E)
16 (A) (B) (C) (D) (E)
17 (A) (B) (C) (D) (E)
18 (A) (B) (C) (D) (E)
19 (A) (B) (C) (D) (E)
20 (A) (B) (C) (D) (E)
21 (A) (B) (C) (D) (E)

22 (A) (B) (C) (D) (E)
23 (A) (B) (C) (D) (E)
24 (A) (B) (C) (D) (E)
25 (A) (B) (C) (D) (E)
26 (A) (B) (C) (D) (E)
27 (A) (B) (C) (D) (E)
28 (A) (B) (C) (D) (E)

29 (A) (B) (C) (D) (E)
30 (A) (B) (C) (D) (E)
31 (A) (B) (C) (D) (E)
32 (A) (B) (C) (D) (E)
33 (A) (B) (C) (D) (E)
34 (A) (B) (C) (D) (E)
35 (A) (B) (C) (D) (E)

36 (A) (B) (C) (D) (E)
37 (A) (B) (C) (D) (E)
38 (A) (B) (C) (D) (E)

# WRITING PRACTICE TEST 2

## SECTION 1: MULTIPLE-CHOICE QUESTIONS

### 38 questions, 30 minutes

*Directions:* The following sentences require you to identify errors in grammar, usage, punctuation, and capitalization. Not every sentence has an error, and no sentence will have more than one. Every sentence error, if there is one, is underlined and lettered. If the sentence does have an error, select the one underlined part that must be changed to make the sentence correct and blacken the corresponding circle on your answer sheet. If the sentence does not have an error, blacken circle E. Elements of the sentence that are not underlined are not to be changed.

*Part A*
*21 questions*

Suggested time: 10 minutes

1. Once the house <u>had been painted</u>, but the sun had blistered the <u>paint and the rains</u> had
   A                                                                              B
   washed it away<u>,</u> the house was <u>as dull and gray as everything</u> else. <u>No error.</u>
   C                                    D                                    E

2. <u>James Simmons,</u> an American hedge fund manager <u>and who</u> has founded a successful
   A                                                    B
   private investment <u>firm, is</u> now giving back to society by donating $150 million
   C
   <u>to Stony Brook University and $38 million to autism research.</u> <u>No error.</u>
   D                                                              E

3. <u>As suggested by its name,</u> <u>Alice's Teacup</u> is a charming restaurant where quirky food
   A                              B
   <u>is served</u> by skilled waiters <u>on mismatched china.</u> <u>No error.</u>
   C                                  D                        E

4. <u>Located in Kansas,</u> the college currently enrolls 7,000 students in 27 baccalaureate and
   A
   9 associate degree programs <u>in its</u> schools of arts and sciences, business, engineering,
   B
   and health sciences, and it has 190 <u>full-time</u> tenure-track faculty, 36 percent of <u>who</u> are
   C                                                                                    D
   untenured. <u>No error.</u>
   E

5. The politician <u>didn't say nothing</u> that the audience had not already heard<u>; therefore,</u>
                          A                                                                              B
   the <u>listeners quickly</u> lost interest in her speech and <u>began to talk</u> among themselves.
              C                                                              D
   <u>No error.</u>
        E

6. For all the sophistry that <u>declares texting while driving kills,</u> we forget everything car-
                                              A
   ries that <u>potential, however,</u> writing a law fining people for living is just that<u>:</u> evidence
                    B                                                                                    C
   of <u>government's inability</u> to stay between the lines. <u>No error.</u>
            D                                                          E

7. The guests <u>felt badly</u> because they arrived <u>an hour late</u> and had neglected to call
                      A                                        B
   <u>ahead, but</u> they felt they should be forgiven <u>their rudeness</u> nonetheless. <u>No error.</u>
        C                                                      D                              E

8. Whether we accept the former secretary of labor Robert <u>Reich's</u> assertion that
                                                                        A
   40 percent of minimum-wage workers are the sole source of income for their <u>families'</u>
                                                                                          B
   or the <u>report's</u> claim that "only 2.8 percent of workers earning less than $5.15 are
              C
   single <u>parents,</u>" we cannot deny that some families do rely on minimum wages. <u>No error.</u>
              D                                                                                    E

9. <u>It's</u> a little-known <u>fact, but</u> when opossums are "playing possum," <u>they have not played:</u>
    A                          B                                                      C
   they are passing out from <u>sheer terror.</u> <u>No error.</u>
                                    D                E

10. The salesperson <u>guaranteed to call</u> my <u>mother and I</u> as soon as the <u>coat went on sale</u> so
                            A                          B                              C
    <u>we could save 50 percent</u> on the purchase. <u>No error.</u>
              D                                          E

11. The light bulbs in the <u>New York subway system</u> screw in clockwise and screw out
                                    A
    <u>counterclockwise</u> (the reverse of traditional light bulbs)<u>;</u> so people who steal them
          B                                                          C
    <u>can't</u> use them. <u>No error.</u>
        D              E

12. <u>Although nearly over,</u> we left the concert <u>earlier</u> <u>than</u> we had planned because we
              A                                        B        C
    <u>were concerned</u> about our sick puppy. <u>No error.</u>
            D                                        E

13. My father <u>lays down</u> <u>on the sofa</u> every afternoon to take a <u>nap, but</u> my mother never
                    A            B                                        C
    lets him rest <u>undisturbed.</u> <u>No error.</u>
                          D            E

**14.** In many languages <u>other than</u> English, the object possessed is named first, <u>following</u> by
                 A                                                      B
the <u>person or thing that possesses</u> it, as in <u>"This is the office of Spencer."</u> <u>No error.</u>
     C                                 D            E

**15.** <u>When the results</u> from the Students First Grants for Teaching are combined with a
     A
complex array of other initiatives funded by the Title III Strengthening Institutions
<u>award we</u> expect that the campus culture <u>will have been transformed</u> into the type of
   B                                   C
robust learner-centered institution worthy of <u>its</u> new mission as a comprehensive
                                      D
four-year polytechnic college. <u>No error.</u>
                     E

**16.** The suburban homeowner <u>who</u> is saddled with a significant <u>mortgage, car loan, and</u>
                    A                                        B
<u>credit card bills</u> is <u>frequent</u> hard-pressed for <u>sufficient funds</u> to set aside for retirement.
  C                                    D
<u>No error.</u>
  E

**17.** When tea was first introduced in the <u>American colonies,</u> many <u>people, not</u> knowing
                               A                  B
what to do with the <u>stuff served</u> the tea leaves with sugar or syrup and <u>threw</u> away the
                 C                                    D
water they had been boiled in. <u>No error.</u>
                      E

**18.** The cell phone <u>ringed</u> during dinner<u>;</u> however<u>,</u> Vanessa ignored it because she knew
             A             B    C
the telemarketers <u>always called</u> around 6:00 P.M. <u>No error.</u>
           D                     E

**19.** The main library at <u>Indiana University</u> <u>sinking more than an inch every year</u><u>,</u> because
                  A               B                C
when it was built, <u>engineers failed to take into account</u> the weight of all the books that
                                  D
would occupy the building. <u>No error.</u>
                  E

**20.** <u>In reviewing Debbie's checkbook,</u> <u>hundreds of errors</u> involving major and minor errors
         A                          B
in arithmetic—<u>especially addition and subtraction</u>—<u>were identified.</u> <u>No error.</u>
                   C                      D     E

**21.** <u>Alphabetic writing</u> is basically <u>phonetic,</u> no <u>alphabet</u> has <u>ever perfectly</u> represented a
     A                  B        C       D
language. <u>No error.</u>
      E

*Part B*
*17 questions*

Suggested time: 20 minutes

*Directions:* Choose the best version of the underlined portion of each sentence. Choice A is the same as the underlined portion of the original sentence. If you think that the original sentence is better than any of the suggested revisions, choose A. Otherwise, choose the revision you think is best. Answers and explanations follow the questions.

22. <u>In view of the fact that</u> Saturday morning dawned fresh and clear and the trees were in bloom, Tom Sawyer did not want to waste his time painting his Aunt Polly's fence.

    (A) In view of the fact that
    (B) Due to the fact that
    (C) Because
    (D) Insomuch as
    (E) As a result of the fact that

23. After spending a month searching in vain for a decent apartment at an affordable price, I was glad that the landlord gave <u>my family and I</u> a year's extension on our lease.

    (A) my family and I
    (B) me and my family
    (C) I and my family
    (D) we
    (E) my family and me

24. When a seaman did put up at the Admiral Benbow (as now and then some did, making by the coast road for Bristol), he would look in at him through the curtained door before <u>he entered the parlor he was</u> always sure to be as silent as a mouse when any such was present.

    (A) he entered the parlor he was
    (B) he entered the parlor, he was
    (C) he entered the parlor was
    (D) he entering the parlor he was
    (E) he entered the parlor, and he was

25. Many people consider the medical field a service rather than a profession: they expect doctors to give unselfishly, to offer unending care with little or no concern for compensation, and <u>working long hours</u> seven days a week.

    (A) working long hours
    (B) to work long hours
    (C) worked long hours
    (D) had been working long hours
    (E) will work long hours

**26.** <u>Being that</u> mosquitoes have killed more people than all the world's wars combined, we can conclude that it is vital to eradicate these insects.

(A) Being that
(B) Being
(C) If
(D) Because
(E) Yet

**27.** <u>Dashing to make the subway, the new murals on the walls were seen</u>, in all their glorious colors.

(A) Dashing to make the subway, the new murals on the walls were seen
(B) Dashing to make the subway, the new murals on the walls were seen by the commuters
(C) The new murals on the walls were seen dashing to make the subway
(D) As the commuters dashed to make the subway, they saw the new murals on the walls
(E) Dashing to make the subway, the new murals on the walls had been seen

**28.** <u>The house approaching by graveled</u> driveways that wound through wide-spreading lawns and under the interlacing boughs of tall poplars, shading great stables, long grape arbors, green pastures, orchards, and berry patches.

(A) The house approaching by graveled
(B) The house was approached by graveled
(C) The house approached by graveled
(D) The house being approached by graveled
(E) The house having been approached by graveled

**29.** Worldwide, there are more statues of Joan of Arc than of anyone <u>else France</u> alone has about 40,000 of them.

(A) else France
(B) else; France
(C) else, France
(D) else, yet France
(E) else, because France

**30.** <u>Nobody in the community speak</u> well of them, likely because of their raucous parties and unkempt yard.

(A) Nobody in the community speak
(B) Nobody in the community speaked
(C) Nobody in the community speaking
(D) Nobody in the community speaked
(E) Nobody in the community speaks

**31.** <u>For the reason that</u> the class involves a great deal of reading as well as writing, the instructor decided to be relatively lenient on grading.

(A) For the reason that
(B) As a result of the fact that
(C) Since
(D) In which case
(E) As a direct consequence of the situation that

**32.** But his strength ebbed, his eyes glazed, and he knew nothing when the train was flagged and the two men <u>throw him</u> into the baggage car.

(A) throw him
(B) throwing him
(C) threw him
(D) throwing him
(E) throw he

**33.** After his bachelor party, C.J. was not feeling <u>good, so he decided to lie</u> down on the sofa for the afternoon.

(A) good, so he decided to lie
(B) good, so he decided to lay
(C) good, so he decided to lies
(D) well, so he decided to lay
(E) well, so he decided to lie

**34.** <u>That there</u> is the lake where the entire community enjoys spending weekends picnicking, swimming, and playing sports.

(A) That there
(B) That
(C) This here
(D) That their
(E) That they're

**35.** The supervisor <u>doesn't</u> care if her employees come to work late, as long as they get all their tasks completed for the day and the work is satisfactory.

(A) doesn't
(B) don't
(C) kind of don't
(D) sort of don't
(E) can't help but not

36. Edith <u>Whartons' word pictures' of society's upper reaches</u> remain unsurpassed; her glimpse into the mystery and misery of the human heart still has the ability to reach our own souls.

    (A) Edith Whartons' word pictures' of society's upper reaches
    (B) Edith Whartons' word pictures' of societys' upper reaches
    (C) Edith Wharton's word picture's of society's upper reaches'
    (D) Edith Wharton's word pictures of society's upper reaches
    (E) Edith Wharton's word pictures of societys' upper reache's

37. <u>Each of the teachers donate</u> his or her time as well as expertise to the successful school open house.

    (A) Each of the teachers donate
    (B) Each of the teachers donating
    (C) Each of the teachers having donating
    (D) Each of the teachers donating
    (E) Each of the teachers donates

38. By 1770, Ben Franklin was the chief spokesman for the <u>colonies in 1757 he</u> was elected to the Second Continental Congress.

    (A) colonies in 1757 he
    (B) colonies; in 1757, he
    (C) colonies, in 1757, he
    (D) colonies, in 1757 he
    (E) colonies in 1757, he

# STOP. This is the end of Section 1: Multiple-Choice Questions.

# SECTION 2: ESSAY

## 30 minutes

*Directions:* Write an essay on the following topic. You will not receive any credit for writing on a topic other than the one given here. Plan your essay carefully and be sure to include specific examples and details that illustrate your point. Write your essay on your own paper. (On the real Praxis PPST test, paper for writing your essay will be provided.)

**You will not receive credit if you write on any other topic. For your response to be scored, you must write in English. You cannot write in a foreign language.**

Read the opinion stated:

A classic is something that everybody wants to have read and nobody wants to read.
—MARK TWAIN

In an essay, agree or disagree with this statement. Be sure to support your opinion with specific examples from readings, your experiences, your observations, or the media.

The space below is for your notes.

**Test Hint:** If your writing is difficult to read, consider printing. Don't use all capital letters, though. Instead, use the accepted mix of uppercase and lowercase letters.

# WRITING PRACTICE TEST 2: ANSWERS

## SECTION 1: MULTIPLE-CHOICE QUESTIONS

*Part A*

> **Note: This part of the test does *not* require you to correct the sentence, only to identify the error that it may or may not contain. However, to help you learn more about grammar and usage to earn a higher score on the entire Praxis writing test (including Part B and the essay), as well as to improve your teaching, all errors are corrected and the relevant grammar and usage rules explained.**

**1. C**   This sentence has an error in structure. As written, it is a run-on because the two independent clauses are joined incorrectly; a comma is not sufficient between two complete sentences. Here are two ways to correct the sentence:

- *Once the house had been painted, but the sun had blistered the paint and the rains had washed it away, <u>so</u> now the house was as dull and gray as everything else.*
- *Once the house had been painted, but the sun had blistered the paint and the rains had washed it away; <u>as a result</u>, the house was as dull and gray as everything else.*

**2. B**   This sentence has an error in wordiness. There is no reason to add the word *and*.

> **Test Hint:** Trying to learn all the rules of grammar in a day, a week, or even a month is impossible, but it is not impossible to learn enough grammar in a short time to make a big difference in your test grade. Therefore, set realistic goals, such as one rule a day or one rule every two days. Then stick with your schedule. You'll soon find that you have learned enough grammar to make a huge difference.

**3. D** This sentence has an error in usage: it contains a misplaced modifier. As written, it states that the waiters are on mismatched china. The sentence should read: *As suggested by its name, Alice's Teacup is a charming restaurant where quirky food is served on mismatched china by skilled waiters.*

**Test Hint:** Practice makes perfect, so here's another misplaced modifier to use as practice:

*The judge sentenced the killer to die in the electric chair for the third time.*

(Error: You can only die in the electric chair once, unless you're a cat with nine lives.)

Corrected sentence: *For the third time, the judge sentenced the killer to die in the electric chair.*

**4. D** This sentence has an error in case. Use the objective case (*whom*) as the object of the preposition *of*. *Case* is the form of a noun or pronoun that shows how it is used in a sentence. English has three cases: nominative, objective, and possessive. The following chart shows the pronouns and their forms in the three cases.

| Nominative | Objective | Possessive |
|---|---|---|
| I | me | my, mine |
| you | you | your, yours |
| he | him | his |
| she | her | her, hers |
| it | it | its |
| we | us | our, ours |
| they | them | their, theirs |
| who | whom | whose |
| whoever | whomever | whoever |

**5. A** This sentence has an error in usage; it contains a double negative. The correct form is *didn't say anything* or *said nothing*.

**6. B**    This sentence has an error in structure. As written, it is a run-on, meaning two sentences run together without the correct punctuation. There are several ways to correct this sentence; here are two grammatically correct versions:

- *For all the sophistry that declares texting while driving kills, we forget everything carries that potential; however, writing a law fining people for living is just that: evidence of government's inability to stay between the lines.*
- *For all the sophistry that declares texting while driving kills, we forget everything carries that potential. However, writing a law fining people for living is just that: evidence of government's inability to stay between the lines.*

**Test Hint:** Words such as *however* are called conjunctive adverbs. A semicolon and a comma are used when a conjunctive adverb separates two main clauses. The conjunctive adverb may look like a coordinate conjunction (*and, or, so, but, for*), but it is not as strong, which is why a semicolon is needed. The sentence structure looks like this:

| Tommy was ill | ; | however, | he stayed at work. |
|---|---|---|---|
| *independent clause* | *semicolon* | *conjunctive adverb* | *independent clause* |

Other conjunctive adverbs include:

| | | | | |
|---|---|---|---|---|
| accordingly | furthermore | moreover | similarly | further |
| also | hence | namely | still | meanwhile |
| anyway | however | nevertheless | then | undoubtedly |
| besides | incidentally | next | thereafter | otherwise |
| certainly | indeed | nonetheless | therefore | likewise |
| consequently | instead | now | thus | finally |

**7. A**    This sentence has an error in usage. Use an adjective, not an adverb, after a linking verb. The correct form is: *The guests felt bad.*

**8. B**   This sentence has an error in plural forms. The error occurs in choice B, because the correct plural form of *family* is *families*. There is no reason to use an apostrophe because the word is plural, not possessive. This is shown in choice D. Choices A and C use apostrophes correctly to show ownership.

---

**Test Hint:** Practice makes perfect, so here are some items to use for additional practice with apostrophes. Add apostrophes as necessary to show the plural form of each noun.

1. the antics of Bozo
2. the laundry of the men
3. the room of Charles
4. the gills of the tadpole
5. the wages of Leroy
6. the tantrums of the children

*Answers:*

1. Bozo's antics
2. men's laundry
3. Charles's room
4. tadpole's gills
5. Leroy's wages
6. children's tantrums

---

**9. C**   This sentence has an error in tense use. Don't switch tenses in midsentence. The sentence should read: *It's a little-known fact, but when opossums are "playing possum," they are not playing: they are passing out from sheer terror.*

**10. B**   This sentence has an error in case. The salesperson is doing the action and my mother and me are receiving the action, so use the objective case (*me*) rather than the nominative case (*I*). In the objective case, the pronoun is used as a direct object, indirect object, or object of a preposition. The pronoun receives the action. Here are some examples:

- Pronoun as direct object

  *The elaborate meal pleased me.* (not *I*)

  *The thunderstorm frightened the dog and them.* (not *they*)

- Pronoun as indirect object

  *The power outage gave us a scare.*

  *My brother sent me some perfume from Paris.*

- Pronoun as the object of a preposition

  *Sit          by          me.*

              preposition    pronoun

  *I refuse to speak          to          her.*

              preposition    pronoun

**11. C**  This is a question on sentence structure. There is no reason to use a semicolon with the coordinating conjunction *so*, since a coordinating conjunction and a semicolon fulfill the same function—to connect two independent clauses. Place a comma before the coordinating conjunction. The correct sentence reads: *The light bulbs in the New York subway system screw in clockwise and screw out counterclockwise (the reverse of traditional light bulbs), so people who steal them can't use them.*

You'll find it easier to solve test items involving long sentences if you break the sentences into their independent clauses. You can cross out intervening phrases to make it easier to see the complete units of thought. Here is an example:

Light bulbs ~~in the New York subway system~~ screw in clockwise and screw out coun-
     *intervening phrase*      *independent clause*

terclockwise ~~(the reverse of traditional light bulbs)~~, people who steal them can't use them.
     *intervening phrases*     *independent clause*

Putting the sentence back together: *The light bulbs screw in clockwise and screw out counterclockwise, so people who steal them can't use them.*

**12. A**  This sentence has an error in usage. As written, it contains a misplaced modifier. The way this sentence is structured, the phrase "Although nearly over" illogically modifies *we*, the pronoun directly following it. The sentence should read: *Although the concert was nearly over, we left earlier than we had planned because we were concerned about our sick puppy.*

---

**Test Hint:** Here's another misplaced modifier to use as practice:

*Please take some time to look over the letter that is enclosed with your union representative.*

(Error: How would they fold your union representative to be enclosed with a letter?)
Corrected sentence:

*Please take some time with your union representative to look over the letter that is enclosed.*

---

**13. A** This sentence has an error in usage: *lie* versus *lay*. Use the verb *lie* to mean "to be in a horizontal position, to recline." The correct word in this sentence is *lies*. Since this is a tricky usage point, here's additional explanation:

*Lie*

- *Lie* means "to recline."
- *Lie* is an intransitive verb, which means it never takes a direct object. For example: *If you are tired, you should lie down.*
- *Lie* means that the subject is doing something to himself or herself. It is a complete verb. When accompanied by subjects, complete verbs tell the whole story.

*Lay*

- *Lay* means "to put down."
- *Lay* is a transitive verb, which means it always takes a direct object. For example: *Please lay the book on the table.*
- *Lay* means that the subject is acting on something or someone else; therefore, it requires a complement to make sense. This is why it always takes a direct object.

Here are the principal tenses of *lie* and *lay*:

| Word | Meaning | Examples |
|------|---------|----------|
| Lie | To recline | Present tense: Fido lies down. Past tense: Fido lay down. Future tense: Fido will lie down. Perfect tense: Fido has lain down. |
| Lay | To put down | Present tense: Lay your cards down. Past tense: He laid the cards down. Future tense: He will lay the cards down. Perfect tense: He has laid the cards down. |

**14. B** This sentence has an error in sentence structure. It is a fragment because the verb is in the wrong form. The correct sentence reads: *In many languages other than English, the object possessed is named first, followed by the person or thing that possesses it, as in "This is the office of Spencer."*

**15. B** This sentence has an error in punctuation: comma usage. Use a comma after an introductory clause. In this sentence, the introductory clause is: *When the results from the Students First Grants for Teaching are combined with a complex array of other initiatives funded by the Title III Strengthening Institutions award.* Don't be confused because the sentence is so long; as suggested in this book, break it up into logical units (clauses and phrases) and study each one separately.

**16. C**   This sentence has an error in usage. Use an adverb to modify (describe) an adjective. The adverb here is *frequently*; the adjective is *hard-pressed*.

    *Adverbs* are words used to describe a verb, an adjective, or another adverb. By so doing, they give the verb, adjective, or other adverb a more precise and specific meaning. To identify adverbs, ask yourself these questions:

| Where? | move <u>aside</u> |
| | adverb |
| When? | arrived <u>yesterday</u> |
| | adverb |
| In what manner? | talked <u>smoothly</u> |
| | adverb |
| To what extent? | <u>partly</u> understand |
| | adverb |

Many adverbs end in *-ly*, but not all. Here are some examples of adverbs:

| **Adverbs That End in -*ly*** | **Adverbs That Don't End in -*ly*** |
| --- | --- |
| brightly | very |
| slowly | never |
| quickly | seldom |
| easily | always |
| nicely | somewhat |
| extremely | just |
| amazingly | more |
| fairly | almost |

**17. C**   This sentence has an error in punctuation: commas. Set off nonessential information with commas. Here, the nonessential phrase is *not knowing what to do with the stuff*.

**18. A**   This sentence has an error in usage: the sentence requires the past tense "rang."

---

**Test Hint:** As you read the sentence, concentrate on the underlined portion. If it doesn't sound right, how would you improve it? Look for your improvement (or something similar) in the answer choices. If any of the underlined portions contains punctuation, double-check that the correct mark has been used.

---

**19. B**   This is a sentence error. The sentence is incomplete because the verb *sinking* is in the wrong form, creating a fragment. The verb should be *sinks* or *is sinking*. Here are two versions, both equally correct:

- *The main library at Indiana University sinks more than an inch every year, because when it was built, engineers failed to take into account the weight of all the books that would occupy the building.*
- *The main library at Indiana University is sinking more than an inch every year, because when it was built, engineers failed to take into account the weight of all the books that would occupy the building.*

**20. A**   This sentence has an error in usage. As written, it has a dangling modifier because no one is performing the action. One possible revision involves shifting from the passive voice to the active voice: *The accountant, in reviewing Debbie's checkbook, identified hundreds of errors involving major and minor errors in arithmetic—especially addition and subtraction.*

**21. B**   This is a run-on, meaning two sentences that are joined incorrectly. Here are two correct revisions:

- *Alphabetic writing is basically phonetic, but no alphabet has ever perfectly represented a language.*
- *Alphabetic writing is basically phonetic; no alphabet has ever perfectly represented a language.*

*Part B*

**22. C**  This is a question on wordiness. Generally, you should choose the most concise construction. Choice C is the least wordy answer here; all the other choices are unnecessarily verbose.

Redundancies (wordy phrases) can be grouped as follows:

| Type of Redundancy | Example | Correction |
|---|---|---|
| adjectives | complete and total failure<br>narrow, slender margin | ~~complete and total~~ failure<br>narrow~~, slender~~ margin |
| adverbs | working carefully and methodically<br>completely and totally fail | working carefully ~~and methodically~~<br>~~completely and totally~~ fail |
| adverbs and verbs | completely finish<br>connect together<br>prove conclusively | ~~completely~~ finish<br>connect ~~together~~<br>prove ~~conclusively~~ |
| adverbs and adjectives | totally unique<br>bothersomely annoying<br>completely finished | ~~totally~~ unique<br>~~bothersomely~~ annoying<br>~~completely~~ finished |
| adjectives and nouns | transportation vehicle<br>successful victory<br>alternative choices | ~~transportation~~ vehicle<br>~~successful~~ victory<br>alternative ~~choices~~ |

Here are some ways to improve wordy phrases:

| **Wordy Phrase** | **Concise Phrase** |
|---|---|
| a large number of | many |
| at that point in time | then |
| due to the fact that | because |
| has the ability to | can |
| in the event | that is |
| in close proximity to | near |
| in view of the fact that | because |
| in my own personal opinion | I believe |
| subsequent to | after |
| with reference to the fact that | concerning |

**23. E**  This is a question on *pronoun case*, the form the pronoun takes to show whether it is being used as a subject, as an object, or to show possession. Here, *the landlord* is the subject (performing the action); *my family and me* is the object (receiving the action). Choice B is incorrect because you always put yourself last. Thus, the phrase is written *my family and me*, not *me and my family*. Choice C is wrong because it is in the wrong case; switching the order of the noun and pronoun doesn't change the case. Choice D is wrong because it is the nominative (subject) case rather than the object case, which would be *us*.

**24. E** This is a question about sentence structure. As written, the sentence is a run-on. Adding a coordinating conjunction *(and)* corrects the error by linking the two independent clauses. As you learned earlier, identifying the independent clauses can help you find the error. Here is what the sentence looks like simplified:

> When a seaman did put up at the Admiral Benbow
>
> *dependent clause*
>
> he would look in at him through the curtained door before he entered the parlor
>
> *independent clause*
>
> he was always sure to be as silent as a mouse when any such was present.
>
> *independent clause*

Ignore the dependent clause for the moment and you get:

> he would look in at him through the curtained door before he entered the parlor, and
>
> *independent clause*
>
> he was always sure to be as silent as a mouse when any such was present.
>
> *independent clause*

Adding a comma (choice B) does not correct the error. Rather, it creates a comma splice, a comma used to join two independent clauses. As explained earlier, a comma is not sufficient. Changing the tense (choice D) doesn't correct the error either. Choice C introduces a new error by eliminating the subject.

This is a *compound-complex sentence*, a construction that has at least two independent clauses and at least one dependent clause. The dependent clause can be part of the independent clause.

---

**Test Hint:** If you have to guess, keep it simple. Go for the answer that creates the most direct, least complex sentence.

---

**25. B** This is a question on parallel structure. Make the infinitive (base form of the verb) *to work* parallel with the infinitives *to give* and *to offer*. The corrected sentence is: *Many people consider the medical field a service rather than a profession: they expect doctors to give unselfishly, to offer unending care with little or no concern for compensation, and to work long hours seven days a week.*

**26. D** This is a question on usage. *Being that* is considered substandard usage, so use *because* or *since* instead. Choice B *(being)* does not correct the error. *If* (choice C) and *yet* (choice E) do not make sense in context.

**27. D**   This is a dangling participle. Only choice D corrects the error.

> **Test Hint:** Here's another dangling participle to use as practice:
>
> *Do not sit on the swing set without being assembled.*
>
> (Error: As the sentence reads, it means that the person–not the swing set–isn't fully assembled. This is possible but not likely.)
>
> Corrected sentence: *Do not sit on the swing set until it is assembled.*

**28. B**   As written, this sentence is a fragment because it is missing a complete verb. *Approaching* is not complete. Only choice B corrects the error.

**29. B**   This is a run-on, meaning two sentences that are joined incorrectly. Choices D and E correct the error grammatically but don't make sense logically. Choices A and C don't correct the error.

**30. E**   This is a question on agreement. The singular pronoun *nobody* requires the singular verb *speaks*. Ignore the intervening prepositional phrase *in the community*; it does not affect agreement.

**31. C**   This sentence has an error in style. The phrase *for the reason that* is unnecessarily wordy. Use *since* instead. As explained earlier, clear, direct writing is preferable to wordiness.

**32. C**   This is a question on verb tense. Use the past tense (*threw*) to match the past tense in the first clauses (*ebbed, glazed, knew, was flagged*). Choice E introduces another error, this one in case (how a pronoun is used).

**33. E**   This is a usage question. *Good* is an adjective, so you should never use it after an action verb. Use the adverb *well* instead. *Lie*, which means "to be in a horizontal position, to recline," is correct as used here.

**34. B**   This sentence has an error in usage. *That there* and *this here* are considered substandard usage. Use *that* or *there* alone. Choices D and E are incorrect because they not only maintain the substandard usage, but they also spell *there* wrong.

> **Test Hint:** Consider the basics. The people who make the PPST writing test pose questions about the most common sentence errors rather than obscure writing problems. As a result, look for problems with sentence boundaries (fragments and run-ons), parallel structure, pronoun case, agreement of subject and verb, pronoun reference, degree of comparison, misplaced and dangling modifiers–all the types of questions you have practiced in this book.

**35. A**   The sentence is correct as written.

**36. D**   This sentence has an error in possessives. The word pictures belong to one writer, Edith Wharton, so the correct possessive form is *Wharton's*. The upper reaches belong to society, so the correct form is *society's*. Do not confuse possession (ownership) with plural (adding an *s* or changing the spelling of the noun) construction. There is no reason to add an apostrophe to *pictures* or *reaches*.

**37. E**   This is a question on agreement. The singular pronoun *each* requires the singular verb *donates*. Ignore the intervening prepositional phrase *of the teachers*. Choices C and D create fragments (incomplete sentences).

**38. B**   This is a run-on, meaning two sentences that are joined incorrectly. Only choice B corrects the error.

## Skills Spread

| Specific Content Area | Item Numbers |
|---|---|
| Grammar and usage (14) | 4, 7, 8, 9, 10, 16, 20, 23, 26, 27, 30, 32, 33, 37 |
| Sentence structure (13) | 1, 3, 6, 11, 12, 14, 19, 21, 24, 25, 28, 29, 38 |
| Mechanics—punctuation, capitalization Diction—word choice (11) | 2, 5, 13, 15, 17, 18, 22, 31, 34, 35, 36 |
| Essay | 1 |

# SECTION 2: ESSAY

The following model essay would receive a 6, the highest score, for its specific details, organization, and style (such as appropriate word choice, sentence structure, and consistent facility in the use of language). It is an especially intelligent and insightful response.

*sophisticated diction creates clear voice and style*

While much fuss is made over the annual lists of books that everyone should read, the fact is that most people do not read any classics beyond those they are forced to endure in school. Even that much may well be in doubt, since more than one student has tried to coast through a class solely on a mishmash of movie adaptations, CliffsNotes, and Wikipedia articles. But avoiding the classics is hardly a new phenomenon. A century ago, Mark Twain quipped, "A classic is something that everybody wants to have read and nobody wants to read." (One wonders if he had any idea at the time that his own works would eventually be relegated to this status.) Our attention spans have only decreased since Twain's time, while shortcuts to knowing key quotes and plot points have only increased. So why bother reading the classics at all, when it's so easy to fake the knowledge and skip Twain's little paradox?

*clear argumentative thesis statement*

Here's why people should read the classics: they offer pleasures that can only be discovered by actually reading them yourself.

*first main point*

First, one of the greatest complaints about literature written more than a generation or two before the birth of the reader is that the language is archaic. It's true that it takes patience (and sometimes footnotes) to make our way through Cervantes or Chaucer. But it's the very language that makes these works more rewarding than merely skimming the plot synopsis.

*specific examples prove the thesis*

The bawdiness of the Wife of Bath in *The Canterbury Tales* contrasts with the loftiness of the prose, not only to remind the reader that these ancestors were people with minds as filthy as our own, but also to make the entire passage funnier. What would *Wuthering Heights* be without its broody descriptions of the windswept moor? The flowery epithets applied to the gods of Homer tell us as much about the ancient Greeks themselves as they do about the characters of the story. There is a joy to be found here, along with information that could never be captured in CliffsNotes. To fully understand the book, and to even begin to understand the author, you have to read the book in its original words.

*transition*
*second main point*
*specific examples prove the thesis*

Second, cultural literacy demands that you be familiar with the canon, as references to classic literature abound in everyday speech. Read *Hamlet* for the first time and suddenly you understand where the quotes "Sweets to the sweet" and "To be or not to be"—to mention just two of the many sayings we use daily—came from. Even understanding today's works often requires familiarity with older ones. The novel *Wide Sargasso Sea* retells *Jane Eyre*; Kurosawa's film *Ran* is based on *King Lear*; and the band Iron Maiden has written songs based on everything from *Brave New World* to "The Charge of the Light Brigade." Even *Hamlet* itself is based on older works. To understand newer references and jokes, you have to have read the classics.

transition
third main point

specific examples
prove the thesis

humor creates clear
voice and style

specific examples
prove the thesis

humor creates clear
voice and style

insightful, intelligent
conclusion

But the real reason to read the classics is to be able to authoritatively mock the inevitable Hollywood remake. The entertainment industry has only accelerated its plundering of our cultural heritage in the last few years. You knew that *Troy* was a bad film—but a working knowledge of *The Iliad* would have allowed you to savage it properly when reviewing it for your friends. Reading the original *Alice in Wonderland* will show that the Disney version was quite faithful, but if you were confused by Tim Burton's version, you should feel no shame. A study of "A Scandal in Bohemia" allows you to join the debate on whether Irene Adler was mistreated in either Guy Ritchie's or the British Broadcasting Corporation's version of *Sherlock Holmes*. And only reading the book will ever make the film version of *2001: A Space Odyssey* make any sense at all. Let's face it—snobbishness can be fun, especially when accompanied by snark.

If knowledge is power, understanding your own cultural heritage is the key to appreciating it (or making fun of it, as appropriate). This kind of knowledge cannot be acquired secondhand. No, if you want to be witty, you need to know your Wilde. Besides, the definition of *classic* changes from generation to generation. When Twain wrote his epigram, the classics referred mostly to ancient Greek and Latin texts. Now the classics include not only Twain himself, but writers all the way up to modern-day authors like Gabriel Garcia Marquez and J. M. Coetzee. So bone up on your classics now, before *Twilight* is added to the list.

# MATHEMATICS PRACTICE TEST 2

## Answer sheet

1  Ⓐ Ⓑ Ⓒ Ⓓ Ⓔ
2  Ⓐ Ⓑ Ⓒ Ⓓ Ⓔ
3  Ⓐ Ⓑ Ⓒ Ⓓ Ⓔ
4  Ⓐ Ⓑ Ⓒ Ⓓ Ⓔ
5  Ⓐ Ⓑ Ⓒ Ⓓ Ⓔ
6  Ⓐ Ⓑ Ⓒ Ⓓ Ⓔ
7  Ⓐ Ⓑ Ⓒ Ⓓ Ⓔ

8   Ⓐ Ⓑ Ⓒ Ⓓ Ⓔ
9   Ⓐ Ⓑ Ⓒ Ⓓ Ⓔ
10  Ⓐ Ⓑ Ⓒ Ⓓ Ⓔ
11  Ⓐ Ⓑ Ⓒ Ⓓ Ⓔ
12  Ⓐ Ⓑ Ⓒ Ⓓ Ⓔ
13  Ⓐ Ⓑ Ⓒ Ⓓ Ⓔ
14  Ⓐ Ⓑ Ⓒ Ⓓ Ⓔ

15  Ⓐ Ⓑ Ⓒ Ⓓ Ⓔ
16  Ⓐ Ⓑ Ⓒ Ⓓ Ⓔ
17  Ⓐ Ⓑ Ⓒ Ⓓ Ⓔ
18  Ⓐ Ⓑ Ⓒ Ⓓ Ⓔ
19  Ⓐ Ⓑ Ⓒ Ⓓ Ⓔ
20  Ⓐ Ⓑ Ⓒ Ⓓ Ⓔ
21  Ⓐ Ⓑ Ⓒ Ⓓ Ⓔ

22  Ⓐ Ⓑ Ⓒ Ⓓ Ⓔ
23  Ⓐ Ⓑ Ⓒ Ⓓ Ⓔ
24  Ⓐ Ⓑ Ⓒ Ⓓ Ⓔ
25  Ⓐ Ⓑ Ⓒ Ⓓ Ⓔ
26  Ⓐ Ⓑ Ⓒ Ⓓ Ⓔ
27  Ⓐ Ⓑ Ⓒ Ⓓ Ⓔ
28  Ⓐ Ⓑ Ⓒ Ⓓ Ⓔ

29  Ⓐ Ⓑ Ⓒ Ⓓ Ⓔ
30  Ⓐ Ⓑ Ⓒ Ⓓ Ⓔ
31  Ⓐ Ⓑ Ⓒ Ⓓ Ⓔ
32  Ⓐ Ⓑ Ⓒ Ⓓ Ⓔ
33  Ⓐ Ⓑ Ⓒ Ⓓ Ⓔ
34  Ⓐ Ⓑ Ⓒ Ⓓ Ⓔ
35  Ⓐ Ⓑ Ⓒ Ⓓ Ⓔ

36  Ⓐ Ⓑ Ⓒ Ⓓ Ⓔ
37  Ⓐ Ⓑ Ⓒ Ⓓ Ⓔ
38  Ⓐ Ⓑ Ⓒ Ⓓ Ⓔ
39  Ⓐ Ⓑ Ⓒ Ⓓ Ⓔ
40  Ⓐ Ⓑ Ⓒ Ⓓ Ⓔ

# MATHEMATICS PRACTICE TEST 2

## 40 items, 60 minutes

*Directions:* Select the best choice for each item and mark the answer on your answer sheet.

1. If the scale on a dollhouse is 1 inch = 3 feet, and a doorframe is 2.5 yards high, how high would you make a dollhouse-scale doorframe?

   (A) 0.5 inches
   (B) 1 inch
   (C) 2.5 inches
   (D) 5 inches
   (E) 2.5 feet

2. The room shown has 8-foot-high walls. One gallon of paint will cover 100 square feet. How many gallons of paint are needed to paint the entire room?

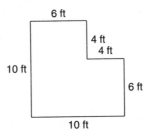

   (A) 3.2
   (B) 4
   (C) 8
   (D) 4.8
   (E) 10

3. Which formula describes the relationship between $X$ and $Y$?

   | $X$ | $Y$ |
   | --- | --- |
   | 2 | 2 |
   | 6 | 4 |
   | 14 | 8 |
   | 18 | 10 |
   | 22 | 12 |

   (A) $Y = X$
   (B) $Y = 2X - 10$
   (C) $Y = 3X - 4$
   (D) $Y = X/2 + 1$
   (E) $Y = 2X + 2$

4. If $A = \frac{1}{9}r + 9$ and $r = 18$, then $A =$

(A) 3
(B) 11
(C) $2\frac{2}{9}$
(D) 27
(E) 18

5. The wall of a room is 13 feet by 8 feet. Part of the wall includes two windows that each measure 3 feet by 5 feet. If 1 quart of paint covers 20 square feet, how many quarts of paint are needed to paint the room?

(A) 4
(B) 3.7
(C) 7.4
(D) 8.9
(E) 4.45

6. Which pairs of decimals and fractions are equivalent?

     I.   $0.30, \frac{1}{3}$
    II.  $0.65, \frac{13}{20}$
   III. $0.55, \frac{3}{5}$
   IV. $0.65, \frac{33}{50}$

(A) I only
(B) II only
(C) I and IV
(D) II and III
(E) II and IV

7. Three friends go to a restaurant for dinner. When the bill comes, the tax on it is $8.15. If the tax rate is 7.625 percent, approximately how much should you leave as a 15 percent tip?

(A) $8.00
(B) $9.50
(C) $7.75
(D) $16.00
(E) $12.50

**8.** On the speedometer shown, the arrow most likely indicates a speed of:

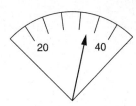

(A) 23.5 mph
(B) 24 mph
(C) 34 mph
(D) 36 mph
(E) 38 mph

**9.** Which of these fractions is the greatest?

(A) $\frac{4}{7}$
(B) $\frac{9}{5}$
(C) $\frac{20}{13}$
(D) $\frac{14}{5}$
(E) $\frac{11}{6}$

**10.** If $A = 5x + 2$, and $A = 22$, then $x =$

(A) 7
(B) 20
(C) 2.75
(D) 4
(E) 110

**11.** Elena catered a birthday gala and made 200 cupcakes. The party planners were expecting 98 people to come to the party. About how many cupcakes did Elena estimate each person would eat?

(A) 1
(B) 1.5
(C) 2
(D) 2.5
(E) 3

**12.** Based on the estimate in the previous question, if 53 more people were expected at the party, how many more cupcakes should Elena make?

(A) 25
(B) 50
(C) 75
(D) 100
(E) 150

**13.** I know that 20 percent of the partygoers are on diets and will eat only one cupcake each. Another 10 percent will not eat any. Approximately how many cupcakes should Elena make based on this information?

(A) 300
(B) 250
(C) 200
(D) 100
(E) 150

**14.** The following pie chart refers to purchases made at a store. If there were 400 purchases in total, how many were toys?

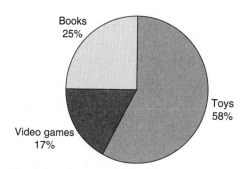

(A) 58
(B) 232
(C) 240
(D) 180
(E) 174

**15.** If the average price of video games is $26.00, what is the approximate total of video game sales in this example?

(A) $4,640
(B) $2,500
(C) $3,400
(D) $1,768
(E) $5,000

**16.** Which point on the following graph do the coordinates (–4,–2) refer to?

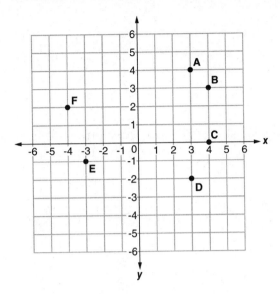

(A) F
(B) B
(C) E
(D) D
(E) none of the above

**17.** A pizza is cut into eight equal pieces. How would you represent the area of the pizza that one slice represents?

(A) $\frac{1}{8}\pi$
(B) $2\pi r \times 8$
(C) $\pi r^2/8$
(D) 3.14159/8
(E) $8 \times \pi r^2$

**18.** Using the rulers shown, approximately how much longer is line A than line B?

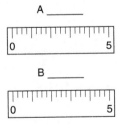

(A) $1\frac{1}{4}$
(B) $3\frac{1}{4}$
(C) 0
(D) $2\frac{1}{4}$
(E) $1\frac{1}{2}$

**19.** If $4z = 2x - y$, define $x$ in terms of $y$ and $z$.

(A) $y - z$
(B) $2z + y/2$
(C) $(y - z)/2$
(D) $y/2 + 2z$
(E) $z + y + 2$

**20.** A bird flies 30 yards from its nest in a tree to a second tree. It then changes direction and flies at a 90-degree angle to a third tree that is 40 yards away. How far will it fly to go directly from the third tree back to its nest?

(A) 900 feet
(B) 1,200 feet
(C) 1,500 feet
(D) 2,100 feet
(E) 2,400 feet

**21.** This graph represents one week of a store's performance. If the store opts to close two days a week, which two days would result in the fewest lost sales?

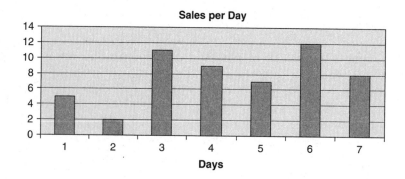

(A) days 1 and 2
(B) days 1 and 5
(C) days 2 and 5
(D) days 4 and 7
(E) days 3 and 6

**22.** A map is drawn to a scale of 1 inch = 5 miles. If the distance between two points on the map is 2.6 inches, what is the actual distance?

(A) 0.5 mile
(B) 5.2 miles
(C) 2.6 miles
(D) 13 miles
(E) 5 miles

**23.** If the probability of picking a white sock from your drawer is 0.4, and you randomly pick 20 socks out of the drawer, about how many would be white?

(A) 0
(B) 4
(C) 8
(D) 10
(E) 20

**24.** The graph shows, in hundreds, the number of lunches sold in one week. What is the mean number sold?

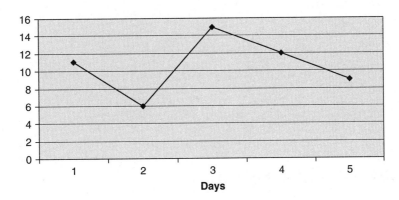

(A) 1,500
(B) 1,060
(C) 840
(D) 1,100
(E) 600

**25.** If there are 1,650 potential lunch customers each day in the preceding problem, how many do not buy lunch on day 4?

(A) 1,200
(B) 150
(C) 900
(D) 1,050
(E) 450

**26.** To convert centimeters to meters, you should

(A) divide by 10
(B) multiply by 10
(C) divide by 100
(D) multiply by 100
(E) divide by 1,000

**27.** Last week, you spent $26 on cups of coffee. This week, you spent $30. If you know coffee costs $2 a cup, what is the percent increase in the number of cups you purchased?

(A) 13.3 percent

(B) 15.4 percent

(C) 26.0 percent

(D) 86.7 percent

(E) 115.4 percent

**28.** Using the ruler shown, approximately how long is the line?

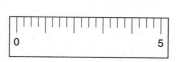

(A) $3\frac{1}{2}$

(B) $4\frac{1}{4}$

(C) 5

(D) 17

(E) 11

**29.** Which answer is closest to $1.987 \times 17{,}888$?

(A) 3,600,000

(B) 3,700,000

(C) 36,000,000

(D) 37,000,000

(E) 370,000,000

**30.** If you roll 2 six-sided dice, what is the probability that the combined total shown will be greater than 4?

(A) $\frac{5}{6}$

(B) $\frac{5}{36}$

(C) $\frac{11}{12}$

(D) $\frac{8}{9}$

(E) $\frac{1}{6}$

**31.** In a deck of 52 cards, 13 of them are hearts. What fraction represents the cards that are hearts?

(A) $\frac{1}{4}$

(B) $\frac{2}{5}$

(C) $\frac{4}{13}$

(D) $\frac{13}{4}$

(E) $\frac{13}{100}$

**32.** The ruler shows measurement in feet, so the arrow most likely indicates how many inches?

(A) 150
(B) 18
(C) 6
(D) $1\frac{1}{2}$
(E) 15

**33.** Which number falls between $\frac{1}{3}$ and $\frac{3}{7}$?

(A) 61%
(B) 0.1147
(C) 0.4144
(D) $\frac{9}{21}$
(E) $\frac{1}{2}$

**34.** How many cubic feet of air are in a spherical balloon with a diameter of 12 feet?

(A) $9\pi$
(B) $27\pi$
(C) $36\pi$
(D) $216\pi$
(E) $288\pi$

**35.** Five waitresses received the following tips. Whose was the most?

(A) 15 percent of $150
(B) 15 percent of $175
(C) 10 percent of $200
(D) 20 percent of $150
(E) 18 percent of $150

**36.** Which point on the graph is located at (–3,2)?

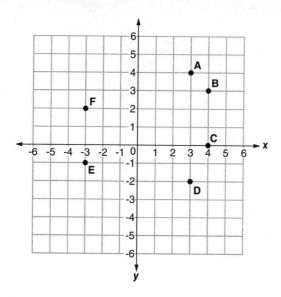

(A) A
(B) B
(C) C
(D) D
(E) F

**37.** If Joe's bowling score is greater than Sue's, and Sue's is less than Ted's, which of the following statements is true?

(A) Ted's score is less than Joe's.
(B) Joe's score is equal to Ted's.
(C) Sue's score is the lowest.
(D) Joe's score is the highest.
(E) None of these statements can be proven true.

**38.** Voters at a meeting are broken into three groups. A motion passes by more than 75 percent approval. Which of the following must have voted in favor to pass a motion?

**Meeting Attendees**

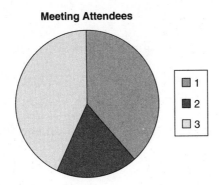

(A) groups 1 and 3
(B) groups 2 and 3
(C) group 1
(D) group 3
(E) groups 1 and 2

**39.** If $x \div 5 = y$, what is $x \div 10$?

(A) $y$
(B) $y \div 2$
(C) $y \div 3$
(D) $2y$
(E) $6y$

**40.** In a jar of marbles, 4 are red, 3 are blue, and 5 are green. What percentage is red?

(A) 4 percent
(B) 12 percent
(C) 25 percent
(D) 33.3 percent
(E) 40 percent

# STOP. This is the end of Mathematics Practice Test 2.

# MATHEMATICS PRACTICE TEST 2: ANSWERS

**1. C** Convert 3 feet to 1 yard, then use equivalent fractions: $1/1 = x/2.5$, therefore $x = 2.5$.

**2. A** This is an area problem. The total wall area is 320 square feet ($80 + 80 + 48 + 32 + 48 + 32$). A total of 3.2 gallons of paint would be needed.

**3. D** Use trial and error. Try all the pairs in each equation and find which one works for all of them.

**4. B** $(\frac{1}{9} \times 18) + 9 = 11$.

**5. B** The wall area is 104 square feet, minus 30 square feet of windows. You need to cover 74 square feet, so divide by 20 square feet per quart of paint.

---

**Test Hint:** To solve some problems, draw a picture on scrap paper to help you visualize the problem and the solution.

---

**6. B** Change fractions to decimals by dividing.

**7. D** Estimate: The tip is approximately double the tax rate, so it should be about $16.00.

**8. C** There are 5 hashes between 20 and 40, so each of the hashes is 4 mph. The arrow is about $3\frac{1}{2}$ hashes away from 20. $20 + (3.5 \times 4) = 34$.

**9. D** $\frac{14}{5}$ is the only fraction greater than 2.

**10. D** Since $22 = 5x + 2$, subtract 2 from both sides to get $20 = 5x$, then divide both sides to get $4 = x$.

---

**Test Hint:** Remember that negative numbers have less value than positive numbers.

---

**11. C** Estimate: About 100 people were expected, so each person would eat 2 cupcakes.

**12. D** Estimate: 53 is about $\frac{1}{2}$ of 100. So Elena would need about $\frac{1}{2}$ more cupcakes, and $200 \times \frac{1}{2} = 100$. (Alternatively, 53 is about 50. If each person eats 2 cupcakes, she would need $50 \times 2$, or 100 more cupcakes.)

**13. B**    Twenty percent of the guests is 30 people, each of whom will eat 1 cupcake, so subtract 30; 10 percent is 15 people, each of whom will eat 0, so subtract another 15. $300 - 30 - 15 = 255$, so 250 is the closest approximation.

**Test Hint:** Look for key words. For addition, look for the words *sum, more than*, and *increased*. For subtraction, look for the words *minus, difference*, and *less than*.

**14. B**    $400 \times 0.58 = 232$.

**15. D**    $0.17 \times 400 \times 26 = 1,768$.

**16. E**    $(-4, -2)$ refers to a point 4 spaces to the left and 2 down, which is not named.

**17. C**    The area of the pie could be expressed as $\Pi r^2$, so one slice would be $\frac{1}{8}$ of that.

**18. C**    Line A measures $1\frac{3}{4}$; line B also measures $1\frac{3}{4}$. They are the same length.

**19. B**    $4z = 2x - y$, $4z + y = 2x$, $2z + y/2 = x$.

**Test Hint:** Make sure you do the correct operation, such as addition or subtraction.

**20. C**    The trip is a right triangle, so use the Pythagorean equation: $30^2 = 900$. $40^2 = 1,600$. $900 + 1,600 = 2,500$. The square root of 2,500 is 500, which then converts to 1,500 feet.

**21. A**    Days 1 and 2 have the fewest sales.

**22. D**    Use equivalent fractions: $5 \times 2.6 = 13$.

**23. C**    $0.4 \times 20$.

**Test Hint:** Base your response only on the data provided on the PPST in Mathematics. Do not include any outside information you may have.

**24. B**    5,300 lunches divided by 5 days.

**25. E**    $1,650 - 1,200 = 450$.

**26. C**    100 centimeters = 1 meter.

**27. B**    $30 - 26 = 4$, $4 \div 26 = 0.154$, or 15.4 percent.

**28. B** There are 20 hashes between 0 and 5, so each of the long hashes is 1 unit and each of the small hashes is $\frac{1}{4}$ unit. The line begins at the $\frac{3}{4}$ hash and ends at 5, and $5 - \frac{3}{4} = 4\frac{1}{4}$.

**29. C** Estimate by rounding to the nearest thousand: $2,000 \times 18,000 = 36,000,000$.

**30. A** There is one combination that adds up to 2 (1, 1), two for 3 (1, 2 and 2, 1), and three for 4 (1, 3; 3, 1; and 2, 2), out of 36 possible combinations. Therefore, there are 30 combinations greater than 4. $\frac{30}{36} = \frac{5}{6}$.

**31. A** $\frac{13}{52}$ reduces to $\frac{1}{4}$.

**32. B** There are 20 hashes between 0 and 5, so each of the long hashes is 1 foot and each of the small hashes is 3 inches. The arrow is 6 short hashes away from 0, which is 18 inches.

**33. C** The number must fall between 0.333 and 0.428, or 33.3 percent and 42.8 percent.

**34. E** This is a volume problem. $V = 4/3\pi r^3$. Radius is half of diameter. $4/3\pi(6)^3 = 288\pi$.

**35. D** Multiply to find each tip; $30 is the most.

**36. E** $(-3,2)$ means 3 to the left and 2 up.

**37. C** Joe's and Ted's scores are higher than Sue's, but we don't know anything about the relationship of their scores to each other. Either one could be greater.

**Test Hint:** Create a number line to help you visualize and figure out "less than" and "greater than." This strategy is especially helpful for word problems.

**38. A** Only the sum of groups 1 and 3 represents more than 75 percent of the circle.

**39. B** $x = 5y$, so $x \div 10 = y \div 2$.

**40. D** As a fraction, $\frac{4}{12}$. Convert fractions to decimals by dividing: $\frac{4}{12} = 0.333$. $0.333 = 33.3$ percent.

# TEST 3

8  Ⓐ Ⓑ Ⓒ Ⓓ Ⓔ
9  Ⓐ Ⓑ Ⓒ Ⓓ Ⓔ
10 Ⓐ Ⓑ Ⓒ Ⓓ Ⓔ
11 Ⓐ Ⓑ Ⓒ Ⓓ Ⓔ
12 Ⓐ Ⓑ Ⓒ Ⓓ Ⓔ
13 Ⓐ Ⓑ Ⓒ Ⓓ Ⓔ
14 Ⓐ Ⓑ Ⓒ Ⓓ Ⓔ

15 Ⓐ Ⓑ Ⓒ Ⓓ Ⓔ
16 Ⓐ Ⓑ Ⓒ Ⓓ Ⓔ
17 Ⓐ Ⓑ Ⓒ Ⓓ Ⓔ
18 Ⓐ Ⓑ Ⓒ Ⓓ Ⓔ
19 Ⓐ Ⓑ Ⓒ Ⓓ Ⓔ
20 Ⓐ Ⓑ Ⓒ Ⓓ Ⓔ
21 Ⓐ Ⓑ Ⓒ Ⓓ Ⓔ

29 Ⓐ Ⓑ Ⓒ Ⓓ Ⓔ
30 Ⓐ Ⓑ Ⓒ Ⓓ Ⓔ
31 Ⓐ Ⓑ Ⓒ Ⓓ Ⓔ
32 Ⓐ Ⓑ Ⓒ Ⓓ Ⓔ
33 Ⓐ Ⓑ Ⓒ Ⓓ Ⓔ
34 Ⓐ Ⓑ Ⓒ Ⓓ Ⓔ
35 Ⓐ Ⓑ Ⓒ Ⓓ Ⓔ

36 Ⓐ Ⓑ Ⓒ Ⓓ Ⓔ
37 Ⓐ Ⓑ Ⓒ Ⓓ Ⓔ
38 Ⓐ Ⓑ Ⓒ Ⓓ Ⓔ
39 Ⓐ Ⓑ Ⓒ Ⓓ Ⓔ
40 Ⓐ Ⓑ Ⓒ Ⓓ Ⓔ

# READING PRACTICE TEST 3

## 40 questions, 60 minutes

*Directions:* Each of the following passages is followed by a question and five answer choices. Answer every question based on what is stated directly or suggested in each passage. You are not expected to have any prior knowledge of the information in the passages.

*Questions 1–2*

Charter schools are public schools that operate with freedom from many of the local and state regulations that apply to traditional public schools. Although the local school district approves the charter school, such a school is self-managed.

Charter schools allow parents, community leaders, educational entrepreneurs,
(5) and others the flexibility to innovate and provide students with increased educational options within the public school system. Parents, teachers, community leaders, and colleges or universities help create and control them. Charter schools do not have to follow many educational mandates, except for those concerning nondiscrimination, health and safety, and accountability.

1. Which of the following is an unstated opinion the author of this passage makes?

   (A) Charter schools require more governmental oversight than traditional schools to ensure that they provide an appropriate education for all students.
   (B) Charter schools are a trendy fad that will fade away once people realize they cost significantly more than traditional schools.
   (C) Charter schools have many significant and important advantages over traditional public schools.
   (D) Teachers' unions and elected public officials oppose charter schools for invalid reasons.
   (E) Traditional public schools in educationally disadvantaged areas should be replaced by charter schools.

2. According to this passage, all of the following are characteristics of charter schools EXCEPT that they are

   (A) controlled by a variety of different people
   (B) open to all students
   (C) able to operate under their own management
   (D) sanctioned by community school districts
   (E) exempt from all educational regulations

*Questions 3–6*

  I am writing to you because a very unsettling situation has occurred. My fiancée
departed Lagos via British Airways and was detained by immigration officials at
London's Heathrow Airport. I received a telephone call from an immigration officer
who told me that she was being detained for expired documents and that she was going
(5) to be deported unless I, as her fiancé and sponsor, paid $2,500 in total fines for violating
immigration law. The officer said that if I could raise the money before the deportation
paperwork was done, they would release her and provide her with new documents so
that she could continue her travel to the United States.
  The officer contacted me again later, and we began discussing the total amount of
(10) the fines. She stated that the actual fine for the violation was $1,500. I said I thought
I could raise that. She said if I did, then my fiancée could still be released with new
documents and continue her journey.
  On October 9, I collected $1,200 and sent the money electronically via the Money
Gram Store. I was happy to send the money because I thought the immigration officials
(15) would release my fiancée.
  Since October 12, I have not heard from the immigration officer or my fiancée.
I have attempted to contact her via telephone, but she never answers.
  Subsequently, I have been very distraught, worrying and hoping that my fiancée will
be released and allowed to continue on to the United States to be with me. I have not
(20) heard from her since this ordeal began. I want to know if she is in good health and that
she is okay. Please help me resolve this ghastly situation. I thank you, in advance, for
any help you may provide.

3. Which of the following BEST describes the organization of this passage?

(A) The advantages and disadvantages of a situation are described.
(B) A series of related events are arranged chronologically.
(C) An economic theory is postulated and then shown to be invalid.
(D) A problem is described from the most important details to the least.
(E) An unanticipated problem is described, evaluated, and then rejected.

4. Which of the following words, if substituted for the word *ghastly* in line 21, would introduce the LEAST change in the meaning of the sentence?

(A) terrible
(B) ghostly
(C) grisly
(D) unfair
(E) costly

**5.** What is the BEST statement of the main idea of the first paragraph?

(A) The writer's fiancée traveled to England from Lagos, Nigeria, on British Airways.

(B) The writer is experiencing a troubling situation that has greatly baffled and upset him.

(C) The writer must pay $2,500 to British officials so his fiancée will be allowed to leave England and travel to America.

(D) The writer's fiancée is currently being held at Heathrow Airport in London, England.

(E) The writer is sponsoring his fiancée for American citizenship.

**6.** Which of the following is the most logical conclusion you can draw from this passage?

(A) Travelers must be extremely scrupulous to ensure that all their official documents are in order, especially when they venture overseas.

(B) Modern travel is extremely arduous as a result of terrorism threats, but these difficulties are the price we pay to be safe.

(C) Some British immigration officials are dishonest, because they try to extort money from naive foreign travelers.

(D) This entire situation is hypothetical, as the writer is trying to extort money from his credulous readers.

(E) England's immigration laws, among the harshest in the world, are extremely unfair and must be overturned.

*Questions 7–9*

Treatment for people with chronic diseases and conditions accounts for about 75 percent of the more than $2 trillion spent annually on medical care in the United States. According to a 2007 report from the Milken Institute on the economic burden of chronic disease, even modest weight loss (10 to 20 pounds) and exercise (15 minutes a day) could lead to
(5)  40 million fewer cases of illness and a savings of more than $1 trillion by 2023.

**7.** The author would be LEAST likely to agree with which of the following statements about diseases?

(A)  Chronic conditions drain an undue share of American health care dollars.
(B)  People should make every effort to live a healthier lifestyle.
(C)  Risk factors for many chronic diseases are well known.
(D)  Even small changes in lifestyle can have far-reaching health effects.
(E)  Most of the health care resources expended in the United States occur at the end stages of a person's life.

**8.** The primary purpose of this passage is to

(A)  instruct consumers how to care properly for chronic illnesses
(B)  convince people to reduce their risk factors for chronic diseases
(C)  persuade readers that the United States needs affordable universal health care
(D)  describe the work of the Milken Institute vis-à-vis public health
(E)  advocate for a reallocation and rationing of health care resources

**9.** The word *modest* in line 4 most nearly means

(A)  reserved
(B)  unpretentious
(C)  small
(D)  plain
(E)  reticent

*Questions 10–16*

It was in 1868, when I was nine years old or thereabouts, that while looking at a map of Africa and putting my finger on the blank space then representing the unsolved mystery of that continent, I said to myself, with absolute assurance and an amazing audacity that are no longer in my character, "When I grow up, I shall go there."

(5)    Of course, I thought no more about it until, after a quarter of a century or so, an opportunity arose for me to go there—as if the sin of childish audacity were to be visited on my mature head. Yes, I did go, *there* being the region of Stanley Falls, which in '68 was the blankest of blank spaces on the earth's figured surface. And the manuscript of *Almayer's Folly*, carried about me as if it were a talisman or a treasure, went there

(10)    too. That it ever came out again seems a special dispensation of Providence, because a good many of my other possessions, infinitely more valuable and useful to me, remained behind through unfortunate accidents of transportation. I call to mind, for instance, an especially awkward turn of the Congo between Kinchassa and Leopoldsville—more particularly when one had to take it at night in a big canoe with only half the proper

(15)    number of paddlers. I got round the turn more or less alive, though I was too sick to care, and always with *Almayer's Folly* among my diminishing baggage, I arrived at that delectable capital, Boma. Here, before the departure of the steamer that was to take me home, I had the time to wish myself dead over and over again with perfect sincerity.

At that time, there were only seven chapters of *Almayer's Folly* in existence, but

(20)    the next chapter in my history was that of a long, long illness and very dismal convalescence. Geneva, or more precisely the hydropathic establishment of Champel, is rendered forever famous by the termination of the eighth chapter in the history of Almayer's decline and fall. The events of the ninth are inextricably mixed up with the details of the proper management of a waterside warehouse owned by a certain city

(25)    firm whose name does not matter. But that work, undertaken to accustom myself again to the activities of a healthy existence, soon came to an end. The earth had nothing with which to hold me for very long. And then that memorable story, like a cask of choice Madeira, was carried for three years to and fro upon the sea. Whether this treatment improved its flavor or not, I would not like to say. As far as appearance is

(30)    concerned, it certainly did nothing of the kind. The whole manuscript acquired a faded look and an ancient, yellowish complexion. It finally became unreasonable to suppose that anything in the world would ever happen to Almayer and Nina. And yet something most unlikely to happen on the high seas was to wake them up from their state of suspended animation.

**10.** *Almayer's Folly* is most likely a

(A) novel
(B) city in Africa
(C) waterside warehouse
(D) failed business venture
(E) cask of choice Madeira

**11.** Who must Almayer and Nina be?

(A) the narrator's close friends
(B) totally fictional creations
(C) the narrator's parents
(D) the owners of the waterside warehouse
(E) elderly people with ancient, yellowish complexions

**12.** The speaker's travels through Africa are BEST described as

(A) unique and intriguing
(B) protracted and costly
(C) terrifying and treacherous
(D) humorous and enjoyable
(E) noble and altruistic

**13.** Which of the following words, if substituted for the word *audacity* in line 3, would introduce the LEAST change in the meaning of the sentence?

(A) impudence
(B) cowardice
(C) ignorance
(D) immaturity
(E) intelligence

**14.** This passage is primarily concerned with

(A) discussing the advantages of traveling to unexplored parts of the world
(B) explicating the narrator's life and times to educate readers
(C) achieving revenge on people who impeded the narrator's progress
(D) describing a watershed moment in the narrator's life
(E) educating readers about life in Africa in the latter part of the nineteenth century

**15.** What is the narrator's tone in this passage?

    (A) deeply depressing
    (B) lightly ironic
    (C) truly horrified
    (D) eerily detached
    (E) deliberately neutral

**16.** What was the ultimate effect of the narrator's trip?

    (A) Almayer and Nina were reunited with the narrator.
    (B) Africa became the narrator's permanent home.
    (C) The narrator moved to Boma, a capital city.
    (D) A waterside warehouse was finally properly managed.
    (E) The narrator achieved a goal he had long sought.

*Questions 17–18*

> A glaciologist's goal is to be able to measure the "mass balance" of a given ice sheet; that is, how much ice the sheet accumulates from snowfall over the course of a year minus how much it loses due to melt and the periodic calving off of large ice chunks. Ice sheets can be good indicators of what the climate is like in a given region. This is
> (5) because changes in climate can cause changes in the earth's ice sheets. This simple fact points to the ultimate question facing glaciologists today: As the globe warms, will Antarctica's ice mass remain in balance? Or will the southern continent gain or lose ice mass over time?

17. Which sentence from the passage BEST states the author's overall main idea?

   (A) A glaciologist's goal is to be able to measure the "mass balance" of a given ice sheet.
   (B) Ice sheets can be good indicators of what the climate is like in a given region.
   (C) This is because changes in climate can cause changes in the earth's ice sheets.
   (D) This simple fact points to the ultimate question facing glaciologists today: As the globe warms, will Antarctica's ice mass remain in balance?
   (E) Or will the southern continent gain or lose ice mass over time?

18. According to the author, scientists who study glaciers debate all of the following issues EXCEPT

   (A) global warming
   (B) if Antarctica will lose ice mass over time
   (C) if Antarctica will gain ice mass over time
   (D) changes in Antarctica, the southern continent
   (E) whether or not Antarctica's ice mass will remain in balance

*Questions 19–22*

Because of Check 21 and other check-system improvements, your checks may be processed faster—which means money may be deducted from your checking account more quickly. Before you write a check, make sure your account has enough money to cover it.

(5)   You may be one of the majority of consumers who do not receive their canceled checks with their account statements. Instead, you may get digital images of your checks, a list of paid checks, or a combination of the two. Check 21 will have little or no effect on these practices.

On the other hand, if you do get your canceled checks back in your regular state-
(10)   ments, you may notice some changes under Check 21. For example, your bank or credit union may start sending you a combination of original checks and substitute checks. You may use a canceled substitute check as proof of payment just as you would use a canceled original check.

The account agreement you have with your banking organization governs whether
(15)   you receive canceled checks with your statements. If you currently get canceled checks back, you will continue to receive them unless your bank notifies you that it is changing your account agreement.

You may receive substitute checks in other limited circumstances. For example, your bank may give you a substitute check if you ask to have a particular canceled
(20)   check back to prove a payment. Also, your bank may provide a substitute check when returning a bounced check that you deposited into your account.

By law, your bank may not pay a check from your account unless you authorized that payment. In other words, you are protected from your bank paying the same check from your account more than once or from it paying the wrong amount for a check.
(25)   Check 21 does not change these protections. However, it does give you special rights if you receive a substitute check from your bank.

**19.** This excerpt would most likely be published in a(n)

(A) economics textbook for high school students
(B) white paper for national banking officials
(C) government web page for general consumers
(D) brochure for people who use banks rather than credit unions
(E) newspaper article on raising your credit rating

**20.** Which of the following BEST describes the organization of this passage?

(A) A series of economic events are arranged in chronological order.
(B) An assumption is followed by specific proof of its validity.
(C) The ideas are arranged from most important to least important.
(D) An important policy is stated and then fully explained.
(E) The information is arranged in chronological order.

**21.** The people who will see the MOST changes to their banking situation under Check 21 are those

(A) with excellent credit ratings
(B) who get their canceled checks back in their regular account statements
(C) who do not receive their canceled checks with their account statements
(D) do not keep enough money in their checking accounts to cover their checks
(E) receive digital images of their checks, a list of paid checks, or a combination of the two

**22.** What is the BEST title for this passage?

(A) Why Was Check 21 Instituted?
(B) What Is Check 21?
(C) Why Use Checks Rather Than Debit Cards?
(D) Check 21 and U.S. Law Today
(E) How Does Check 21 Affect You?

*Questions 23–27*

**Ear with Cochlear Implant**

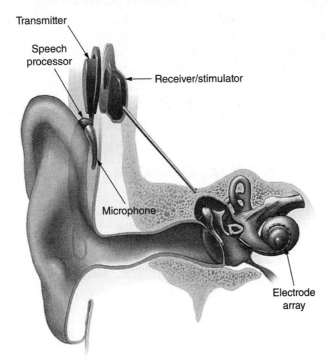

Credit: NIH Medical Arts

A cochlear implant is a small, complex electronic device that can help to provide a sense of sound to a person who is profoundly deaf or severely hard of hearing. The implant consists of an external portion that sits behind the ear and a second portion that is surgically placed under the skin (see figure).

(5)      An implant has the following parts:

- A microphone that picks up sound from the environment
- A speech processor that selects and arranges sounds picked up by the microphone
- A transmitter and receiver/stimulator that receive signals from the speech processor and convert them into electric impulses
(10) • An electrode array, or a group of electrodes, that collects the impulses from the stimulator and sends them to different regions of the auditory nerve

An implant does not restore normal hearing. Instead, it can give a deaf person a useful representation of sounds in the environment and help him or her to understand speech.
     Children and adults who are deaf or severely hard of hearing can be fitted for
(15) cochlear implants. According to the U.S. Food and Drug Administration (FDA), as of December 2010, approximately 219,000 people worldwide have received implants. In the United States, roughly 42,600 adults and 28,400 children have them.

Adults who have lost all or most of their hearing later in life can often benefit from cochlear implants. They learn to associate the signal provided by an implant with
(20) sounds they remember. This often provides recipients with the ability to understand speech solely by listening through the implant, without requiring any visual cues such as those provided by lip-reading or sign language.

Cochlear implants, coupled with intensive postimplantation therapy, can help young children to acquire speech, language, and social skills. Most children who receive
(25) implants are between two and six years old. Early implantation provides exposure to sounds that can be helpful during the critical period when children learn speech and language skills. In 2000, the FDA lowered the age of eligibility to 12 months for one type of cochlear implant.

**23.** A cochlear implant has all the following parts EXCEPT

(A) a microphone
(B) a transmitter
(C) a micrometer
(D) an electrode array
(E) a speech processor

**24.** Which of the following words, if substituted for the word *profoundly* in line 2, would introduce the LEAST change in the meaning of the sentence?

(A) extremely
(B) completely
(C) tragically
(D) irreversibly
(E) philosophically

**25.** Which of the following is the most logical conclusion you can draw from this passage?

(A) There is a great deal of controversy about whether or not cochlear implants are destroying the unique elements of deaf culture worldwide.
(B) Every person with severe hearing impairment should be fitted with a cochlear implant, which is why so many people have already received these devices.
(C) Cochlear implants do not restore the quality of hearing a hearing person is born with, and the surgery is costly, painful, and disruptive.
(D) By 2010, about 220,000 people around the world had received cochlear implants, about a third of them in America.
(E) Cochlear implants show the greatest results when implanted early in a deaf person's life, but hearing-impaired people of any age may benefit from the device.

**26.** Which part of the cochlear implant is placed inside a person's ear canal?

    (A) the electrode array
    (B) the transmitter
    (C) the receiver/stimulator
    (D) the microphone
    (E) the speech processor

**27.** What is the primary function of the diagram that accompanies this article?

    (A) It persuades readers that cochlear implants are effective.
    (B) It makes the article more attractive and interesting to read.
    (C) It helps readers visualize how the cochlear implant functions.
    (D) It shows how relatively simple the parts of a cochlear implant are.
    (E) It illustrates the ease with which a cochlear implant can be placed inside the ear.

*Questions 28–32*

According to the National Heart, Lung, and Blood Institute of the National Institutes of Health, more than 12.5 million Americans have coronary heart disease (CHD), and more than 500,000 die from it each year. That makes CHD one of the leading causes of death in the United States.

(5)    The Food and Drug Administration has required that saturated fat and dietary cholesterol be listed on food labels since 1993. With trans fat added to the Nutrition Facts panel in 2006, you now know how much saturated fat, trans fat, and cholesterol are in the foods you choose. Identifying all three on the food label gives you information you need to make food choices that help reduce the risk of CHD, and this information is of (10) particular interest to people concerned about high cholesterol and heart disease.

However, everyone should be aware of the risk posed by consuming too much saturated fat, trans fat, and cholesterol. Hydrogenation increases the shelf life and flavor stability of foods containing these fats. A small amount of trans fat is found naturally, primarily in dairy products, some meat, and other animal-based foods. Trans fat, like (15) saturated fat and dietary cholesterol, raises the low-density lipoprotein (LDL), or "bad cholesterol," that increases your risk for CHD. Americans consume an average of four to five times more saturated fat than trans fat in their diets. Although saturated fat is the main dietary culprit that raises LDL, trans fat and dietary cholesterol also contribute significantly.

**28.** Which of the following BEST describes the organization of this passage?

(A)  A series of health issues are arranged from most to least significant.

(B)  A thesis statement is supported by specific reasons and examples.

(C)  A controversial theory is put forth and then thoroughly debunked.

(D)  A hidden problem is exposed to intense and justified public scrutiny.

(E)  A government policy is explained and then shown to be invalid.

**29.** The passage states that everyone should be aware of the risk posed by consuming too much saturated fat, trans fat, and cholesterol, chiefly because

(A)  hydrogenation increases the shelf life and flavor stability of foods containing these fats

(B)  a small amount of trans fat is found in many of the foods we eat, especially in dairy products, some meat, and other animal-based foods

(C)  Americans consume an average of four to five times more saturated fat than trans fat in their diets

(D)  eating too much of these substances dramatically raises your risk of dying prematurely of coronary heart disease

(E)  these substances can be hard to discern in the food we eat because they are not marked on food labels

**30.** This passage is primarily concerned with

    (A) educating consumers about the importance of making healthy food choices
    (B) explaining the many deleterious effects of saturated fat, trans fat, and cholesterol
    (C) prescribing a natural, healthful diet that all Americans should follow
    (D) comparing different harmful substances in the food we eat
    (E) persuading people that the federal government meddles in our lives

**31.** The author would be LEAST likely to agree with which of the following statements about coronary heart disease?

    (A) If not directly caused by poor food choices, CHD is at least partially exacerbated by what we eat.
    (B) People cannot be sure if they will suffer from CHD, so they should take preventive measures by paying attention to the ingredients in processed foods.
    (C) Studies have shown that CHD is genetically based and thus cannot be prevented, so people should eat, drink, and be merry because life is brief.
    (D) Manufacturers deliberately add saturated fat, trans fat, and cholesterol to many of the processed foods we eat to make the foods last longer and taste better.
    (E) It is not a bad idea to try to eat fewer processed foods, such as potato chips, cookies, and pre-made meals, opting instead for fresh fruits and vegetables.

**32.** The word *culprit* in line 18 most nearly means

    (A) grease
    (B) chemical
    (C) criminal
    (D) compound
    (E) substance

*Questions 33–37*

Petroglyph National Monument's visitor center was once the home of an extraordinary lady. Dr. Sophie Aberle, known as "Measuring Lady" by the Native Americans with whom she worked, was the first practicing applied anthropologist in the United States. Her research focused mainly on women's lives at the pueblos, including pregnancy,

(5) childbirth, child care, diet, and healing. Because of her position as superintendent of the United Pueblos Agency, she was able to implement practices that led to better conditions in the villages.

Sometime around 1954 to 1956, Dr. Aberle and her husband, attorney William Brophy, purchased an adobe-style home on what is now known as Albuquerque's

(10) West Mesa. The home was first built by Colonel Alexander Stewart in about 1948 as a homestead property. In 1990, Dr. Aberle agreed to sell her West Mesa home to the Department of the Interior as part of the establishment of Petroglyph National Monument. On July 11, 1996, the monument staff celebrated Dr. Aberle's hundredth birthday by inviting her back to her home. She was genuinely pleased and thought it

(15) appropriate that her home, which had hosted so many tribal and federal representatives, would now be included as part of a national monument dedicated to the preservation and interpretation of petroglyphs.

Today, the visitor center is the first stop for tourists from around the country and around the world. The building also houses the Western National Parks Association

(20) bookstore, where a selection of more than 250 items are available for purchase. From Memorial Day through Labor Day, demonstrations by local native artisans take place on the visitor center patio each weekend.

33. Dr. Sophie Aberle was most likely nicknamed "Measuring Lady" by the Native Americans because she

(A) was a skilled bench chemist as well as being the first practicing applied anthropologist in America

(B) lived to be a centenarian, a landmark achievement that is easily measured

(C) recorded her accomplishments in notebooks and published widely in professional journals

(D) served as superintendent of the United Pueblos Agency and helped the Native Americans in the region

(E) took and recorded statistics about the lives of the women in the area over many decades

34. According to the passage, Dr. Aberle is admirable for all of the following reasons EXCEPT

(A) she had hosted many tribal and federal representatives in her home, bringing people closer together

(B) she was a trailblazer in women's rights, working as the first practicing applied anthropologist in America, as well as an attorney

(C) she used her official position to help improve women's lives at the pueblos

(D) she helped set up Petroglyph National Monument in Albuquerque to preserve and interpret petroglyphs

(E) she served as superintendent of the United Pueblos Agency

**35.** Which of the following is an unstated opinion the author of this passage makes?

(A) Petroglyphs are worth preserving.
(B) Many other women became anthropologists because of Dr. Sophie Aberle.
(C) Native American women in New Mexico revere Dr. Sophie Aberle even today.
(D) Every educated person has heard of Dr. Aberle's work among the pueblo women.
(E) Life is easier in the Southwest, which is why people live longer there than in more urban areas.

**36.** Which of the following words, if substituted for the word *artisans* in line 21, would introduce the LEAST change in the meaning of the sentence?

(A) residents
(B) performers
(C) volunteers
(D) craftspeople
(E) Native Americans

**37.** What is the tone of this passage?

(A) scientific
(B) neutral
(C) admiring
(D) feminine
(E) personal

*Question 38*

Architecturally, the buildings and monuments of Washington, DC, can be powerful, often handsome, sometimes controversial, but they are most important in what they say about us. We read in each the changing concerns, attitudes, and tastes of the culture that built them. Beyond the sites and structures, beyond the events and people they
(5) commemorate, are the truths they embody: justice, equality, courage, and honor—the tools of a free society. Just as the Mall is the symbolic heart of Washington, the city is more than simply the governmental center of the United States. It gives shape to our common heritage and to the diverse culture that is our source of renewal, making it one of those places that help define us as a people.

**38.** Based on this introduction, you can infer that the essay that follows will

(A) persuade the government to change the Smithsonian's policy of free entrance to a sliding scale of admission fees, especially for foreign visitors

(B) argue that American culture reached its pinnacle during the construction of Washington, DC, and has been in decline ever since

(C) focus on specific buildings in Washington, DC, providing examples to illustrate associations between each structure and the values it embodies

(D) explain how none of the great world capitals are as grand and glorious as Washington, DC, showing our superiority to other cultures

(E) demand that more funding be allocated to our nation's capital to support the upkeep of its buildings

*Questions 39–40*

Sneezing, a sore throat, a stuffy nose, coughing—everyone knows the symptoms of the common cold. It is probably the most widespread illness in the country. In the course of a year, people in the United States suffer 1 billion colds.

(5) You can get a cold by touching your eyes or nose after you touch surfaces with cold germs on them. You can also inhale the germs. Symptoms usually begin 2 or 3 days after infection and last 2 to 14 days. Washing your hands and staying away from people with colds will help you avoid illness.

According to the National Institute of Allergy and Infectious Diseases (part of the National Institutes of Health), there is no cure for the common cold. For symptom relief,
(10) you can try these methods:

- Getting plenty of rest
- Drinking fluids
- Gargling with warm salt water
- Using cough drops or throat sprays
(15) - Taking over-the-counter pain or cold medicines

However, do not give aspirin to children, and do not give cough medicine to children under age four.

**39.** To evaluate the validity of the author's claim regarding the danger posed by giving aspirin and cough medicine to young children (lines 16–17), it would be helpful to know which of the following?

(A) how aspirin and cough medicines affect young children
(B) what medicines you can give young children to relieve their symptoms
(C) at what age a child can be given aspirin and cough medicines
(D) how many experiments have been done concerning this problem
(E) when the deleterious affects of giving aspirin and cough medicine to young children were first noticed

**40.** To relieve the misery of the common cold, people can try all of the following methods EXCEPT

(A) gargling with warm salt water
(B) getting a lot of sleep, including taking naps
(C) drinking a lot of fluids, such as chicken soup, water, and juice
(D) washing their hands and staying away from people with colds
(E) sucking on cough drops or using nonprescription throat sprays

# STOP. This is the end of Reading Practice Test 3.

# READING PRACTICE TEST 3: ANSWERS

**1. C**   Recall that "unstated opinion" questions require you to draw a conclusion or make an inference. Here, you can infer that the author supports charter schools from the following sentence: *Charter schools allow parents, community leaders, educational entrepreneurs, and others the flexibility to innovate and provide students with increased educational options within the public school system.* There is no support for choices A, B, and D, although some people may hold these opinions. Choice E overstates the case and also introduces an element (socioeconomic class) not in the passage. Be sure to base your response on information in the passage, not any personal opinions or outside reading.

**2. E**   From the word *except* in the question stem, you know that you are looking for the exception, the one choice that is *not* true. The process of elimination works well here, so skim the passage and look for sentences that match each choice. The answer is E because the passage says that charter schools "operate with freedom from many of the local and state regulations that apply to traditional public schools," but this does not mean they are exempt from all such regulations. The key word is *many*. All the other choices are included in the passage, so they can be eliminated.

You can determine that choice A is true from the sentence, *Parents, teachers, community leaders, and colleges or universities help create and control them.* Choice B is true because charter schools are described as "public schools," so they must be open to all students. Choice C is true from this sentence: *Although the local school district approves the charter school, these public schools are self-managed.* Finally, choice D is true from the phrase: "Although the local school district approves the charter school."

**3. B**   The narrator relates events chronologically. In effect, the article is a story. Choice A is incorrect because the narrative has no advantages; there is no upside to this situation. Choice C is incorrect because the author is writing about an economic problem, not an economic theory. Do not be misled by the discussion of money. Choice D is only partly correct; the author does describe a problem but does not arrange the information from the most to the least important details. Finally, choice E is wrong because an unanticipated problem *is* described, but it is not "evaluated and then rejected."

**Test Hint:** With test items that require you to find the organization of a passage, look for signal words. Focus especially at the beginning and end of sentences or paragraphs. For instance, here are some words that are clues to chronological (time order) organization:

| | |
|---|---|
| specific dates (like 1492) | first, second, third, etc. |
| now | after |
| then | finally |
| later | in the end |
| before | |

**4. A**   Since *ghastly* doesn't have a root, prefix, or suffix, use context clues to define it. The words *distraught, worrying,* and *ordeal* suggest that something ghastly is very upsetting. The closest synonym is *terrible* (choice A). While both g*hostly* (choice B) and *grisly* (choice C) also start with *g*, neither is a synonym for *ghastly*. The situation is *unfair* (choice D) and *costly* (choice E), but neither of those words is a synonym for *ghastly*. Remember to base your answer on word parts and context clues.

**Test Hint:** Use the following method when you're solving vocabulary questions:

1.  **Read the sentence all the way through to get a sense of its meaning.** Ask yourself, "What does the sentence mean overall?"

2.  **Anticipate the answer.** Ask yourself, "What word or words would best fill in the blank?" Think of some terms that might fit.

3.  **Pick the best choice.** Find the closest match, the answer choice that is the best synonym for the answer you anticipated.

4.  **Read all the choices.** Even if you think you've found the answer immediately, read all the choices. You might find a better choice later in the list.

5.  **Use the process of elimination.** If you have to guess, first eliminate choices that do not make sense. Also, look for answer choices that have the same meaning. If any of the choices mean almost the same thing, such as *superb* and *excellent*, then it is highly unlikely that either word will be the correct choice.

6.  **Check your answer.** Read the entire sentence with the word(s) that you chose in place. This will help you make sure the sentence makes sense.

**5. C**   A main idea question is a summary question, so you have to put together all the clues, or details, in the first paragraph to get the big picture. Only choice C summarizes the paragraph. You can eliminate choices A and D because they are details, not the main idea. Choices B and E are too general.

**6. D**   You can conclude that the writer is a con artist because he does not provide any details to legitimize his claims that his fiancée has been unfairly detained or, indeed, that his fiancée even exists! (The writer may be a woman or even a consortium of writers.) While choice A is a good idea—*Travelers must be extremely scrupulous to ensure that all their official documents are in order, especially when they venture overseas*—that is not the main idea of the passage. Choice B has nothing to do with the passage, as the writer does not talk about terrorism. Choice C assumes the writer is telling the truth and thus misses the main idea of the passage. Finally, choice E is not valid because it cannot be determined from the passage. Indeed, England's immigration laws might be lax and eminently fair.

**7. E**   The directions tell you that you must find the exception, the choice that is *not* true. Choice E is not the topic of the passage, nor does the passage discuss it, so it cannot be inferred from the information given. Thus, it is the statement the author is least likely to endorse. All the other choices can be supported by information in the passage.

**8. B**   You can infer the author's purpose, which is to persuade readers to reduce the risk factors for chronic diseases, from the last line. There is no support for choice A (instructing consumers how to properly care for chronic illnesses). Choice C is too far afield from the topic of the passage, as the author does not touch on the issue of the United States getting affordable universal health care. Choice D (describing the work of the Milken Institute vis-à-vis public health) is too narrow. Finally, choice E (advocating for a reallocation and rationing of health care resources) has the same error in logic as choice C; it is too far off the topic to be the author's purpose.

**9. C**   *Modest* has multiple meanings, so you have to use context clues to find the correct answer. The author is talking about small changes. This is directly stated by the details "10 to 20 pounds" (of weight loss) and "15 minutes a day" of exercise. Thus, the best choice is C, *small*. None of the other synonyms fit the context.

---

**Test Hint:** One way to approach vocabulary questions is by reading the sentence with the key word omitted. Instead of the vocabulary word, insert "blank" as you read. Predict the best synonym. Then check the answer choices to find the word that matches your guess most closely.

---

**10. A**   This is an inference question, so you have to put together clues in the passage to draw a conclusion. The words *manuscript* and *chapters* suggest that *Almayer's Folly* must be a literary work of some sort. Only choice A fits this context clue.

**11. B**   You can infer that Almayer and Nina must be totally fictional creations from the last paragraph. The juxtaposition of the phrase "the manuscript" and the sentence *It finally became unreasonable to suppose that anything in the world would ever happen to Almayer and Nina* suggests that Almayer and Nina are fictional characters. Choice E indicates a misreading of the passage; the manuscript has "an ancient, yellowish complexion," not the characters. There is no support for any of the other choices.

**12. C**    This is a literal question, as the details in the passage clearly describe a horrifying, dangerous voyage. Examples include:

- The phrase "as if the sin of childish audacity were to be visited on my mature head," which suggests the horror of the trip.
- "I got round the turn more or less alive, though I was too sick to care."
- "I arrived at that delectable capital, Boma. Here, before the departure of the steamer that was to take me home, I had the time to wish myself dead over and over again with perfect sincerity."

While the trip may have been "unique and intriguing" (choice A), the author clearly describes the dangers he faced, making choice C more accurate. Choice B is only partly correct, as the trip was three years long ("protracted"), but the cost is never mentioned. There is no support for choices D and E.

---

**Test Hint:** If you're having difficulty answering a reading question, try to identify its type. For instance, is it a literal recall question or one that requires you to make an inference? Once you identify the type of question you must answer, you'll know whether you can find the specific fact you need in the passage or whether you'll have to draw a conclusion from the details.

---

**13. A**    As you have learned from this book, to answer vocabulary questions, you need to find the word in the passage and see if it contains parts that you know. If it doesn't contain a root, prefix, or suffix, try context clues. Since *audacity* doesn't have a word part that you can use, try this method to discover the context:

- Find the sentence that contains the vocabulary word.
- Read the sentence with "blank" for the vocabulary word.
- Substitute your own synonym for the word.
- Look at the answers to see which one is the closest.

Here is the sentence: *Of course, I thought no more about it until, after a quarter of a century or so, an opportunity arose for me to go there—as if the sin of childish audacity were to be visited on my mature head.* The author is describing his youthful overconfidence. The best synonym for *overconfidence* is *impudence* (choice A). *Cowardice* is the antonym, so choice B is wrong. *Ignorance* (choice C) isn't specific enough to capture the author's tone here. *Immaturity* (choice D) is close, but *impudence* more accurately reflects the tone. Finally, *intelligence* (choice E) doesn't match with the context clue of "as if the sin of childish audacity were to be visited on my mature head."

**14. D**    This is a main idea question, so look first at the topic sentences. These sentences (the first one in each paragraph) tell you that the narrator is describing a critical event in his life: his trip to Africa and the novel that he wrote as a result. Choices A and E are too general. Choice B is too vague, and there is no support in the passage for choice C.

**15. B**   *Tone* is the author's attitude toward the subject matter. Thus, identifying tone is an inference skill. To find the tone of a passage, look at the connotations of words and details and the mood or feeling they convey. Sentences such as *Whether this treatment improved its flavor or not, I would not like to say* show the narrator's lightly ironic, self-mocking tone (choice B). The passage is not deeply depressing (choice A) or truly horrifying (choice C), although some of his experiences are. The narrator is deeply invested in the experience and the novel that resulted from it, so eerily detached (choice D) cannot be valid. Finally, the sentences *That it ever came out again seems a special dispensation of Providence, because a good many of my other possessions, infinitely more valuable and useful to me, remained behind through unfortunate accidents of transportation* and *I got round the turn more or less alive, though I was too sick to care whether I did or not, and always with* Almayer's Folly *among my diminishing baggage, I arrived at that delectable capital, Boma. Here, before the departure of the steamer that was to take me home, I had the time to wish myself dead over and over again with perfect sincerity* certainly show that he is not deliberately neutral (choice E).

---

**Test Hint:** Restate difficult questions in your own words to make them easier to understand. Paraphrasing like this helps you check your understanding as well.

---

**16. E**   Combining the information in the last two lines with the word *manuscript* reveals that as a result of his trip, the author was able to complete his project, a goal that he had long sought. Choices A (Almayer and Nina's reunion with the narrator) and D (proper management of a waterside warehouse) are misreadings of the passage. The narrator clearly states that he left Africa after three years, so choices B (in which Africa became the narrator's permanent home) and C (in which the narrator moved to Boma) are incorrect.

**17. A**   To find the author's main idea, look for the most general statement, the one that serves as an "umbrella" for the rest of the information in the passage. As a further guideline, in expository paragraphs, the main idea will usually be stated in the first or last sentence. Here, it is the first sentence, which states the author's thesis by defining a glaciologist's goal: *A glaciologist's goal is to be able to measure the "mass balance" of a given ice sheet.*

---

**Test Hint:** Refer to the passage to check your answers. This is especially useful with questions that test recall.

---

**18. A**   The word *except* in the question stem indicates that you have to find the one item that does not fit. Thus, the process of elimination is an effective test strategy.

- You can eliminate choices B and C because of the last sentence, which indicates that scientists do debate the issue: *Or will the southern continent gain or lose ice mass over time?*
- You can eliminate choices D and E because of the following sentence, which indicates that scientists do debate the issue: *As the globe warms, will Antarctica's ice mass remain in balance?*

The following sentence shows that scientists accept global warming as a fact, so they do not debate it: *This simple fact points to the ultimate question facing glaciologists today: As the globe warms, will Antarctica's ice mass remain in balance?* This shows that choice A is correct.

**19. C**   This is an inference question, so you have to draw a conclusion. You can infer that choice C is correct. This excerpt would most likely be published on a government web page for general consumers because the language and content are aimed at a wide variety of people, not students (choice A) or national banking officials (choice B). Since both credit unions and banks are mentioned, choice D cannot be correct. Choice E is off the topic.

**20. D**   This is a literal recall question, and the information is located in the passage and does not have to be inferred from clues the writer provides. The author states a policy about checks and then explains it. Here is the policy: *Because of Check 21 and other check-system improvements, your checks may be processed faster—which means money may be deducted from your checking account more quickly.*

- Choice A is incorrect because the subject of the passage is based in economics, but the organization is not.
- Choice B is incorrect because the author presents a fact, not an assumption. The fact is presented in the first paragraph and establishes the organizational pattern for the entire passage.
- Choice C is incorrect because the ideas are *not* arranged from most to least important. Rather, they are arranged point by point.
- Choice E is incorrect because the information is *not* arranged in chronological (time) order.

---

**Test Hint:** If you can't figure out the organization of a passage, try to draw a quick diagram for yourself, such as an outline or flowchart.

---

**21. B**   This is a literal recall question, and the answer is directly stated in the third paragraph: *On the other hand, if you do get your canceled checks back in your regular statements, you may notice some changes under Check 21.* None of the other choices answer the question.

**22. E**   This is the best answer because it summarizes the main idea of the passage. Choices A, B, and D are too narrow; choice C is off the topic.

**23. C**   This is a recall question. Since you are looking for the exception (as you know from the word *except* in the question stem), return to the passage and use the process of elimination to cross out the parts of the cochlear implant listed. Skimming the list after paragraph 1, you will see that a cochlear implant does not have a micrometer. As a result, choice C is correct.

**24. A**   Return to the passage to find the sentence that contains the word *profoundly*. Here is the sentence: *A cochlear implant is a small, complex electronic device that can help to provide a sense of sound to a person who is profoundly deaf or severely hard of hearing.* Then use context clues to infer the correct meaning, since *profoundly* has multiple meanings. You will find a definition/synonym context clue: someone who is *profoundly deaf* is "severely hard of hearing." Thus, choice A is the best choice, as *extremely* means "severely."

**Test Hint:** To improve your vocabulary, connect words with their meanings by creating memorable mental associations. For example, *stalactite* and *stalagmite* are often confused. Here's how you can remember the meaning of each word and distinguish between them:

- A stalactite is a geological formation that hangs from the ceiling within a cave. Here's your clue: the word contains a *c* for *ceiling*.
- A stalagmite is a geological formation that is deposited on the ground within a cave. Here's your clue: the word contains a *g* for *ground*.

**25. E**   Choice E is the correct answer because it draws a logical conclusion from the information in the last three paragraphs, especially from the final one.

- Choice A may be true, but it cannot be determined from the information in the passage.
- Choice B overstates the case. The passage states that *Children and adults who are deaf or severely hard of hearing can be fitted for cochlear implants*, but saying that every deaf person can benefit is not supported by this statement.
- Choice C cannot be correct because only the first half the statement is right; the second, in contrast, cannot be determined from the information in the passage.
- Choice D contains paraphrased information that is directly stated in the passage, so it is not a conclusion.

**Test Hint:** Beware of statements and answer choices that contain "absolute" words such as *all, none, each, every,* and so on. Such statements are rarely valid, since situations are rarely absolute.

**26. A**   This question tests your ability to interpret visuals. The diagram clearly shows that only the electrode array is placed inside the ear canal.

**27. C**   By showing the parts of the cochlear implant in a cutaway diagram of the ear, the illustration helps you see how the implant functions. The diagram does not persuade (choice A), nor is it merely decorative (choice B). The parts of the implant have been drawn to appear simple, but their labels show that this is not the case, so choice D is incorrect. The same logic applies to choice E.

---

**Test Hint:** Don't get rattled by unfamiliar words. Chances are that they are not essential to your understanding of the passage. Skip over them as you read; you can always define them from context clues later on if you need to know what they mean.

---

**28. B**   This passage gives a thesis (main idea) statement in the middle of the second paragraph: *Identifying [saturated fat, trans fat, and cholesterol] on the food label gives you information you need to make food choices that help reduce the risk of CHD.* This thesis is supported by examples. Choice E may seem like a good choice because the first part is correct, but the second part is not, so it can be eliminated. The passage describes only one health issue, so choice A is incorrect. There is nothing controversial about this theory, so you can eliminate choice C. The problem is not hidden, so choice D is also wrong.

**29. D**   The passage directly states that everyone should be aware of the significant health risk posed by consuming too much saturated fat, trans fat, and cholesterol. The passage provides two statements in support of this:

- *Identifying [saturated fat, trans fat, and cholesterol] on the food label gives you information you need to make food choices that help reduce the risk of CHD [coronary heart disease].*
- *However, everyone should be aware of the risk posed by consuming too much saturated fat, trans fat, and cholesterol.*

Choices A, B, and C are facts from the passage, but they do not explain why everyone should be aware of the risk posed by diet. Choice E is simply untrue.

**30. A**  This is a literal recall question. The writer's goal is to persuade readers to avoid foods that contain too much saturated fat, trans fat, and cholesterol; hence the reason for listing the amounts of these substances on food labels. The purpose is directly stated in this sentence: *Identifying [saturated fat, trans fat, and cholesterol] on the food label gives you information you need to make food choices that help reduce the risk of CHD.*

- Choice B is close, but the writer gives only one harmful effect of saturated fat, trans fat, and cholesterol (an increased risk of CHD), not *many* effects.
- Choice C is wrong because the writer does not prescribe or even describe a specific diet.
- Choice D is wrong because the author does not *compare* different harmful substances food in the food we eat. Rather, the author *discusses* the substances.
- Choice E takes the information in the passage much too far by making an unsupported value judgment.

**Test Hint:** If you can't figure out an answer, use the process of elimination. Then skim the passage to find the facts and details you need.

**31. C**  This is an inference question, requiring you to read between the lines to draw a conclusion. To do so, look at all the details to see what they suggest about the author's bias or beliefs. You can infer that the author would not agree with choice C because the passage focuses on the importance of reading food labels to become aware of the amount of saturated fat, trans fat, and cholesterol in the foods we choose, as these substances increase the risk of developing CHD. All the other choices can be inferred from the information in the passage.

**32. C**  You can infer that *culprit* must be something negative from the context, since it "raises low-density lipoprotein," which is bad. This eliminates every choice but C, since the other answers do not have uniformly negative meanings or connotations.

**Test Hint:** As you solve vocabulary questions on the Praxis, consider a vocabulary word's connotation (emotional overtones) as well as its denotation (dictionary meaning). Think about the connotations of these words, as examples: *cheap, stingy, miserly, penny-pinching, mean,* and *parsimonious* all have negative connotations. On the other hand, *thrifty, economical, frugal, prudent,* and *economical* have more positive connotations. Yet all the words have the same denotation—careful with money.

**33. E**  This is a drawing conclusions question, so put together details in the passage to make an inference. The nickname Measuring Lady suggests that Dr. Sophie Aberle took measurements of some kind. From the details in the first paragraph, you can conclude that she took recorded data related to women's lives at the pueblos. Choice C seems logical, but there's no proof of it in the passage. Neither is there any proof that she was a chemist (choice A). Choice B would have occurred long *after* she received her nickname. Finally, choice D is too vague.

**34. B**  The word *except* tells you to find the one choice that is the exception. Choice B is a misreading of the passage: Aberle's husband worked as an attorney; she did not.

**35. A**  You can conclude that the petroglyphs are worth preserving by the fact that Petroglyph National Monument was established. The success of the park, as shown by the visitor information provided, further indicates that many people support the preservation of the petroglyphs. The other choices are too big a leap, as there is insufficient evidence in the passage to reach any of these conclusions.

**Test Hint:** Consider working in sections. For instance, try to complete every question in a reading set, even if you have to make an educated guess. You will lose a lot of time if you have to go back and reread the passage to answer one or two questions.

**36. D**  You can sometimes figure out what a word means by taking it apart and looking for roots, prefixes, suffixes, and smaller words within it. The word *artisans* contains the smaller word *art*. Combining this with context clues tells you that an artisan must be an artist. The closest synonym is *craftspeople* (choice D).

**37. C**  The author deeply admires Dr. Sophie Aberle, which you can infer from the details about her achievements. Don't confuse the topic—the science of anthropology (choice A) and Dr. Aberle's focus on women's lives at the pueblos (choice D)—with the tone. Choice E overstates the case. The tone is relaxed and familiar rather than personal.

**38. C**  Based on this introduction, you can infer that the essay that follows will focus on specific buildings in Washington, DC, and provide examples to illustrate associations between each structure and the values it embodies. You can draw this conclusion from the topic sentence and the laudatory tone.

- Choice A lacks any support in the passage, as the Smithsonian isn't even mentioned, much less its policy of free entrance.
- Choice B is too big a stretch, given the information in the passage.
- Similarly, choice D lacks support, as none of the great world capitals are mentioned.
- Finally, you can eliminate choice E because the author does not suggest that the buildings are in disrepair and thus require funding. In fact, the opposite appears to be the case.

**39. A** To evaluate the author's claims, you would need to know how aspirin and cough medicine affect young children. How dangerous are these medicines? Do they cause major or minor problems? None of the other choices would help you make such a judgment.

**40. D** This is a recall question. Every answer except D is a recommended method of relieving the misery of a cold. Since you are looking for the exception, choice D is the correct answer. It is a way to prevent a cold.

## Skills Spread

|  | **Item Numbers** |
| --- | --- |
| Literal (18) | 2, 3, 5, 9, 10, 12, 16, 17, 18, 20, 21, 23, 26, 28, 29, 30, 34, 40 |
| Inferential (22) | 1, 4, 6, 7, 8, 11, 13, 14, 15, 19, 22, 24, 25, 27, 31, 32, 33, 35, 36, 37, 38, 39 |

# WRITING PRACTICE TEST 3

## Answer sheet

1 Ⓐ Ⓑ Ⓒ Ⓓ Ⓔ
2 Ⓐ Ⓑ Ⓒ Ⓓ Ⓔ
3 Ⓐ Ⓑ Ⓒ Ⓓ Ⓔ
4 Ⓐ Ⓑ Ⓒ Ⓓ Ⓔ
5 Ⓐ Ⓑ Ⓒ Ⓓ Ⓔ
6 Ⓐ Ⓑ Ⓒ Ⓓ Ⓔ
7 Ⓐ Ⓑ Ⓒ Ⓓ Ⓔ

8 Ⓐ Ⓑ Ⓒ Ⓓ Ⓔ
9 Ⓐ Ⓑ Ⓒ Ⓓ Ⓔ
10 Ⓐ Ⓑ Ⓒ Ⓓ Ⓔ
11 Ⓐ Ⓑ Ⓒ Ⓓ Ⓔ
12 Ⓐ Ⓑ Ⓒ Ⓓ Ⓔ
13 Ⓐ Ⓑ Ⓒ Ⓓ Ⓔ
14 Ⓐ Ⓑ Ⓒ Ⓓ Ⓔ

15 Ⓐ Ⓑ Ⓒ Ⓓ Ⓔ
16 Ⓐ Ⓑ Ⓒ Ⓓ Ⓔ
17 Ⓐ Ⓑ Ⓒ Ⓓ Ⓔ
18 Ⓐ Ⓑ Ⓒ Ⓓ Ⓔ
19 Ⓐ Ⓑ Ⓒ Ⓓ Ⓔ
20 Ⓐ Ⓑ Ⓒ Ⓓ Ⓔ
21 Ⓐ Ⓑ Ⓒ Ⓓ Ⓔ

22 Ⓐ Ⓑ Ⓒ Ⓓ Ⓔ
23 Ⓐ Ⓑ Ⓒ Ⓓ Ⓔ
24 Ⓐ Ⓑ Ⓒ Ⓓ Ⓔ
25 Ⓐ Ⓑ Ⓒ Ⓓ Ⓔ
26 Ⓐ Ⓑ Ⓒ Ⓓ Ⓔ
27 Ⓐ Ⓑ Ⓒ Ⓓ Ⓔ
28 Ⓐ Ⓑ Ⓒ Ⓓ Ⓔ

29 Ⓐ Ⓑ Ⓒ Ⓓ Ⓔ
30 Ⓐ Ⓑ Ⓒ Ⓓ Ⓔ
31 Ⓐ Ⓑ Ⓒ Ⓓ Ⓔ
32 Ⓐ Ⓑ Ⓒ Ⓓ Ⓔ
33 Ⓐ Ⓑ Ⓒ Ⓓ Ⓔ
34 Ⓐ Ⓑ Ⓒ Ⓓ Ⓔ
35 Ⓐ Ⓑ Ⓒ Ⓓ Ⓔ

36 Ⓐ Ⓑ Ⓒ Ⓓ Ⓔ
37 Ⓐ Ⓑ Ⓒ Ⓓ Ⓔ
38 Ⓐ Ⓑ Ⓒ Ⓓ Ⓔ

# WRITING PRACTICE TEST 3

## SECTION 1: MULTIPLE-CHOICE QUESTIONS

### 38 questions, 30 minutes

*Directions:* The following sentences require you to identify errors in grammar, usage, punctuation, and capitalization. Not every sentence has an error, and no sentence will have more than one error. Every sentence error, if there is one, is underlined and lettered. If the sentence does have an error, select the one underlined part that must be changed to make the sentence correct and blacken the corresponding circle on your answer sheet. If the sentence does not have an error, blacken circle E. Elements of the sentence that are not underlined are not to be changed.

*Part A*
*21 questions*

Suggested time: 10 minutes

1. <u>The elegant elderly gentleman</u> with all the dogs <u>stroll</u> down our block every day<u>, and he</u>
       A                                B                                    C
   pauses to chat with <u>everyone he meets</u> along the way. <u>No error.</u>
                       D                      E

2. Spanish coins, articles of trade, and words were all freely exchanged<u>;</u> 400 years
                                                                      A
   <u>later, the</u> money and spices are <u>musty relics</u>, but all the words <u>nearly</u> remain fresh and
     B                                 C                      D
   useful. <u>No error.</u>
          E

3. <u>During the highly contentious meeting</u>, the contest judges ruled that the singer was a
                        A
   <u>good</u> performer, the juggler was <u>even better</u>, but the ballroom dancers and the
     B                           C
   magician were the <u>most best</u> of all and so awarded them first place. <u>No error.</u>
                   D                                    E

4. <u>After the third quarter</u> of the football game, the candy bowl <u>was empty,</u> but Jack
              A                                                  B
   <u>was sick</u> of eating <u>it</u> anyway. <u>No error.</u>
     C          D        E

5. <u>A family is the best medicine</u> to cure all sickness and illness<u>,</u> I know that people are
             A                                              B
   more likely to become <u>really healthy</u> and stay well <u>if they have a good family</u>. <u>No error.</u>
                          C                         D             E

**6.** Although <u>doctors'</u> do get paid while <u>they complete their</u> residencies and fellowship
            A                      B

<u>training, the</u> salaries are modest and thus go mainly for food and <u>housing, so</u> doctors
    C                                              D

are forced to defer repaying their loans. <u>No error.</u>
                                  E

**7.** Samuel Clemens was born in 1835 in Florida, <u>Missouri but</u> the family <u>moved</u> soon
                                          A                    B

after to the one-horse town of Hannibal, where <u>Samuel's father,</u> John, an
                                                  C

<u>unsuccessful lawyer-turned-merchant</u>, had big plans to make his fortune. <u>No error.</u>
               D                                                    E

**8.** <u>All careers require</u> a breath of knowledge, so learning a wide variety of basic
           A

<u>skills helps</u> students become <u>more effective and agile</u> workers, <u>which helps them</u>
    B                                    C                              D

withstand economic turbulence. <u>No error.</u>
                                E

**9.** <u>The Fair Labor Standards Act</u> establishes a minimum wage—the lowest legal
               A

wage—that <u>Employers</u> can pay their workers<u>;</u> currently, the minimum wage in the
               B                               C

<u>United States</u> is $7.25 per hour. <u>No error.</u>
    D                           E

**10.** If you want to travel overseas this <u>summer, the</u> line at the passport office is
                                          A

usually <u>quite</u> <u>long, so</u> <u>one</u> should set aside sufficient time to procure this document.
        B      C   D
<u>No error.</u>
  E

**11.** <u>Due to</u> the reclining S shape of the <u>Isthmus of Panama,</u> the sun
     A                                B

<u>rise on the Pacific Coast</u> and <u>sets on the Atlantic Coast</u> in this cape. <u>No error.</u>
      C                         D                      E

**12.** <u>My Father</u> and most of the elderly visitors to <u>renowned sites</u> such as the
     A                                      B

<u>Great Wall of China and the Taj Mahal were</u> intrepid <u>travelers, not</u> unwilling tourists.
                        C                          D
<u>No error.</u>
  E

**13.** <u>At the commencement ceremony,</u> Samara <u>was told</u> that she <u>had been granted</u> a
           A                               B               C

lucrative graduate fellowship <u>by her adviser</u>. <u>No error.</u>
                      D       E

**14.** <u>Between you and I</u>, the park across the street has a <u>much better dog walk</u> than the one
     A                                 B
on <u>Clifford Avenue, but</u> the <u>latter</u> does have a magnificent rose garden. <u>No error.</u>
     C           D                          E

**15.** <u>Rotating the tires every winter,</u> the truck unquestionably <u>ran better</u>, especially in the
          A                                 B
<u>region's</u> fierce <u>snowstorms</u>. <u>No error.</u>
   C        D    E

**16.** With the sharp increase in medical costs and the concurrent decline in employment

and subsequent loss of medical insurance, many individuals <u>falsely believe</u> that
                                                   A

<u>doctors</u> should provide free medical services to the <u>indigent, much</u> as lawyers provide
   B                                      C

pro bono assistance <u>to people accused of crimes</u> who cannot afford to pay for legal
                                D

representation. <u>No error.</u>
            E

**17.** <u>"Bloody Mary's"</u> reign lasted only five years before her half-sister Queen Elizabeth
       A

took <u>charge it</u> was enough time to forge a strong link <u>between</u> the <u>English and Spanish</u>
     B                                   C         D
<u>courts.</u> <u>No error.</u>
        E

**18.** According to a recent survey <u>taken by the editors</u> of the Travel Channel, the top
                          A

three <u>most-visited vacation</u> destinations in the world are <u>Paris, New York, and Rome,</u>
            B                                C
<u>respectfully</u>. <u>No error.</u>
   D       E

**19.** The <u>Chamber of Commerce director,</u> Ms. Debbie Holaski, shared with Stephen and
           A

<u>I</u> the blueprints for the <u>new high-density housing</u> in the gentrified <u>downtown area</u>.
B                          C                       D
<u>No error.</u>
  A

**20.** <u>The job applicant expected</u> that she would present her résumé at the interview,
          A                                        B
describe her <u>relevant experiences</u>, and <u>that questions about why she left her previous</u>
           C                                D
<u>job would be asked</u>. <u>No error.</u>
               E

**21.** <u>Us employees</u> donated <u>gently used</u>, unwanted clothing; <u>unwrapped new toys</u>; and bags
     A                 B                     C
of canned goods as part of the <u>company's annual holiday</u> charity drive. <u>No error.</u>
                            D                        E

*Part B*
*17 questions*

Suggested time: 20 minutes
*Directions:* Choose the best version of the underlined portion of each sentence. Choice A is the same as the underlined portion of the original sentence. If you think that the original sentence is better than any of the suggested revisions, choose A. Otherwise, choose the revision you think is best. Answers and explanations follow the questions.

22. An international team of astronomers has identified a candidate for the smallest-known black hole by using data from NASA's Rossi X-ray Timing <u>Explorer the evidence</u> comes from a specific type of x-ray pattern.

    (A) Explorer the evidence
    (B) Explorer, the evidence
    (C) Explorer; the evidence
    (D) Explorer, nor the evidence
    (E) Explorer, so the evidence

23. We were <u>suppose to drive toward the city but turned around; irregardless,</u> we arrived at the movie with plenty of time to spare.

    (A) suppose to drive toward the city but turned around; irregardless,
    (B) suppose to drive toward the city but turned around; irregardless,
    (C) supposed to drive toward the city but turned around; regardless,
    (D) suppose to drive toward the City but turned around; regardless,
    (E) suppose to drive toward the City but turned around; irregardless,

24. Washington Irving (1783–1859) became the first American writer to achieve an international <u>reputation, and he was</u> the central figure in the American literary scene between 1809 and 1865.

    (A) reputation, and he was
    (B) reputation, he was
    (C) reputation and he was
    (D) reputation, or he was
    (E) reputation, yet he was

25. Brandywine Falls is a 60-foot waterfall and the centerpiece of the falls <u>area but not its' only</u> source of interest.

    (A) area but not its' only
    (B) area, but not it's only
    (C) area but not its only
    (D) area, but not its only
    (E) area; but not its only

26. The Internet can be used for many helpful purposes, including to purchase items such as clothing and tickets, to reconnect with old friends and acquaintances, and <u>looking up information on a seemingly endless list of topics</u>.

    (A) looking up information on a seemingly endless list of topics
    (B) you can look up information on a seemingly endless list of topics
    (C) being able to look up information on a seemingly endless list of topics
    (D) on a seemingly endless list of topics you can be looking up information
    (E) to look up information on a seemingly endless list of topics.

27. Julia Dent Grant rejoiced in her husband's fame as a victorious <u>general they entered</u> the White House in 1869 to begin, in her words, "the happiest period" of her life.

    (A) general they entered
    (B) general, they entered
    (C) general, when they entered
    (D) general, they entering
    (E) general, they enter

28. <u>Swimming slowly to shore, the terrifying storm clouds were seen gathering at the horizon</u>.

    (A) Swimming slowly to shore, the terrifying storm clouds were seen gathering at the horizon.
    (B) As Jalen was swimming slowly to shore, he saw the terrifying storm clouds gathering at the horizon.
    (C) As Jalen was swimming slowly to shore, the terrifying storm clouds were seen gathering at the horizon by him.
    (D) The terrifying storm clouds gathering at the horizon were seen by Jalen swimming slowly to shore.
    (E) The terrifying storm clouds, seen by Jalen swimming slowly to shore, gathering at the horizon.

29. Stephen <u>feels bad the next day when he stays up too late reading</u>, but try as he might, he can never put a good novel down until he has finished reading it.

    (A) feels bad the next day when he stays up too late reading,
    (B) feels badly the next day when he stays up too late reading,
    (C) feels bad the next day when he stays up to late reading,
    (D) feels badly the next day when he stay up too late reading,
    (E) feels bad the next day after he stay up too late having read,

30. The package was <u>more heavier</u> than Marc expected, so he decided to get some help carrying it to his truck.

    (A) more heavier
    (B) most heavier
    (C) heavier
    (D) most heavy
    (E) heaviest

31. <u>Despite the fact that higher education is expensive, a large number of people realize that a college degree is a key to success at the present time.</u>

  (A) Despite the fact that higher education is expensive, a large number of people realize that a college degree is a key to success at the present time.
  (B) Although higher education is expensive, a large number of people realize that a college degree is a key to success at the present time.
  (C) Despite the fact that higher education is expensive, many people realize that a college degree is a key to success at the present time.
  (D) Despite the fact that higher education is expensive, a large number of people realize that a college degree is a key to success now.
  (E) Although higher education is expensive, many people realize that a college degree is a key to success now.

32. The chemical compound had to be mixed precisely to be effective, so the scientist was <u>real cautious</u> to measure accurately and check her work often.

  (A) real cautious
  (B) real cautiously
  (C) really cautiously
  (D) real cautiousful
  (E) really cautious

33. The winter <u>solstice, which marks the day when winter officially starts in the Northern Hemisphere and when days start to become incrementally longer, takes</u> place this year on Thursday, December 22, at 12:30 A.M.

  (A) solstice, which marks the day when winter officially starts in the Northern Hemisphere and when days start to become incrementally longer, takes
  (B) solstice which marks the day when winter officially starts in the Northern Hemisphere and when days start to become incrementally longer, takes
  (C) solstice, which marks the day when winter officially starts in the Northern Hemisphere and when days start to become incrementally longer takes
  (D) solstice which marks the day when winter officially starts in the Northern Hemisphere and when days start to become incrementally longer takes
  (E) solstice; which marks the day when winter officially starts in the Northern Hemisphere and when days start to become incrementally longer takes

34. During the seminar at the hotel, the personable, handsome speaker explained how to buy foreclosed homes at bargain-basement prices, how to get cut-rate mortgages, and <u>saving significant money on closing costs.</u>

  (A) saving significant money on closing costs
  (B) one saving significant money on closing costs
  (C) how to save significant money on closing costs
  (D) savvy investors saving significant money on closing costs
  (E) cutting significant money from closing costs

**35.** In the Hoover Library located in West Branch, <u>Iowa, can learn</u> about President Hoover's life and career through manuscripts, photographs, and oral histories.

(A) Iowa, can learn
(B) Iowa, people can learn
(C) Iowa, learning
(D) Iowa, to learn
(E) Iowa, learning can occur

**36.** <u>Jason did bad on the first test, but he did even worst on the second test</u>, so he is contemplating dropping the class and taking it during the summer when he has more time.

(A) Jason did bad on the first test, but he did even worst on the second test,
(B) Jason did bad on the first test, but he did even worse on the second test,
(C) Jason did worse on the first test, but he did even worst on the second test,
(D) Jason did badly on the first test, but he did even worse on the second test,
(E) Jason did worst on the first test, but he did even more badly on the second test,

**37.** Although relatively new, the house was not well built and <u>hadn't no</u> repairs, so it was fast becoming the neighborhood eyesore.

(A) hadn't no
(B) barely no
(C) scarcely no
(D) not quite no
(E) hadn't any

**38.** The National Conservation Training Center (NCTC) Conservation Library includes topics covered in all NCTC training classes, with an emphasis on natural resource conservation, environmental education, and <u>becoming a good leader in the conservation community</u>.

(A) becoming a good leader in the conservation community.
(B) conservation leadership.
(C) to be a good leader in the conservation community.
(D) being a good leader in the conservation community.
(E) conservation community.

# STOP. This is the end of Section 1: Multiple-Choice Questions.

# SECTION 2: ESSAY

## 30 minutes

*Directions:* Write an essay on the following topic. You will not receive any credit for writing on a topic other than the one given here. Plan your essay carefully and be sure to include specific examples and details that illustrate your point. Write your essay on your own paper. (On the real Praxis PPST test, paper for writing your essay will be provided.)

**You will not receive credit if you write on any other topic. For your response to be scored, you must write in English. You cannot write in a foreign language.**

Read the opinion stated below:

People are affected by their environment, in both a good way and a bad way.

In an essay, agree or disagree with this statement. Be sure to support your opinion with specific examples from readings, your experiences, your observations, or the media.
The space below is for your notes.

**Test Hint:** Start your essay with a topic sentence. State your position in the first paragraph, organize your ideas clearly, and use ample details and examples.

# WRITING PRACTICE TEST 3: ANSWERS

## SECTION 1: MULTIPLE-CHOICE QUESTIONS

*Part A*

> **Note:** This part of the test does *not* require you to correct the sentence, only to identify the error that it may or may not contain. However, to help you learn more about grammar and usage to earn a higher score on the entire Praxis writing test (including Part B and the essay), as well as to improve your teaching, all errors are corrected and the relevant grammar and usage rules explained.

**1. B**  This sentence has faulty subject-verb agreement. The subject and verb must agree in number: both must be either singular or plural. The verb agrees with the subject, not with a noun or pronoun in the phrase. Don't be misled by a phrase that comes between the subject and the verb. In this sentence, the subject is the *gentleman*, which is singular. Thus, it takes the singular verb *strolls*, not the plural *stroll*. Ignore the intervening prepositional phrase "with all the dogs."

**2. D**  This sentence has a misplaced modifier. As you learned earlier in this book, *modifiers* are words and phrases that describe. To make your intended meaning clear, place a modifier as close as possible to what it describes. The modifier in this sentence is *nearly*. As the sentence reads, the words almost remain fresh and useful, which is not the writer's meaning. The sentence should read: *Spanish coins, articles of trade, and words were all freely exchanged; 400 years later, the money and spices are musty relics, but nearly all the words remain fresh and useful.*

> **Test Hint:** Here's another misplaced modifier to use as practice:
>
> *Tank had driven with his girlfriend, Bunny, from their home in a Hummer for the football game.* (Error: Do Bunny and Tank live in a Hummer? Perhaps, but it's not likely.)
>
> Corrected sentence: *Tank had driven in a Hummer from their home with his girlfriend, Bunny, for the football game.*

**3. D**  This sentence has a faulty comparison. Use the comparative form (*more* or *-er*) to compare two things. Use the superlative form (*most* or *-est*) to compare three or more things. Never use *more* or *most* with *-er* or *-est*; you get one or the other. The sentence should read: *During the highly contentious meeting, the contest judges ruled that the singer was a good performer, the juggler was even better, but the ballroom dancers and the magician were the best of all and so awarded them first place.*

**4. D**  This sentence has a faulty pronoun reference. Always make sure that a pronoun has a clear *antecedent*, the word to which it refers. Here, the pronoun *it* refers to the candy bowl, which clearly does not make sense, as Jack is not eating the candy bowl. In these instances, use the noun instead of the pronoun to avoid confusion. The sentence should read: *After the third quarter of the football game, the candy bowl was empty, but Jack was sick of eating candy anyway.*

**5. B**  This is a run-on sentence, meaning two complete sentences (independent clauses) are joined incorrectly. As you've already learned, two sentences can be joined with a coordinating conjunction (*for, and, nor, but, or, yet, so*) or with a semicolon. They can also be divided into two sentences by using a period. Here are some ways to correct the sentence:

- Add a coordinating conjunction

  *A family is the best medicine to cure all sickness and illness, and I know that people are more likely to become really healthy and stay well if they have a good family.*

- Use a semicolon in place of the comma

  *A family is the best medicine to cure all sickness and illness; I know that people are more likely to become really healthy and stay well if they have a good family.*

- Create a complex sentence rather than a compound sentence

  *A family is the best medicine to cure all sickness and illness, because I know that people are more likely to become really healthy and stay well if they have a good family.*

- Create two sentences

  *A family is the best medicine to cure all sickness and illness. I know that people are more likely to become really healthy and stay well if they have a good family.*

**Test Hint:** As you study, focus on the grammar errors that you are most likely to find on the Praxis. At the end of each practice writing test in this book, you will find a chart that shows the array of skills being tested. Use these charts to identify common errors.

Then focus even more closely on the types of errors you typically make. If you have a particular problem area, take the time to find out why. Learn the specific rule that applies, so you don't make the same kind of mistake again. This will help you earn a higher score on the Praxis and become a better teacher.

**6. A**  This sentence has an error with apostrophes. Do not use apostrophes to show plurals. Rather, use an apostrophe with a noun (never with a pronoun!) to show ownership. Since the doctors do not own anything, there is no reason to use an apostrophe. The word should be *doctors.*

**7. A**  This sentence has an error in punctuation. Use a comma before a coordinating conjunction (*but*) that joins two complete sentences.

**8. E**  This sentence does not have an error. It is correct as written.

**9. B**    This sentence has an error in capitalization. There is no reason to capitalize *employers*, as it is not a proper noun or the title of anything.

> **Test Hint:** Try working backward from the answer choices. If you're unsure which choice is correct, try reading the sentence again, substituting each of the answers for the underlined portion. Which one sounds best?
>
> Look for the revision that is also the best writing. It will be direct and clear. It will not have any unnecessary words.

**10. D**    This sentence has a shift in pronoun case. The sentence starts with the pronoun *you* and then shifts to the pronoun *one*. Stay with the same pronoun throughout a sentence.

**11. C**    This sentence has an error in subject-verb agreement. The singular verb *sun* requires the singular verb *rises*, not the plural *rise*. Because this test item has so many proper nouns, it is easy to overlook the agreement issue. Be sure to read each sentence carefully.

**12. A**    This sentence has an error in capitalization. Capitalize titles showing family relations when the title is used with the person's name (such as Aunt Margaret). However, do not capitalize the title when it comes after a possessive noun or pronoun, as is the case here. Thus, the phrase should be "My father," not "My Father."

**13. D**    This sentence has a misplaced modifier. The modifier in this sentence is by "her adviser." As the sentence reads, we don't know if the adviser did the telling or the awarding. The sentence should read: *At the commencement ceremony, Samara was told by her adviser that she had been granted a lucrative graduate fellowship.*

**14. A**    This sentence has an error in case. Both pronouns are objects of the preposition *between* and so should be in the objective case: "Between you and me." Case is a difficult grammatical issue and a common topic on the Praxis writing test.

> **Test Hint:** Here's a hint for solving questions on pronoun case. To help you "hear" the correct answer, make "you and me" plural and then read the sentence: *I believe that this issue should remain between us.* (not between *we*)

**15. A**    This is a dangling participle. A *present participle* is a verb ending in *-ing*; it dangles when the subject of the verb and the subject of the sentence do not agree. You can correct the sentence this way: *By rotating the tires every winter, Luke found that the truck unquestionably ran better, especially in the region's fierce snowstorms.*

**16. E**    The sentence is correct as written.

> **Test Hint:** Some test takers are afraid to choose the answer that doesn't change the sentence. But if you're certain that the sentence does not contain an error, go ahead and pick that answer.

**17. B** This is a run-on sentence, meaning two complete sentences (independent clauses) are joined incorrectly. Here are two possible ways of correcting the sentence.

> *"Bloody Mary's" reign lasted only five years before her half-sister Queen Elizabeth took charge, but it was enough time to forge a strong link between the English and Spanish courts.*
>
> *Even though "Bloody Mary's" reign lasted only five years before her half-sister Queen Elizabeth took charge, it was enough time to forge a strong link between the English and Spanish courts.*

**18. D** This is a usage error. *Respectfully* means "with respect or full of respect" (*The reporters listened respectfully to the senator's speech.*). *Respectively* means "each in the order given." This is the word needed to complete the meaning of the sentence in this example.

**19. B** This is an error in pronoun case. "Ms. Debbie Holaski" is the subject because she is doing the action. Therefore, "Stephen and I" are the objects, requiring the pronoun to be in the objective case (*me*). To "hear" the error, replace the object with the pronouns:

- Incorrect nominative case

    *The Chamber of Commerce director, Ms. Debbie Holaski, shared with <u>we</u> the blueprints for the new high-density housing in the gentrified downtown area.*

- Correct objective case

    *The Chamber of Commerce director, Ms. Debbie Holaski, shared with <u>us</u> the blueprints for the new high-density housing in the gentrified downtown area.*

In the nominative case, the pronoun is used as a subject of a verb or a predicate nominative. This means the pronoun does the action. Here are some examples:

- Who goes there? (*Who* is the subject of the verb *goes*.)
- She planned to go to the rave. (*She* is the subject of the verb *planned*.)
- Jack and I do most of the cooking. (*I* is the subject of the verb *cooking*.)

The *predicate nominative* is the noun or pronoun that follows a linking verb. It identifies or renames the subject. Here are some examples:

It      <u>is</u>      <u>I</u>.      (not *It is me.*)
      *linking verb*    *pronoun*

It      <u>is</u>      <u>they.</u>      (not *It is them.*)
      *linking verb*    *pronoun*

The winners      are      Leroy and      he.      (not *him*)
      *linking verb*               *pronoun*

In compound structures (those with two pronouns or a noun and a pronoun), drop the other word for the moment. Then you can see which case you need. For example:

Bob and (I, me) travel a lot.

I travel a lot.

This tells you the answer is *I*, the nominative case.

**20. D**   This sentence has faulty parallel structure. As you have already learned, *parallel structure* means using the same pattern of words to show that two or more ideas have the same level of importance. This can happen at the word, phrase, or clause level. The correct sentence should read: *The job applicant expected that she would present her résumé at the interview, describe her relevant experiences, and answer questions about why she left her previous job.*

The clauses "present her résumé at the interview," "describe her relevant experiences," and "answer questions about why she left her previous job" are now all parallel.

**21. A**   This is an error in pronoun case. The subject case is *we* because *we* are doing the action. Read the sentence without the noun to hear the error: *we* sounds correct; *us* sounds awkward.

*Part B*

**22. C**   This is a run-on sentence, meaning two sentences are run together without the correct punctuation. Choices D and E use coordinating conjunctions correctly in relation to grammar, but they don't make sense logically. Of the choices offered here, only C correctly and logically joins the two sentences. The correct sentence reads: *An international team of astronomers has identified a candidate for the smallest-known black hole by using data from NASA's Rossi X-ray Timing Explorer; the evidence comes from a specific type of x-ray pattern.*

**Test Hint:** When in doubt, go for the most logical and obvious answer. If that doesn't fit, look more deeply into the question and see if you can find an answer that matches your line of thought.

**23. C**   This sentence has errors in tense and usage. First, the word *suppose* should be *supposed.* Second, the word *irregardless* is considered substandard usage. It is not used in standard English. In its place, use *regardless.* Only choice C corrects both errors.

- Choice B is incorrect because *suppose* should be *supposed.* Further, the sentence still contains the substandard word *irregardless.*
- Choice D is incorrect because *suppose* should be *supposed.* Further, *city* should not be capitalized because it is a common noun, not a proper noun.
- Choice E has *suppose* instead of *supposed, city* incorrectly capitalized, and *irregardless* rather than *regardless.*

**24. A**   This sentence is correct as written. Choice B is incorrect because removing the coordinating conjunction *and* between the two independent clauses creates a run-on sentence. Adding a comma between two independent clauses creates a comma splice, as a comma isn't sufficient to join the sentences. A semicolon is needed. Choice C is wrong because a comma is needed before a coordinating conjunction in a compound sentence. Choices D and E are correct grammatically because *or* and *yet* are coordinating conjunctions (needed to join two independent clauses), but they do not make logical sense in the context.

**25. D**  This sentence has two errors: one in pronoun use and one in commas. First, *it's* is a contraction for the phrase "it is," and the sentence requires the possessive pronoun *its*. Second, a comma is required before a coordinating conjunction in a compound sentence. Only choice D corrects both errors. The correct sentence reads: *Brandywine Falls is a 60-foot waterfall and the centerpiece of the falls area, but not its only source of interest.*

- Choice A is wrong because *its'* is not a word.
- Choice B is wrong because the sentence requires the pronoun *its*, not the contraction *it's*.
- Choice C is wrong because it is missing the comma before the coordinating conjunction.
- Choice E is wrong because the sentence does not require both a semicolon and a coordinating conjunction. Both are used to connect two independent clauses in a compound sentence, so only one is required.

Here's a quick review: The coordinating conjunctions are *for*, *and*, *nor*, *but*, *or*, *yet*, and *so*, and they are used to link two or more independent clauses.

Study the following chart to help you distinguish between contractions and possessive pronouns:

| Contractions | Possessive Pronouns |
| --- | --- |
| it's | its |
| you're | your |
| they're | their |
| who's | whose |

**26. E**  This sentence has faulty parallel structure. The correct sentence should read: *The Internet can be used for many helpful purposes, including to purchase items such as clothing and tickets, to reconnect with old friends and acquaintances, and to look up information on a seemingly endless list of topics.* With this revision, the infinitive phrases "to purchase," "to reconnect," and "to look up" are parallel because they are in the same grammatical form.

**27. C**  This is a run-on sentence, meaning two sentences that are joined incorrectly. Two independent clauses (complete sentences) can be joined with a coordinating conjunction (*for*, *and*, *nor*, *but*, *or*, *yet*, *so*) or a semicolon. Or one of the sentences can be made into a dependent clause by using a subordinating conjunction (such as *when*, *although*, *because*, or *since*). Choice C does this. Here is how the sentence looks deconstructed:

Julia Dent Grant rejoiced in her husband's fame as a victorious general
>    *independent clause*

they entered the White House in 1869 to begin, in her words, "the happiest period" of her life
>    *independent clause*

And here is the sentence recombined:

Julia Dent Grant rejoiced in her husband's fame as a victorious general
>    *independent clause*

when they entered the White House in 1869 to begin, in her words, "the happiest period" of her life
>    *dependent clause*

Notice the subordinating conjunction *when* in the second part of the sentence. It starts the dependent clause.

**28. B**   This sentence contains a dangling participle. In this sentence, the subject is "the terrifying storm clouds," but the clouds are not doing the swimming. The correct sentence should read: *As Jalen was swimming slowly to shore, he saw the terrifying storm clouds gathering at the horizon.*

- Choice A is wrong because it is the same as the original.
- Choices C and D create passive constructions. In the passive voice, the action is done to the subject. The active voice, where the subject does the action, is more direct and concise. Thus, it is better writing.
- Finally, choice E is incorrect because it is not a complete sentence. It does not have a complete verb and thus does not express a complete thought. A complete verb in this instance would be *were gathering*.

**29. A**   This sentence is correct as written. The confusion over *bad* and *badly* has been going on for decades and is not likely to be resolved soon, but you can do your part to help use these two words correctly. Let's look at verbs to understand how they are modified.

   A *verb* is a word that expresses time while showing an action, a condition, or the fact that something exists.

- Verb that shows action: walk
- Verb that shows condition: will
- Verb that shows existence: were

   A *linking verb* is a verb that connects a noun or a pronoun at or near the beginning of a sentence with a word at or near the end of the sentence. The most common linking verb is *to be*; others include *appear, become, fell, grow, look, remain, seem, smell, sounds, stay, taste,* and *turn.*
   Use *bad* (an adjective) with linking verbs. For example:

- Rob feels bad that he missed the concert.
- Stephen always feels bad the next day when he stays up too late reading.

   Use *badly* (an adverb) with action verbs. For example:

- Rob smells badly. (Rob cannot smell well.)

**30. C**   This sentence has an error in case. In the comparative case, you compare two people, places, or things. Use *-er* or *more* to create the comparison—never both.

**31. E**   This sentence has an error in style. It is verbose, filled with wordy phrases that should be pared down to create a clearer and more concise sentence. The following chart shows the existing word phrases and the more concise revisions.

| Wordy Phrase | Revision |
| --- | --- |
| despite the fact that | although |
| a large number of | many |
| at the present time | now |

   Only choice E replaces all three wordy phrases with more direct options.

**32. E** This sentence has an error in usage. Use an adverb to modify (describe) a verb, adjective, or other adverb. Use an adjective to modify nouns and pronouns. The word *cautious* is an adverb, so you need an adverb to modify it. *Real* is an adjective, and *really* is an adverb. Hint: Many adverbs are formed by adding *-ly* to an adjective.

**33. A** This sentence is correct as written because the clause "which marks the day when winter officially starts in the Northern Hemisphere and when days start to become incrementally longer" is not necessary to the meaning of the sentence. Therefore, it is a nonessential clause and can be set off by commas.

---

**Test Hint:** Don't use the length of the sentence element to determine whether or not the sentence is complete. Rather, decide whether the sentence element is necessary to the sentence or not.

---

**Here is the rule:** Surround nonessential words, phrases, and clauses with commas. (*Nonessential* refers to words, phrases, and clauses that interrupt the sentence without changing the essential meaning.)

**Here is the test:** If you can enclose the words, phrases, and/or clauses with parentheses or put the element somewhere else in the sentence, it is not essential. If you can't do this, then the element should not be set off with commas. Here is another example. The nonessential element is underlined:

- The Cuyahoga Valley's waterfalls, <u>among the most popular attractions in the national park,</u> once powered a thriving village.
- <u>Among the most popular attractions in the national park,</u> the Cuyahoga Valley's waterfalls once powered a thriving village.

**34. C** This sentence has faulty parallel structure. The correct sentence should read: *During the seminar at the hotel, the personable, handsome speaker explained how to buy foreclosed homes at bargain-basement prices, how to get cut-rate mortgages, and how to save significant money on closing costs.* The infinitive "how to" phrases are parallel.

When you are confronted by a long sentence, reduce it to its bare bones so you can determine what needs to be done. Here is how the sample sentence looks simplified:

- *how to buy*
- *how to get*
- *how to save*

**35. B**    This sentence is a fragment because it is missing the subject. As a result, it does not express a complete thought or make sense. To figure out the error, ask yourself, "*Who* can learn about President Hoover?" Only choice B provides a subject. Choice E recasts the sentence into the passive voice, but it still doesn't provide a subject, someone to perform the action.

---

**Test Hint:** Be creative but don't overthink. Sometimes the answer isn't obvious, so you have to think outside the box by looking at the question from different angles to analyze it. You have to use creative-thinking skills by inferring, analyzing, and drawing conclusions. But when you think creatively, be sure not to overanalyze your answers and create relationships that don't really exist. This may also cause you to get hopelessly lost.

---

**36. D**    This sentence has faulty comparison. With regular adjectives and adverbs, use the comparative form to compare two things.

- Use *-er* or *-est* to form the comparative and superlative degree of most one- and two-syllable modifiers. Thus, you would use *fast, faster, faster* and *heavy, heavier, heaviest*.
- Use *more* or *most* to form the comparative and superlative degree of all modifiers of three or more syllables. Thus, you would use *popular, more popular, most popular*.
- Use *more* or *most* to form the comparative and superlative degree of all adverbs that end in *-ly*, regardless of the number of syllables they contain. Thus, you would use *quickly, more quickly, most quickly*.

Some modifiers are irregular, which means they form the comparative and superlative forms in other ways. The word *bad* is one of these. The following chart lists the most common irregular modifiers:

| Positive | Comparative | Superlative |
| --- | --- | --- |
| bad | worse | worst |
| badly | worse | worst |
| far | farther | farthest |
| far | further | furthest |
| good | better | best |
| ill | worse | worst |
| late | later | last or latest |
| little (amount) | less | least |
| many | more | most |
| much | more | most |
| well | better | best |

Now, back to our sentence. Here, we use *badly* because the sentence requires an adverb to modify the verb *did*. We use *worse* to compare two things, the two tests. The corrected sentence reads: *Jason did badly on the first test, but he did even worse on the second test, so he is contemplating dropping the class and taking it during the summer when he has more time.*

**37. E** This sentence contains a double negative, as the words *barely* and *no* are both negative. Use a single negative word to convey negation (choice E). Negative words include *no, not, nothing, none, nowhere,* and *none.*

---

**Test Hint:** Pace yourself to avoid making careless errors. During the Praxis, make sure you wear a watch or can see a clock. This will help you keep working at the right pace. You want to work quickly—but not so quickly that you throw away points by being careless. It's an awful feeling to lose points on questions that you really can answer.

---

**38. B** The error here is faulty parallel structure (also called parallelism). As you have already learned in this book, *parallel structure* means using the same grammatical pattern of words to show that two or more ideas have the same level of importance. This can be done at the word, phrase, or clause level. The pattern in this sentence is adjective-noun, as follows:

| natural resource | conservation |
|---|---|
| adjective | noun |

| environmental | education |
|---|---|
| adjective | noun |

This pattern has to continue for the sentence to have parallel structure. When you look for an answer that has this pattern, only choice B fits the bill:

| conservation | leadership |
|---|---|
| adjective | noun |

Choice E looks correct, but it cannot be because it changes the meaning of the sentence by omitting anything about leadership.

## Skills Spread

| Specific Content Area | Item Numbers |
|---|---|
| Grammar and usage (13) | 1, 3, 4, 10, 11, 13, 14, 18, 19, 21, 30, 32, 36 |
| Sentence structure (14) | 2, 5, 15, 17, 20, 22, 26, 27, 28, 29, 33, 34, 35, 38 |
| Mechanics—punctuation, capitalization | 6, 7, 8, 9, 12, 16, 23, 24, 25, 31, 37 |
| Diction—word choice (11) | |
| Essay | 1 |

# SECTION 2: ESSAY

The following model essay would receive a 6, the highest score, for its specific details, organization, and style (such as appropriate word choice, sentence structure, and consistent facility in the use of language). It is an especially intelligent and insightful response.

opening provides creative, valid parallel to topic

Gardeners know that the composition of the soil affects the flowers they plant. The results can be dramatic, as the ostentatious hydrangea demonstrates, for acidic soil causes some varieties of hydrangeas to turn blue; conversely, neutral to alkaline soil produces pink blooms. Other levels of soil chemicals produce purple flowers or even a mixture of blue and pink on the same hydrangea plant.

clear thesis statement directly links to the topic given

Similarly, we are all influenced in significant ways by our families, the "soil" in which we grow. But unlike growing flowers, raising children is far from an exact science. The effect of being raised in an unstable family, in poverty, is a case in point.

first main point

humor relieves the tragedy that follows

transition to main idea

specific examples prove the thesis

Growing up in an impoverished single-parent family can cause some children to become criminals. As Leonard Bernstein and Stephen Sondheim joked in the famous song "Gee, Officer Krupke" from *West Side Story*, "Dear kindly Sergeant Krupke, You gotta understand, It's just our bringin' up-ke, That gets us out of hand." But the case of Lee Boyd Malvo, the teenaged sniper who teamed up with adult John Allen Muhammad in the "Beltway sniper attacks," is no joke. Malvo grew up in a highly unstable family, and his mother abandoned him to Muhammad. Soon after, Malvo and Muhammad ended up in a homeless shelter. Muhammad convinced the teenager to join him in his murderous 2002 rampage, which resulted in the death of 10 people. Prior to these attacks, the duo had committed robbery and murder in Louisiana and Alabama. Malvo clearly "went bad" and is currently serving a life sentence without parole. Most people would agree that his tragic life was most likely caused by his poor family environment; however, growing up in a poor, single-parent family can cause other children to become brain surgeons.

second main point

specific examples prove the thesis

thoughtful analysis

Benjamin Carson was raised by a single, illiterate mother who toiled as a cleaning woman. As a young child, Carson was a poor student and at the bottom of his class; some of his classmates mocked him as "the dumbest child in the fifth grade, maybe in the whole world." Not until high school did Carson hit his stride, doing so well that he gained entrance to Yale University. Perhaps his success is due in part to his mother. Although she could not read, she insisted that her son do so, pretending to read along with him. Today, Carson is a world-famous neurosurgeon at Johns Hopkins Hospital, one of the top medical centers in the country. He is honored around the world for his work separating conjoined twins.

insightful, intelligent conclusion; elegant parallel structure

summary avoids facile response

Both Malvo and Carson were raised by single mothers. Both grew up in deep poverty. Both are male. Yet the former became a vicious murderer who stole lives; the latter, a compassionate surgeon who saves them. There is no doubt that environment can have a powerful effect on someone's life—for evil and for good.

# MATHEMATICS PRACTICE TEST 3

## Answer sheet

1 Ⓐ Ⓑ Ⓒ Ⓓ Ⓔ
2 Ⓐ Ⓑ Ⓒ Ⓓ Ⓔ
3 Ⓐ Ⓑ Ⓒ Ⓓ Ⓔ
4 Ⓐ Ⓑ Ⓒ Ⓓ Ⓔ
5 Ⓐ Ⓑ Ⓒ Ⓓ Ⓔ
6 Ⓐ Ⓑ Ⓒ Ⓓ Ⓔ
7 Ⓐ Ⓑ Ⓒ Ⓓ Ⓔ

8 Ⓐ Ⓑ Ⓒ Ⓓ Ⓔ
9 Ⓐ Ⓑ Ⓒ Ⓓ Ⓔ
10 Ⓐ Ⓑ Ⓒ Ⓓ Ⓔ
11 Ⓐ Ⓑ Ⓒ Ⓓ Ⓔ
12 Ⓐ Ⓑ Ⓒ Ⓓ Ⓔ
13 Ⓐ Ⓑ Ⓒ Ⓓ Ⓔ
14 Ⓐ Ⓑ Ⓒ Ⓓ Ⓔ

15 Ⓐ Ⓑ Ⓒ Ⓓ Ⓔ
16 Ⓐ Ⓑ Ⓒ Ⓓ Ⓔ
17 Ⓐ Ⓑ Ⓒ Ⓓ Ⓔ
18 Ⓐ Ⓑ Ⓒ Ⓓ Ⓔ
19 Ⓐ Ⓑ Ⓒ Ⓓ Ⓔ
20 Ⓐ Ⓑ Ⓒ Ⓓ Ⓔ
21 Ⓐ Ⓑ Ⓒ Ⓓ Ⓔ

22 Ⓐ Ⓑ Ⓒ Ⓓ Ⓔ
23 Ⓐ Ⓑ Ⓒ Ⓓ Ⓔ
24 Ⓐ Ⓑ Ⓒ Ⓓ Ⓔ
25 Ⓐ Ⓑ Ⓒ Ⓓ Ⓔ
26 Ⓐ Ⓑ Ⓒ Ⓓ Ⓔ
27 Ⓐ Ⓑ Ⓒ Ⓓ Ⓔ
28 Ⓐ Ⓑ Ⓒ Ⓓ Ⓔ

29 Ⓐ Ⓑ Ⓒ Ⓓ Ⓔ
30 Ⓐ Ⓑ Ⓒ Ⓓ Ⓔ
31 Ⓐ Ⓑ Ⓒ Ⓓ Ⓔ
32 Ⓐ Ⓑ Ⓒ Ⓓ Ⓔ
33 Ⓐ Ⓑ Ⓒ Ⓓ Ⓔ
34 Ⓐ Ⓑ Ⓒ Ⓓ Ⓔ
35 Ⓐ Ⓑ Ⓒ Ⓓ Ⓔ

36 Ⓐ Ⓑ Ⓒ Ⓓ Ⓔ
37 Ⓐ Ⓑ Ⓒ Ⓓ Ⓔ
38 Ⓐ Ⓑ Ⓒ Ⓓ Ⓔ
39 Ⓐ Ⓑ Ⓒ Ⓓ Ⓔ
40 Ⓐ Ⓑ Ⓒ Ⓓ Ⓔ

# MATHEMATICS PRACTICE TEST 3

## 40 items, 60 minutes

*Directions:* Select the best choice for each item and mark the answer on your answer sheet.

1. "Some multiples of 5 are perfect squares." According to this statement, which of the following statements is true?

   (A) Five is a perfect square.
   (B) All perfect squares are multiples of 5.
   (C) All numbers greater than 5 are perfect squares.
   (D) Some perfect squares are multiples of 5.
   (E) No perfect squares are multiples of 7.

2. Andrew left New York with a full tank of gas. He drove to Washington, DC, and then refilled his tank. The tank took 8.3 gallons of gas. Andrew looked at the map and saw that he had gone approximately 250 miles. What is a good estimate of his miles per gallon?

   (A) 20
   (B) 23
   (C) 25
   (D) 28
   (E) 30

3. Using the data from the previous problem, if Andrew expected to drive another 300 miles, about how much more gas would he need?

   (A) 10 gallons
   (B) 12 gallons
   (C) 15 gallons
   (D) 18 gallons
   (E) 20 gallons

4. My car is more fuel-efficient than Andrew's; I get 35 miles to the gallon. If I travel the 250 miles from New York to Washington, about how many gallons of gas do I need?

   (A) 6
   (B) 7
   (C) 8
   (D) 10
   (E) 15

**5.** On the speedometer shown here, the arrow most likely indicates a speed of

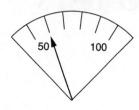

(A) 55 mph
(B) 60 mph
(C) 65 mph
(D) 75 mph
(E) 90 mph

**6.** A wall is 9 feet high and 22 feet long. A window that is 3 feet high and 4 feet wide is set into the wall. If 1 quart of paint covers 15 square feet, about how many quarts of paint are needed to cover the wall?

(A) 10
(B) 12
(C) 13
(D) 14
(E) 15

**7.** A gallon of paint costs $14; a quart of paint costs $4. If these are the only sizes of cans available, what is the minimum amount I must spend to have enough paint to cover the wall in the previous question?

(A) $28
(B) $42
(C) $52
(D) $46
(E) $48

**8.** The following chart tracks the number of employees the Hobart Company has at work on each of five days. On which day are 39 employees at work?

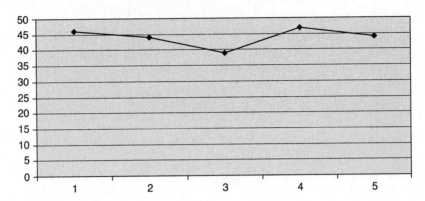

(A)  day 1
(B)  day 2
(C)  day 3
(D)  day 4
(E)  day 5

**9.** Which of the following numbers is three-quarters of 100,000?

(A)  30,000
(B)  100,000/4 × 3
(C)  30,000/40,000
(D)  100,000/3
(E)  100,000 × 0.25%

**10.** Using the ruler shown here, approximately how long is the line?

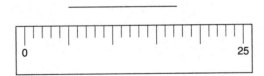

(A)  18
(B)  11
(C)  13
(D)  $10\frac{3}{5}$
(E)  $2\frac{3}{5}$

**11.** The line shown here is how much longer than the one in the previous question?

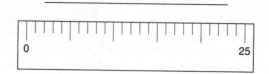

(A) 5

(B) 21

(C) 11

(D) 8

(E) $1\frac{1}{5}$

**12.** Which formula describes the relationship between $X$ and $Y$ shown in the table?

| $X$ | $Y$ |
| --- | --- |
| 2 | 6 |
| 6 | 14 |
| 13 | 28 |
| 17 | 36 |
| 22 | 46 |

(A) $Y = 2X + 1$

(B) $Y = 2(X - 1)$

(C) $Y = 3X - 4$

(D) $Y = 2(X + 1)$

(E) $Y = X + 4$

**13.** To convert meters to millimeters, you should

(A) multiply by 10

(B) divide by 100

(C) multiply by 100

(D) multiply by 1,000

(E) divide by 1,000

**14.** If I have 9 red socks, 7 black socks, and 6 white socks in my drawer, and I pick one at random, what is the probability that I'll pick a white sock?

(A) $\frac{3}{11}$

(B) $\frac{6}{17}$

(C) $\frac{1}{6}$

(D) $\frac{2}{21}$

(E) $\frac{11}{15}$

**15.** According to the graph, which employee made half as many sales as Allen?

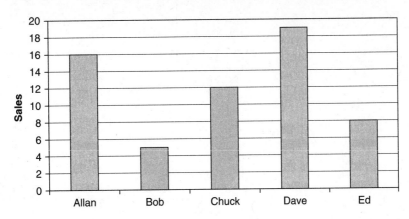

(A) Bob
(B) Chuck
(C) Dave
(D) Ed
(E) none of them

**16.** Which decimal is least?

(A) 0.00121
(B) 0.000453
(C) 0.0299
(D) 0.00354
(E) 0.000419

**17.** In a box of donuts, 4 are frosted, 2 are plain, and 6 have sprinkles. What percentage is frosted?

(A) 4 percent
(B) 25 percent
(C) 33.3 percent
(D) 40 percent
(E) 66.6 percent

**18.** If the following scale shows a load of iron ore, how much more is needed to raise the load to 250?

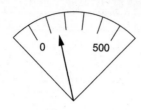

(A) 100
(B) 150
(C) 250
(D) 50
(E) 200

**19.** If there are 3 feet in a yard and 1,760 yards in a mile, how would you find the number of feet in 5 miles?

(A) Divide 3 by 12, then divide the answer by 1,760
(B) Divide 5 by 3, then multiply the answer by 1,760
(C) Multiply 5 by 1,760, then multiply the answer by 3
(D) Multiply 5 by 1,760, then divide the answer by 3
(E) Multiply 3 by 1,760, then divide the answer by 5

**20.** Which point on the graph is located at (4,3)?

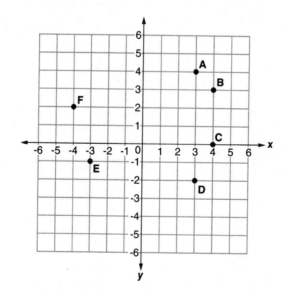

(A) A
(B) B
(C) F
(D) D
(E) E

**21.** Which answer is closest to $6{,}865 \times 1{,}015$?

    (A)  6,000,000

    (B)  7,000,000

    (C)  10,000,000

    (D)  12,000,000

    (E)  14,000,000

**22.** Which of these fractions is the smallest?

    (A)  $\frac{3}{4}$

    (B)  $\frac{7}{9}$

    (C)  $\frac{17}{23}$

    (D)  $\frac{4}{5}$

    (E)  $\frac{10}{19}$

**23.** If $A = 9r - 5$, and $r = 4$, then $A =$

    (A)  4

    (B)  14

    (C)  20

    (D)  31

    (E)  36

**24.** If you roll 2 six-sided dice, what is the probability that the combined total shown will not be 7?

    (A)  $\frac{5}{6}$

    (B)  $\frac{31}{36}$

    (C)  $\frac{7}{12}$

    (D)  $\frac{33}{36}$

    (E)  $\frac{15}{18}$

**25.** Your utility bill for June was \$250, but your electric bill for July was \$285. Assuming you used the same amount of power both months, what is the percent increase in the cost of electricity?

    (A)  12.3 percent

    (B)  14.0 percent

    (C)  25.0 percent

    (D)  87.7 percent

    (E)  114.0 percent

**26.** Which of these problems have the same numerical answer?

    I.   If a box holds 12 eggs, how many boxes do you need to hold 40 eggs?

    II.  If bus fare is $3, how many people can ride for $40?

    III. If I need 12 cups of flour to make one batch of brownies, how many full batches can I make with 40 cups of flour?

(A) I and II

(B) I and III

(C) II and III

(D) I, II, and III

(E) none of the above

**27.** If the probability of picking a red jellybean from a bag is 0.35, then if you randomly picked 40 jellybeans out of the bag, about how many would be red?

(A) 10

(B) 13

(C) 14

(D) 35

(E) 40

**28.** Number of books owned:

    Sammi 📖📖📖📖

    Vanessa 📖📖

    Andrew 📖📖📖📖📖

Each 📖 represents 8 books. How many more books does Sammi own than Vanessa?

(A) 2

(B) 8

(C) 12

(D) 16

(E) 24

**29.** If $x \div 8 = y$, what is $x \div 2$?

(A) $y$

(B) $y \div 2$

(C) $y \div 4$

(D) $2y$

(E) $4y$

**30.** Which answer is closest to $0.0005 \times 250$?

(A) 125
(B) 1.25
(C) 0.125
(D) 0.0125
(E) 0.000125

**31.** How many square feet of carpet would you need to carpet the room pictured here if a 6-foot by 8-foot area is tiled and would not be covered with carpet?

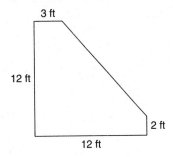

(A) 96
(B) 51
(C) 45
(D) 48
(E) 60

**32.** The following pie chart shows the percentage of items a store has available for sale. If there are 150 books on the shelves, how many video games does the store have?

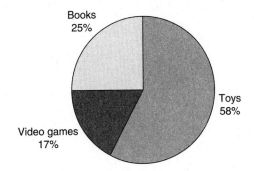

(A) 17
(B) 34
(C) 102
(D) 116
(E) 25

**33.** In a class of 22 students, 5 received an A this term. What percentage of the students did not receive an A?

(A) 77 percent
(B) 23 percent
(C) 67 percent
(D) 72 percent
(E) 17 percent

**34.** I went bicycling in a straight line 8 miles from my home, then made a 90-degree right turn and biked straight for another 6 miles. If I could ride straight home from there, how far would I have to go?

(A) 14 miles
(B) 10 miles
(C) 8 miles
(D) 6 miles
(E) 24 miles

**35.** How many square inches of wrapping paper are needed to exactly cover a cylinder-shaped box that is 10 inches tall and has a 4-inch radius?

(A) $12\pi$
(B) $80\pi$
(C) $112\pi$
(D) $14\pi$
(E) $56\pi$

**36.** Five salespeople earned the following commissions. Whose was the greatest?

(A) 8 percent of $120
(B) 5 percent of $200
(C) 7 percent of $160
(D) 6 percent of $150
(E) 10 percent of $105

**37.** Which number does not fall between $\frac{1}{4}$ and $\frac{2}{5}$?

(A) $\frac{1}{3}$
(B) 0.38
(C) 37%
(D) $\frac{3}{15}$
(E) 0.395

**38.** Which pairs of decimals and fractions are equivalent?

      I.  0.25, $\frac{1}{4}$

     II.  0.45, $\frac{9}{17}$

    III.  0.2, $\frac{2}{5}$

    IV.  0.05, $\frac{5}{10}$

(A) I only

(B) IV only

(C) I and IV

(D) I and III

(E) I, III, and IV

**39.** 660,000 is how many times 0.66?

(A) 100

(B) 1,000

(C) 10,000

(D) 100,000

(E) 1,000,000

**40.** On the following scale drawing of a room, 1 inch = 5 feet. What is the widest dimension of the actual room?

3 in.

3.5 in.

(A) 32.5 feet

(B) 16.5 feet

(C) 17.5 feet

(D) 15 feet

(E) 10.5 feet

# STOP. This is the end of Mathematics Practice Test 3.

# MATHEMATICS PRACTICE TEST 3: ANSWERS

**1. D**    If some perfect squares are multiples of 5, then some are not. You don't know anything else about perfect squares.

**2. E**    Estimate: He bought a bit more than 8 gallons of gas, so $250 \div 8 = 31.25$.

**3. A**    Estimate: 300 is 20 percent more than 250. He'd need about 10 gallons of gas, about 20 percent more than 8 gallons. (Or divide 300 by 30.)

**Test Hint:** Be sure to erase stray marks that might be misread.

**4. B**    Estimate: $250 \div 35 = 7.1$.

**5. B**    There are 4 hashes between 50 and 100, so each of the hashes is 10 mph. The arrow is 1 hash away from 50, and $50 + 10 = 60$ mph.

**6. B**    The wall is 198 square feet minus 12 square feet of window. To cover 186 square feet at 15 square feet per quart of paint, you will need $186 \div 15 = 12.4$ quarts of paint.

**7. D**    Twelve quarts is 3 gallons of paint. Three gallons of paint costs $42, plus one more quart at $4.

**8. C**    The point for day 3 is 39 on the chart.

**Test Hint:** To relieve "chart anxiety," figure out what the data presented mean before you look at the question and answer choices.

**9. B**    $(100{,}000 \div 4) \times 3 = 75{,}000$.

**10. C**    There are 25 hashes between 0 and 25, so each of the long hashes is 5 units, and each of the small hashes is 1 unit. The line begins at the 5 hash and ends at 18, and $18 - 5 = 13$.

**11. D**    This line starts at the 2 hash and ends at the 23 hash, so it is 21 units long: $21 - 13 = 8$.

**12. D**    Trial and error. Try all of the pairs in each equation and find which one works for all of them.

**13. D**    1 meter = 1,000 millimeters.

**14. A**    You have 6 choices out of a possible 22 $(9 + 6 + 7)$.

**15. D**    Ed made 8; Allen made 16.

**16. E**   Find the number with the most leading zeros; if two are tied, compare the first nonzero place.

**17. C**   As a fraction, $\frac{4}{12}$. Convert fractions to decimals by dividing: $\frac{4}{12} = 0.333 = 33.3$ percent.

**18. A**   There are 5 hashes between 0 and 500, so each of the hashes is 100 units. The arrow is about 1½ hashes away from 0, and $1.5 \times 100 = 150$. Thus, 250 would be between the next two hash marks, or 100 additional pounds.

> **Test Hint:** Always check your calculations to make sure you haven't made a computational error or misplaced a decimal.

**19. C**   Multiply 5 miles by 1,760 yards/mile, then multiply the answer by 3 feet/yard.

**20. B**   (4,3) means 4 to the right and 3 up.

**21. B**   Estimate by rounding to the nearest thousand: $7,000 \times 1,000 = 7,000,000$.

**22. E**   Convert all fractions to decimals and compare the answers.

**23. D**   $(9 \times 4) - 5 = 31$.

**24. A**   Six combinations add up to 7, out of 36 possible combinations. Therefore, 30 do not add up to 7. $\frac{30}{36}$ reduces to $\frac{5}{6}$.

**25. B**   $285 - 250 = 35$; $35 \div 250 = 0.14$.

**26. E**   This is a remainder interpretation problem. I is 4 boxes; II is 13, with $1 left over; and III is 3 batches.

> **Test Hint:** Make educated guesses after you have used the process of elimination.

**27. C**   $0.35 \times 40$.

**28. D**   Each 📖 = 8, and Sammi has 4 of them: $8 \times 4 = 32$. Vanessa has 2 of them: $8 \times 2 = 16$. $32 - 16 = 16$.

**29. E**   $x = 8y$, so $x \div 2 = 4y$.

**30. C**   Multiply; then count the spaces past the decimal point: $0.0005 \times 250 = 0.125$.

**31. B**   This is an area problem. The room is a $12 \times 12$ square, minus a 9 (12 – 3) by 10 (12 – 2) triangle, minus the 48 square feet of tiled area: $(12 \times 12) - (\frac{1}{2} \times 9 \times 10) - 48 = 99 - 48 = 51$.

---

**Test Hint:** Estimate the answer. This will help you make sure that your answer is reasonable.

---

**32. C**   The 150 books represents 25 percent of the total items. Use equivalent fractions: $\frac{150}{25} = x/17$; $25x = 2{,}550$. $x = 102$.

**33. A**   Seventeen students did not receive an A. As a fraction, $\frac{17}{22}$. Convert fractions to decimals by dividing: $\frac{17}{22} = 0.77$; $0.77 = 77$ percent.

**34. B**   Drawing a picture may be helpful here. I have bicycled the two legs of a right triangle, so use the Pythagorean equation: $8^2 + 6^2 = 64 + 36 = 100 = 10^2$.

**35. C**   This is a surface area problem: $SA = 2\pi r(h + r)$; $SA = 2\pi \times 4(10 + 4) = 112\pi$.

---

**Test Hint:** Consider working backward to solve problems. Start with the possible answers and work backward through the problem. This technique is especially helpful with algebra-based problems, where you are trying to find a variable. Use each possible answer choice in place of the variable to see which one works.

---

**36. C**   Multiply to find each commission; $11.20 is greatest.

**37. D**   The number must fall between 0.25 and 0.4, or 25 percent and 40 percent.

**38. A**   $0.45 = \frac{9}{20}$, $0.2 = \frac{1}{5}$, and $0.05 = \frac{1}{20}$. Change fractions to decimals by dividing.

**39. E**   $0.66 \times 1{,}000{,}000 = 660{,}000$.

**40. C**   The widest dimension is 3.5 inches; this is the same as 17.5 feet.